LONDON LITERATURE FESTIVAL

29 JUNE - 12 JULY 2007

Hear authors read, discuss and perform work from children's literature to dub poetry, visit our riverside book market, discover the newly reopened Saison Poetry Library and take part in debates and events across Southbank Centre at our new festival this summer.

WH Auden celebration with Simon Armitage, John Mark Ainsley & Kwame Kwei-Armah Pat Barker | The Caine Prize | Lauren Child Kate Grenville | Armando Iannucci, AL Kennedy & Martin Rowson explore freedom of expression Barbara Kingsolver | Linton Kwesi Johnson presents a night of dub poetry | Roger McGough & Brian Patten in *40-Love* | Michael Rosen Wole Soyinka delivers the Southbank Centre lecture | Jacqueline Wilson & much more.

TICKETS 0871 663 2500
WWW.SOUTHBANKCENTRE.CO.UK

SOUTHBANK CEN

GRANTA

GRANTA 98, SUMMER 2007
www.granta.com

EDITOR   Ian Jack
DEPUTY EDITOR   Matt Weiland
MANAGING EDITOR   Fatema Ahmed
ASSOCIATE EDITOR   Liz Jobey
EDITORIAL ASSISTANT   Helen Gordon

CONTRIBUTING EDITORS   Diana Athill, Simon Gray, Isabel Hilton,
Sophie Harrison, Blake Morrison, John Ryle, Sukhdev Sandhu, Lucretia Stewart

FINANCE   Geoffrey Gordon, Morgan Graver
SALES DIRECTOR   Brigid Macleod
PUBLICITY   Pru Rowlandson
MARKETING AND SUBSCRIPTIONS   Gill Lambert
IT MANAGER   Mark Williams
TO ADVERTISE CONTACT   Kate Rochester, ksrochester@granta.com
PRODUCTION ASSOCIATE   Sarah Wasley
PROOFS   Lesley Levene

PUBLISHER   Sigrid Rausing

GRANTA PUBLICATIONS, 2-3 Hanover Yard, Noel Road, London N1 8BE
Tel +44 (0)20 7704 9776 Fax +44 (0)20 7704 0474
e-mail for editorial: editorial@granta.com
This selection copyright © 2007 Granta Publications.
In the United States, Granta is published in association with Grove/Atlantic Inc,
841 Broadway, 4th Floor, New York, NY 10003

TO SUBSCRIBE go to www.granta.com
or call +44(0)20 7704 0470 or e-mail subs@granta.com
A one-year subscription (four issues) costs £27.95 (UK), £35.95 (rest of Europe)
and £42.95 (rest of the world).

Granta is printed and bound in Italy by Legoprint. The paper used in this publication meets the
minimum requirements of American National Standard for Information Sciences—Permanence of
Paper for Printed Library Materials, ANSI Z39.48-1984.

Design: Slabmedia.
Front and back cover photographs: Gourock's swimming pool by Martin Parr

ISBN 978-0903141-94-9

P08.8
R 53939U

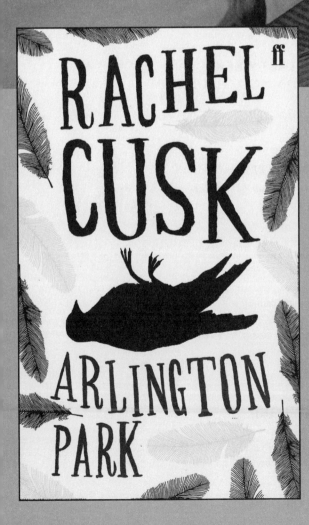

Shortlisted for the
Orange Broadband
Prize for Fiction 2007

RACHEL ff
CUSK

ARLINGTON
PARK

'It seems
there is not
one aspect of
the lunacy of
motherhood
that she
cannot distil
into elegant,
evocative
prose.'
Sarah Vine, *The Times*

Reading guide at
faber.co.uk/bookclub

THE DEEP END

GRANTA

'Gowdy writes as if she's on a sinking boat and needs to throw out all the dead weight. The only words that survive are the ones that matter'

New York Times

BARBARA GOWDY

'She writes like an angel' CAROL SHIELDS

Helpless

A provocative, gripping story of an unthinkable act and a mother's heroic love for her child.

www.littlebrown.co.uk

CONTRIBUTORS

Chimamanda Ngozi Adichie grew up in Nigeria. She is the author of *Purple Hibiscus* (HarperPerennial/Anchor Books) and, most recently, *Half of a Yellow Sun* (Fourth Estate/Knopf). Her short story 'Jumping Monkey Hill' appeared in *Granta 95*.

Diana Athill's books include the memoirs *Yesterday Morning* (Granta Books) and *Stet: An Editor's Life* (Granta/Grove Atlantic). For fifty years she was the editorial director of André Deutsch, where her authors included Jean Rhys, Gitta Sereny and V. S. Naipaul. 'Somewhere Towards the End' is taken from her new memoir which will be published by Granta Books in January 2008.

Louise Carpenter is the author of *An Unlikely Countess: Lily Budge and the 13th Earl of Galloway* (HarperCollins). She lives in Dorset and writes for the London *Daily Telegraph* and the London *Observer*.

Javier Cercas is the author of three novels: *Soldiers of Salamis*, which won the 2005 *Independent* Foreign Fiction Prize, *The Speed of Light* and *The Tenant & The Motive*, all published by Tusquets Editores in Spain and by Bloomsbury in the UK and US. 'Agamemnon's Truth' is taken from the collection *La verdad de Agamenón: crónicas, artículos, ensayos y un cuento* (*Agamemnon's Truth: Columns, Articles, Essays and One Story*) published by Tusquets Editores.

Gerard Donovan was born in Ireland and currently lives in the United States. His recent novel, *Julius Winsome*, is published by Faber in the UK and by Overlook Press in the US. His first novel, *Schopenhauer's Telescope* (Scribner/Overlook Press), was longlisted for the Man Booker Prize in 2003.

Ian Jack is the editor of *Granta*.

Jackie Kay's short story collection *Wish I Was Here* (Picador) has just won a British Book Award. *Darling*, a collection of her new and selected poems, will be published later this year by Bloodaxe Books. 'The Lord in His Wisdom', an extract from her memoir-in-progress, appeared in *Granta 93*.

Thomas Lynch's most recent books include a collection of essays, *Booking Passage* (Vintage/W. W. Norton), and a collection of poetry, *Still Life in Milford* (W. W. Norton). *Late Fictions*, a collection of stories, will be published by W. W. Norton in 2008. He lives in Michigan and in West Clare, Ireland.

Todd McEwen was born a mere twenty miles from the movie capital of the world. He has never stopped running. He last appeared in the magazine with 'Cary Grant's Suit' in *Granta* 94.

Anne McLean has translated writings by, among others, Julio Cortázar, Tomás Eloy Martínez and Carmen Martín Gaite. Her translations of *Soldiers of Salamis*, *The Speed of Light* and *The Tenant & The Motive* by Javier Cercas are published by Bloomsbury in the UK and US.

Martin Parr is a photographer, curator and editor. His most recent book is *Parking Spaces* (Chris Boot) and he is the author, with Gerry Badger, of the two-volume *The Photobook: a History* (Phaidon Press). He is currently working towards a large show at the Scottish National Gallery of Modern Art, Edinburgh where 'Clydeside' and other Scottish photographs will be shown in 2009.

Hugh Raffles lives in New York where he teaches at the New School for Social Research. He is the author of *In Amazonia: a Natural History* (Princeton). 'Cricket Fighting' is taken from his new book, *The Illustrated Insectopedia*, which will be published by Pantheon in 2009.

Jeremy Seabrook's books include *Consuming Cultures: Globalization and Local Lives* (New Internationalist) and, most recently, *Cities* (Oxfam and Pluto Press). He is a contributor to *The Statesman* in Kolkata, *Third World Resurgence* in Malaysia and the London *Guardian*. A piece about his mother and brother, 'Twins', appeared in *Granta* 95.

Helen Simpson is the author of four collections of short stories including *Hey Yeah Right Get a Life* (Vintage), published as *Getting a Life* by Vintage in the US, and *Constitutional* (Jonathan Cape), published as *In the Driving Seat* by Knopf in the US. In 1993 she was chosen as one of *Granta*'s Best of Young British Novelists. She lives in London.

Paul Theroux's short story about a mother, 'Mother of the Year', appeared in *Granta* 88. His latest book, *The Elephanta Suite*, is set in India and is published by Hamish Hamilton in the UK and by Houghton Mifflin in the US. Recently he retraced his journey from *The Great Railway Bazaar* (Penguin/Mariner Books) for a travel book to be published in 2008.

INTRODUCTION

Later this year *Granta* will move from its present address to new offices in west London. After the next issue the familiar words '2/3 Hanover Yard, Noel Road, London N1 8BE' will no longer appear on the imprint page. To a reader, this won't matter: who cares where a magazine is put together, so long as it's successfully put together? Does anyone still mourn the passing of Scribner from Fifth Avenue or Cape from Bedford Square, or every London newspaper from Fleet Street?

To people who have worked here for a few years, it matters a little. You get used to offices. You can even become fond of them. Many people (including me, at one time) spend more of their waking hours in offices among their colleagues than they do in their homes among their family, and for this reason sometimes know them better. I can look around this office and its heaps of manuscripts and remember trivial—though not at the time trivial—moments in literary history. To those who know where to look the place is stained by evidence of an old and now-proscribed way of life. The black mark on the blue carpet is where my colleague Robert Winder set a waste bin on fire after throwing away his still-burning Camel Light. The dark brown marks on my desk show where cigarettes have fallen from the edges of ashtrays. Over five or six years, the ceiling above my head turned from white to buff, just like (I used to imagine) the plasterwork of the Cafe Royal, which became famously stained by decades of smoke from writers' cigars: Frank Harris and Oscar Wilde, puffing and quipping. Perhaps the most surprising thing about Hanover Yard is that it hasn't burned down.

Granta came to this yard behind an Islington pub in 1990 from rooms above a hairdressing salon in Cambridge. Islington wasn't then as expensive or fashionable as it's since become—Brad Pitt has been sighted in another nearby pub—and in the geography of London publishing our offices were rather out of the way. I like the neighbourhood: as well as working in it, I've also lived in Islington for nearly forty years. I tell visitors that the office used to be a piano factory, which somebody told me once and may be true (cheap upright pianos, unlike other musical instruments, were a branch of the furniture trade, which, needing stacks of timber, grew up beside the canal wharves of north and east London). I also tell them that, until anti-German feelings ran high in the First World War, Noel Road was called Hanover Road: the patriotic renaming authority simply forgot

Ian Jack

to change the name of the yard that's attached to it. If they seem interested in literature, which some do, I say that on their way back to the Tube station they should look high on the right, where a plaque on one of Noel Road's Georgian terraced houses remembers that in 1967 the playwright Joe Orton was hammered to death in the top flat by his jealous lover, Kenneth Halliwell, who then killed himself with Nembutals. The woman in the downstairs flat remembers the police knocking at her door that August morning. She is Elena, the oldest and most distinguished restaurant hostess in London (Elena's L'Etoile is named after her) and occasionally I meet her in the street on her way to or from work. She uses a stick now—she must be well into her eighties—but still catches the bus to her restaurant. She once said to me, 'I liked Joe but I never cared much for that Halliwell.'

She and her husband Aldo came from Emilia-Romagna to Soho before the war, and when I meet Aldo, who always looks like a man sauntering his way happily towards a game of cards, he sometimes says, 'You need to cheer up!' I count this among the worst reprimands a person can hear and immediately wonder what is making me look so miserable, abstracted or anxious. A disappointing submission by a writer? Some interpersonal difficulty in the office? My own inadequacy? Offices, and especially small offices, contain lots of emotion. One of the best editors ever to work at *Granta* used to say, 'I just want to kill everybody!' when she eventually turned up as a tall storm, just before lunch. But a lot of work has also got done. Making a quarterly magazine may not sound like a lot of work, but somehow it requires a surprising amount, if it's to be any good. I would like to think that after *Granta* moves the memory of all that has happened here will survive spirit-like in the atmosphere: the ghosts of deadlines past, whispers on the stairs at midnight ('We need to cut four pages from Theroux'). But I know it won't be so. I have never heard the noise of old piano-makers joyfully exclaiming at, or cursing, the quality of their wood.

These thoughts are flavoured with a second valediction. *Granta* is leaving Hanover Yard and I am leaving *Granta* as its editor. I wish I could say exactly why I am leaving. My association with *Granta* began as a writer in 1987 and it has become an important part of my life, not to be lightly discarded. The best I can do is to say it just felt right. I've edited the magazine for twelve years and produced forty-eight issues; my predecessor, Bill Buford, lasted sixteen years and did fifty issues (though he had other things on his mind, such as funds, which were rarely a crisis in my time). You can do a thing too long— inflict your taste and judgement too often in the process of commissioning, selecting, rejecting and editing. You begin to worry that you are missing things. *Granta* is, after all, 'the magazine of new writing' and as such needs perpetual enthusiasm for what 'new writing' may bring. All you can do—all I have done—is to obey your instincts for the original, the interesting and the true. These instincts cannot be faked, though in the hoopla of the publishing industry, where huge talents are discovered every week, it is sometimes hard to hold fast to them. Also, in holding fast, you can make mistakes. What seemed like a piece of dutiful, unpersuasive invention to you turns out to be a work of lively genius to everyone else. Perhaps I have been too fond of clarity, and of the idea that writing, if it can do nothing else, should at least tell the reader something he didn't know before.

As I've written elsewhere, *Granta* has never had a literary manifesto or mission statement; the editorial in its first issue promised 'a dialogue in prose about prose', but that, thank God, proved to be a lie. When pushed against a wall, as I have been, and asked about the kind of writing *Granta* believes in, I've sometimes said that if it were a cathedral rather than a magazine, then two of its stained-glass windows would be to Anton Chekhov and George Orwell. This is of course pretentious—we haven't had a story from Anton recently—but to me the work of those two writers represents a touchstone for so much of what has appeared in the magazine. Partly this is because they were both masters of the short form to which *Granta* is suited, but partly also because they were so alert to and inquisitive of the world they lived in. Like Bill before me, I've never wanted *Granta* simply to reflect fashions in writing—what other publishers happen to be publishing or what comes into the office willy-nilly—but instead (or as well) to send writers into, forgive me, 'the real world' to describe the interesting or alarming things happening there which have yet to be turned into a book or a manuscript; and sometimes to publish pieces not so much for their aesthetic or 'literary' value but because the experience of their writers means that they have something urgent and important to tell us. *Granta* gets a lot of welcome, worldwide attention for its 'Best of

Ian Jack

Young Novelists' issues, both American and British: the media loves judgements and lists. But they are untypical of the regular run of a magazine which four years ago published an issue on global warming ('This Overheating World', *Granta* 83) and five years ago tackled global perceptions of the United States ('What We Think of America', *Granta* 77). I like to think both were illuminating and prescient.

Granta now has editions in Spanish, Greek and (more occasionally) Italian. A Portuguese edition intended for a Brazilian audience will appear soon. None of these ventures is owned by Granta Publications—they are published under licence by imprints in Madrid, Athens and Rome, and within certain boundaries their editors have the freedom to fashion the magazine as they see fit, publishing original work as well as translations from *Granta* in English. That they exist at all suggests that *Granta* has a reputation like no other literary magazine, which may be because it has always fought shy of 'literary magazine' as a definition of itself. If you wanted a magazine that discussed the state of literary culture or carefully reflected its fashions then, frankly, you have been looking in the wrong place. It's not for me to analyse *Granta*'s enduring success—I can only touch wood— but perhaps the critic on the London *Observer* caught an important part of its attraction when he wrote that *Granta* had 'its face pressed against the window, determined to witness the world'.

To be its editor has been a great privilege and I owe many debts. To the writers who have written for it; to the significant contribution, not only editorially, made by my colleagues and friends; to Rea Hederman, our former owner, whose generosity and commitment to *Granta* were vital over two decades and whose friendship will always be precious to me; to Sigrid Rausing, our new owner, whose equal generosity and commitment have assured *Granta*'s future; finally, to too large a group to be individually named, our readers. In his farewell editorial twelve years ago, Bill Buford described them (I mean, you) as 'the world's smartest and most literate strangers' and I can think of no more accurate compliment. *Granta* needs good readers as well as good writers. We have been lucky to have both.

Ian Jack, May 2007

GRANTA

SOMEWHERE TOWARDS THE END

Diana Athill

All through my sixties I felt I was still within hailing distance of middle age, not safe on its shores, perhaps, but navigating its coastal waters. My seventieth birthday failed to change this because I managed scarcely to notice it, but my seventy-first did change it. Being 'over seventy' is being old: suddenly I was aground on that fact and saw that the time had come to size it up.

This year I shall be ninety. I have lived long enough to have witnessed great changes in being old as far as women are concerned—smaller ones for men, but for them less was needed. In my grandmothers' day a woman over seventy adopted what almost amounted to a uniform. If she was a widow she wore black or grey clothes that disregarded fashion, and even if she still had a husband her garments went a bit drab and shapeless, making it clear that this person no longer attempted to be attractive. My paternal grandmother, who was the older of the two, wore floor-length black garments to her dying day, and a little confection of black velvet and lace on her head, a 'cap' such as full-blown Victorian ladies wore. (Judging by the skimpiness of my own hair in old age, which comes from her side of the family, she had good reason for adhering to that particular fashion.) Even one of my aunts, my mother's eldest sister, never wore anything but black or grey after her husband's death in the Thirties, and deliberately chose unsmart shapes for her garments. The abrupt shortening of skirts in the Twenties contributed to the preservation of this 'uniform', because no one at any age wants to look grotesque, and grotesque is what old legs and bodies would have looked in 'flapper' fashions, so in my youth old women were still announcing by their appearance that they had become a different kind of person.

After the Second World War, however, reaction against the austerity it had imposed led to far greater flexibility. For a while *Vogue* ran a feature called 'Mrs Exeter' to persuade elderly women that they could wear stylish clothes, and this demonstration soon became unnecessary, so pleased were women to choose clothes to suit their shapes and complexions rather then to conform to a convention. Nowadays an old woman would obviously be daft if she dressed like a teenager, but I have a freedom of choice undreamt of by my grandmothers. There have been days when I went shopping in my local Morrison's wearing something a bit eccentric and wondered whether I would see any raised eyebrows, only to conclude that I would probably have to wear a bikini before anyone so much as blinked.

Even more than clothes, cosmetics have made age look, and therefore feel, less old. Until quite recently they could be a danger, because women who had always worn a lot of make-up tended to continue to do so, blind to the unfortunate effect it could have on an inelastic and crepy skin. One of my dearest old friends could never get it into her head that if, when doing herself up for a party, she slapped on a lot of scarlet lipstick, it would soon come off on her teeth and begin to run into the little wrinkles round the edge of her lips, making her look like a vampire bat disturbed in mid-dinner. Luckily today's cosmetics are much better made and more subtle in effect, so that an ancient face that would look absurd if *visibly* painted can be gently coaxed into looking quite naturally better than it really is. Having inherited a good skin from my mother, I still receive compliments for it, but nowadays I know that at least half its 'goodness' is thanks to Max Factor. Appearance is important to old women, not because we suppose that it will impress other people, but because of what we ourselves see when we look in a mirror. It is unlikely that anyone else will notice that the nose on an old face is red and shiny or the broken veins on its cheeks are visible, but its owner certainly will, and will equally certainly feel a lift in her spirits when this depressing sight is remedied. And even if how one sees oneself is not wholly how one is, it does contribute a great deal towards it. I know for sure that I both feel and behave younger than my grandmothers did when they were old.

In spite of this, however, the most obvious thing about moving into my seventies was the disappearance of what used to be the most important thing in life: I might not look, or even feel, all that old, but I had ceased to be a sexual being, a condition which had gone through several stages and had not always been a happy one, but which had always seemed central to my existence.

It had started when I was four or five in a way which no doubt appeared comic to onlookers but which felt serious enough to me, with the announcement that I was going to marry John Sherbroke. He was a little boy who lived a few houses up from us on the street beside Woolwich Common (my father, an officer in the Royal Artillery, was presumably an instructor at the Military Academy there at the time, and John's father was also a gunner). I can't remember John at all, except for his name, and that he was my intended. His successor is clearer in my memory because of his beautiful, sad brown eyes and the glamour bestowed on him by his great age—he was Denis, the gardener's boy at the Hall Farm where we had gone to live under the wing of my mother's parents. I doubt whether I ever spoke to Denis, but I did, with great daring, spit on his head out of the lavatory window when he was working the pump by the back door. He was followed by loves with whom I did communicate—indeed I and my brother spent much time with them: Jack and Wilfred, sons of the head cow-man at the farm, remembered even more clearly than Denis because of the amount of time I put into trying to decide which I loved best.

Those two were the first beneficiaries of my romantic phase, in which love took the form of daydreams. The object of my passion would be placed in a situation of great danger—his house on fire, perhaps, or he was being swept away in a flood—and I would rescue him, the dream's climax being that when he recovered consciousness he would open his eyes to find me leaning over him, my cloud of black hair enveloping him like a cloak (I was a skinny child with a mouse-coloured bob, but I confidently expected to improve with time). Jack and Wilfred lasted until I was nine, when they were ousted by the first love I chose for real reasons: David, who was far kinder, braver and more sensible than the rest of us and was also a familiar friend and companion. He, too, was liable to be rescued, though rather guiltily because of how silly he would have thought it, had he known. He told his mother I was a good sport, which was thrilling at the time, though as I entered my teens it did begin to pall.

Then, at fifteen, I fell in love as an adult. It was with Paul (I called him that in my memoir *Instead of a Letter*, so he can keep the name here), who came during one of his Oxford vacations to earn a bit of money by coaching my brother for an exam. He dispelled daydreams by being the real thing, but he did not dispel romance. I loved, I assumed love equalled marriage, and I was certain that once I was married to the man I loved I would be faithful to him for the rest of my life. I did have the occasional, fleeting daydream about my beautiful white wedding, but to embroider my romanticism beyond that, once I was old enough to hold Paul's attention and we became engaged, was not easy, partly because of how everyone went on at me about how poor we would be and how I would have to learn to be a good housewife. Paul, who had gone into the RAF, was still only a pilot-officer whose pay was £400 a year, which seemed to him and me enough to have a good time on, whatever 'they' said, but still the warnings were sobering; though less so than something which happened about six months after we announced our engagement.

We went, with his sister, to a party with a group of rather louche friends of Paul's—I didn't know where he had picked them up, and was disconcerted by them from the start because they were drinking harder and talking more crudely than anyone I had met hitherto. One of them had brought along an extravagantly sexy-looking girl who made a dead set at Paul the moment she saw him, and to my incredulous dismay he responded. After an extremely uncomfortable hour or two he shovelled the task of seeing me home on to his embarrassed sister, and he ended the evening, I was sure, in bed with that girl.

During the following two weeks I heard nothing from him, and felt too crushed to write or call myself, and when he let me know that he was about to fly down from Grantham to spend the weekend at Oxford with me, as he often did, I was more anxious than relieved. During the Saturday evening we drank too much and he collapsed into almost tearful apology. He had behaved horribly, he was so ashamed of himself he couldn't bear it, I must, must believe that it had meant absolutely nothing, that girl had turned out to be a ghastly bore (what a slip-up! Suppose she hadn't been?). Never again would he do anything like that because I was and always would be the only woman he really loved, and so on and so on. It was better than silence had been, but it was not good.

Next morning we took a taxi to 'our' pub in Appleton and dismissed it before we got there in order to dispel our headaches by walking the last mile, although it was a bitterly cold and windy winter day. Paul seemed relaxed, scanning the fields on either side of the muddy lane for fieldfares; I was dismally silent, mulling over his apology. It had meant nothing: yes, I accepted that. But his declaration that such a thing would never happen again: no, that I was unable to believe. I don't remember being as shocked as I ought to have been at his doing it under my nose, thus betraying a really gross indifference to my feelings. I had a humble opinion of my own importance, carefully fostered by a family which considered vanity a serious sin, so in such a situation I tended to blame myself as not being worthy of consideration, and I wasn't consciously thinking of that although I am now sure that it was gnawing away at me. What I knew I was thinking about was how this flightiness of Paul's must be handled. I remember thinking that once we were married I would have to learn to be *really clever*. 'It will be all right for quite a time,' I thought. 'He will go on coming back to me while we are like we are now. But when I get old—when I'm *thirty*'—and I saw a flash of my own face, anxious and wrinkled under grey hair—'then it will be dangerous, then he could fall in love with one of them.' Would I learn to be clever *enough*? I'd have to. The whole of that day remained dismal, but not for a moment did it occur to me that I might not want to marry him, and soon our relationship was restored to its usual enjoyable state.

So I don't think there was ever a time in my adult life when I didn't realize that men were quite likely to be technically unfaithful to women, although it was not until Paul had finally jilted me that I saw that women, too, could be cheered up by sex without love. I 'recovered' from Paul in that I fell in love again, twice, and heavily, but both times it felt 'fatal', something impossible to avoid, and anyway I longed for it, but which was bound to bring pain. The first time it was with a married man much older than myself, and I never envisaged him leaving his wife for me. No doubt if he had suggested it I would have accepted, but I admired him far too much to expect it: I was his wartime fling, or folly (there's nothing like a whiff of death in the air to intensify desire, the essence of life—I remember him whispering in amazement, 'I'd resigned myself to never feeling like this again'), while she was his good and blameless wife who had just become the mother of their first child, so leaving her would prove him cruel and irresponsible which I was sure he was not. I would not have loved him so much if he had been.

My second after-Paul love was available, even eligible, but his very eligibility seemed to make him too good to be true. He liked me a lot. For a time he almost thought he was in love with me, but he never quite was and I sensed almost from the beginning that it was going to end in tears, whereupon I plunged in deeper and deeper. And it did end in tears quite literally, both of us weeping as we walked up and down Wigmore Street on our last evening together. With masochistic abandon I loved him even more for his courage in admitting the situation and sparing me vain hopes (and in fact such courage, which takes a lot of summoning up, is something to be grateful for, because a broken heart mends much faster from a conclusive blow than it does from slow strangulation. Believe me! Mine experienced both.)

That, for me, was the end of romantic love. What followed, until I met Barry Reckord in my forty-fourth year, was a series of sometimes very brief, sometimes sustained affairs, always amiable (two of them very much so), almost always cheering up (two of the tiny ones I could have done without), and none of them going deep enough to hurt. During those years, if a man wanted to marry me, as three of them did, I felt what Groucho Marx felt about a club willing to accept him: disdain. I tried to believe it was something more rational, but it wasn't. Several of the painless affairs involved other people's husbands, but I never felt guilty because the last thing I intended or hoped for was damage to anyone's marriage. If a wife ever found out—and as far as I know that never happened—it would have been from her husband's carelessness, not mine.

Loyalty is not a favourite virtue of mine, perhaps because André Deutsch used so often to abuse the word, angrily accusing any writer who wanted to leave our list of 'disloyalty'. There is, of course, no reason why a writer should be loyal to a firm which has supposed that it will be able to make money by publishing his work. Gratitude and affection can certainly develop when a firm makes a good job of it, but no bond of loyalty is established. In cases where such a bond exists—loyalty to family, for example, or to a political party—it can become foolishness if betrayed by its object. If your brother turns out to be a murderer or your party changes its policies, standing by him or it through thick or thin seems to me mindless. Loyalty unearned is simply the husk of a notion developed to benefit the bosses in a feudal system. When spouses are concerned, it seems to me that kindness and consideration should be the key words, not loyalty, and sexual infidelity does not necessarily wipe them out.

Fidelity in the sense of keeping one's word, I respect, but I think it tiresome that it is tied so tightly in people's minds to the idea of sex. The belief that a wife owes absolute fidelity to her husband has deep and tangled roots, being based not only on a man's need to know himself to be the father of his wife's child, but also on the even deeper, darker feeling that man *owns* woman, god having made her for his convenience. It's hard to imagine the extirpation of that: think of its power in Islam! And woman's anxious clamour for her husband's fidelity springs from the same primitive root: she feels it to be necessary proof of her value. That I know only too well, having had the stuffing knocked out of me so painfully when Paul chose to marry someone else. But understanding doesn't mean approving. Why, given our bone-deep, basic need for one another, do men and women have to put so much weight on this particular, unreliable aspect of it?

I think now of Isaac Bashevis Singer's story 'The Peephole in the Gate', about a young man who saw his sweetheart home on the eve of their marriage, couldn't resist taking one last look at her through the peephole—and there she was, being soundly and obviously enjoyably kissed by the porter. End of betrothal—though the narrator does slyly remind the young man that he had it off with a serving maid that same afternoon. The story goes on to suggest how much simpler, and probably better, two people's lives would have been if that sexual infidelity had never come to light: a theme which Singer, that wise old bird, returns to several times, always with his characteristic trick of leaving the pronouncement of a moral judgement in the hands of the reader. Given his deep attachment to his religious background, I can't be sure that he would have agreed with the judgement I produce—but after all, he *does* ask for it Yes, there are some things, sexual infidelities among them, that do no harm if they remain unknown—or, for that matter, are known and accepted, and which is preferable depends on the individuals and their circumstances. I only have to ask myself which I would choose, if forced to do so, between the extreme belief that a whole family's honour is stained by an unfaithful wife unless she is killed, and the attitude often attributed to the French that however far from admirable sexual infidelity is, it is perfectly acceptable if *conducted properly*. Vive la France!

This attitude I shared, and still share, with Barry, with whom, after I had finally shed the scars of a broken heart, I eventually settled down into an extraordinarily happy loving friendship, which remained at its best for about eight years until it began to be affected not by emotional complications, but by Time. This was not a sudden event, but its early stage, which took place during my mid- and late fifties, was followed by a reprieve, which made it possible to ignore its significance. Gradually I had become aware that my interest in, and therefore my physical response to, making love with my dear habitual companion was dwindling: familiarity had made the touch of his hand feel so like the touch of my own hand that it no longer conveyed a thrill. Looking back, I wonder why I never talked about this with him, because I didn't. I simply started to fake. Probably this was because the thought of 'working at' the problem together, as I supposed a marriage counsellor would suggest, struck me as unlikely to solve it. Tedious and absurd: that was how I envisaged such a procedure. If something that had always worked naturally now didn't work—well, first you hoped that faking it would bring it back, which sometimes it did, and when that stopped happening you accepted that it was over.

That acceptance was sad. Indeed, I was forced into it, at a time when our household was invaded by a ruthless and remarkably succulent blonde in her mid-twenties and he fell into bed with her. There was one sleepless night of real sorrow, but only one night. What I mourned during that painful night was not the loss of my loving old friend, who was still there, and still is, but the loss of youth: 'What she has, god rot her, I no longer have and will never, never have again.' A belated recognition, up against which I had come with a horrid crunch. But very soon another voice began to sound in my head, which made more sense. 'Look,' it said, 'you know quite well that you have stopped wanting him in your bed, it's months since you enjoyed it, so what are you moaning about? Of course you have lost youth, you have moved on and stopped wanting what youth wants.' And that was the end of that stage.

Soon afterwards came the reprieve, when I found, to my amusement and pleasure, that novelty could restore sex. I described in *Instead of a Letter* how after an early, real and long-lasting sorrow my morale had begun to be restored by an affair with a man I called Felix, which did not involve love but was thoroughly enjoyable otherwise. Now, as I approached my sixties, it happened again, and my life as a sexual being was prolonged by seven years while Barry went his own way, our companionship having become more like that of brother and sister than of lovers. A second man with whom I had little in common won himself a place in memory made warm by gratitude. After him there was no reprieve, nor did I want one.

The last man in my life as a sexual being, who accompanied me over the frontier between late middle age and being old, was Sam, who was born in Grenada in the Caribbean. Whether he had come to England in order to volunteer for the war, or his arrival just happened to coincide with its outbreak, I don't know. He joined the RAF Regiment, in which he worked as a clerk, and in his own time came to know George Padmore and other black elders of that day who were concerned with establishing the black man's rights in Britain. He gained a good deal of experience in broadcasting at this time, which served him well later, when he moved on to Ghana and soon attracted the attention of Kwame Nkrumah, who put him in charge of his government's public relations so that he became in effect a member of it, although he was never a minister. He remained Nkrumah's trusted servant and friend until the coup which brought the Redeemer down, simultaneously putting an end to Sam's palmy days in Africa. Because he was known in Accra as an honest man who took no bribes he escaped prison, but he had to leave the country at four days' notice, taking nothing but his clothes. When I met him, all he had left from those days was a beautiful camel-hair overcoat with a sable collar, and the gold watch on a handsome bracelet given him by Haile Selassie.

Being an impressive-looking man, very tall, with pleasant manners, easygoing but sensible, clearly on the side of good sense and decorum, he had no trouble getting a job almost at once in the British government's organization concerned with race relations. He was just settling into it when we met at a party at which there were several old African hands of one sort and another. My partner at André Deutsch had kick-started a publishing firm in Nigeria during the Sixties and we had some African writers on our list, so the newly independent countries, and race relations, were part of the landscape in which I existed at that time.

In addition to that, in the course of my close and happy relationship with Barry, which had by then lasted about eight years, I had come to feel more at home with black men than with white. Barry, having been educated by English schoolmasters at his Jamaican school and by English dons at Cambridge, used sometimes to say that his fellow Jamaicans saw him as 'a small, square, brown Englishman', and some of them may have done so, but he was black enough to have received his share of insults from white men; and one can't identify with someone of whom that is true without feeling more like him than like his insulters.

The first black person with whom I was ever in the same room was an African undergraduate at a party during my first term at Oxford in 1936. Dancing was going on, and I was deeply relieved at his not asking me for a dance. I knew that if he asked I would have to say yes, and I hadn't the faintest idea why the prospect seemed so appalling. It was just something which would have appalled my parents, so it appalled me. But I am glad to say that when, a week later, a friend said to me, 'I think I would be sick if a black man touched me,' I was shocked. I don't remember thinking about it in the intervening days, but somehow I had taken the first tiny step of seeing that my reaction to the idea of dancing with that man had been disgusting.

After that I must gradually have given the matter enough thought to get my head straight about it, because when I next came in touch with black people, which didn't happen for some years, I was able to see them as individuals. The first time I was kissed by a black man— a friendly peck at the end of a taxi ride from one pub to another—I did note it as an occasion, because the fact that it was just like being kissed by anyone else proved me right in a satisfactory way: I was still feeling pleased with myself for not having racist feelings. But by the time I met Barry, although I had never had occasion to make love with a black man, I had met many black people and worked with some of them, so clicking with him at a party and soon afterwards going to bed with him didn't seem particularly noteworthy except for being much more fun than the last such encounter I'd had, because this time we liked each other so well. It was only after we had settled into togetherness that I started expecting to like black men better than whites. I always might, of course, end up disliking the one or liking the other contrary to expectation, but I did, from then on, start out with a bias towards the black, or at any rate the un-English.

So when at our first meeting Sam made a stately swoop, I was pleased: it was both funny and revivifying to be seen as attractive by this agreeable and sexy person, just after concluding that my love-making days were over. Soon after that he moved into a flat near Putney Bridge, and for the next seven years I spent a night with him there about once a week.

We rarely did anything together except make ourselves a pleasant little supper and go to bed, because we had very little in common apart from liking sex. Sam had an old-fashioned sense of what was proper, but I am sure it had never entered his head to think of sex in connection with guilt. As well as *The Pickwick Papers*, *The Bab Ballads* and several booklets about the Rosicrucians and the Christian Scientists, *The Kamasutra* was among the books permanently entangled in his bed-clothes. We also shared painful feet, which was almost as important as liking sex, because when you start feeling your age it is comforting to be with someone in the same condition. You recognize it in each other, but there is no need to go on about it. We never mentioned our feet, just kicked our shoes off as soon as we could.

To be more serious, the really important thing we had in common was that neither of us had any wish to fall in love or to become responsible for someone else's peace of mind. We didn't even need to see a great deal of each other. We knew that we would give each other no trouble.

So what did we give each other?

I gave Sam sex that suited him. The first, but not most enduring attraction was that I was white and well bred. Sam had nothing against black women (except his wife, whom he saw as a burden imposed on him by his mother before he'd developed the sense to understand what a mistake it was); but since he came to England at the end of the 1930s all his most important women had been white. He had been bettering himself ever since his mother urged him to work hard at school, and claiming a white woman for yourself would, alas, be recognized by most black men from his background, at that time, as part of that process. This was a fact that gave older and/or not particularly glamorous white women an edge with black men that they hadn't got for white ones, which is evidently deplorable although I can't help being grateful for it. Sam was not a man of vulgar instincts so he didn't want to show his woman off, but it gave him private satisfaction to feel that she was worth showing. Then it turned out that physically I was right for him, and that I could be good company. So I was satisfying as a status symbol, agreeable as a companion in so far as he wanted one, and was able and willing to play along with him in a way he enjoyed. He obviously felt he need look no further.

Sam's chief attraction to me was that he wanted me: to be urgently wanted at a time when I no longer expected it cheered me up and brought me alive again—no small gift. Also, I am curious. His background and the whole course of his life, being so different from mine, seemed interesting even when he was being dull. A middle-class Englishman with his nature would have bored me because I would have known too much about him. Sam I wanted to find out about, and what I found out was likeable. Even when I was thinking 'What an old noodle!' I liked him, and what I liked best was the sense I picked up of the boy he used to be.

He had the calm self-confidence and general benevolence bestowed by a secure and happy childhood. A middle-class adoring mother can sometimes damage her child, but in a peasant family she is more likely to make him: she must get him out of this hard life if she possibly can, even if she loses him in the process. Sam's father owned the patch of land on which they lived (and that, too, contributed to self-confidence, because being raised on your own place, however small, is stabilizing), but it was a property too small to support a family, so he had to find work in Trinidad, and then in Venezuela. It was the mother who ran the home, and she gave her son unquestioned precedence over her two daughters (Barry's mother did the same thing and her daughter never quite forgave her).

'We didn't know it,' Sam told me, 'but the food we ate was just what everyone says nowadays is the healthiest: fish, fruit and vegetables, we were never short of those.' They lived right on the sea, so escaped the common West Indian over-dependence on root vegetables. 'And all that air and exercise. I thought nothing of running five miles to school and five miles back—long-distance running was a craze with us boys, we ran everywhere.' They rode, too. Most people kept a horse (this surprised me) and if a boy wanted to get somewhere in a hurry he could jump on to some neighbour's bare-backed nag without having to ask. And they swam as much as they ran. He marvelled when he remembered how no one fussed when they used to swim out to a little islet about two miles off-shore. A very tall, good-looking, even-tempered boy, good at all the local pastimes, crammed with healthy food and plunged by his fond mother into herb baths of which she knew the secrets, Sam was evidently secure among his friends as a leader. When he recalled those happy times he seemed to bring glimpses of them into the room—a whiff of nutmeg-scented sea breeze, very endearing.

His mother lost him of course—that wife was her big mistake. He begot two children on her, then could stand it no longer, left for England and his mother never saw him again. She died asking for him; people wrote and told him that. He spoke of it solemnly but placidly: it was a mother's fate, he implied, sad but inevitable.

He did not consider himself a bad son, husband or father for having left. He had kept in touch, sent money, seen to it that his children were educated: he had done what was proper. His son became a doctor and moved to the United States, and they saw each other from time to time. His daughter was unforgiving, 'a stupid girl'. And his wife... Thirty-five years after he left Grenada he returned for the first time, for a three-week visit at the invitation of the prime minister. He didn't let his wife know he was coming, but after the first week it occurred to him to drop in on her, still without warning. 'So what happened?' I asked. He shook his head, clicked his tongue, and said slowly and disapprovingly, 'That's a very *cantankerous* woman.' This made me laugh so much that he took offence and provided no more details. Not that he would have been able to provide any of real interest, since he obviously had no conception of the life to which he had condemned that 'stupid' daughter and that 'cantankerous' wife: a convenient ignorance shared by a great number of West Indian husbands and 'baby-fathers'—though many of the women left behind seem to take it calmly.

Our relationship ended gently, the gaps between our meetings becoming gradually longer. The last time we met, after an especially long one (so long that, without regret, I had thought it final), he was slower than usual and seemed abstracted and tired, but not ill. Although we had agreed already that our affair was over, he said, 'What about coming to bed?' but I could see he was relieved when I said no. 'The trouble with me,' I said, 'is that the spirit is willing but the flesh is weak. My body has gone against it.' He didn't say, 'Mine too,' he wouldn't want to go as far as that, but he did say, 'I know, the body does go against things. You can't do anything about that.' And the next thing I heard about him, not very much later, was that he had died suddenly of a heart attack.

You can't miss someone grievously if you haven't seen them or wanted to see them for several months and they had touched only a comparatively small corner of your life, but after his death Sam became more vivid in my mind than many of my more important dead. I saw him with photographic clarity—still can. His gestures, his expressions, the way he walked and sat, his clothes. The seven years of him played through my head with the immediacy of a newsreel: all we said, all we did; perhaps the pattern of our meetings was so repetitive that I couldn't help learning him by heart. I particularly remember the feel of him. His skin was smooth and always seemed to be cool and dry, a pleasant, healthy skin, and his smell was pleasant and healthy. I feel him lying beside me after making love, both of us on our backs, hands linked, arms and legs touching in a friendly way. His physical presence is so clear, even now, that it is almost like a haunt (an amiable one).

The faith Sam had decided to favour was in the transmigration of souls because, he said, how else could one explain why one person had a good life and another a horrid one: they were getting what they had earned in their previous lives, it was obvious. He was displeased when I said that if that were so, how odd that so many black people must have been very wicked in the past. He refused to take it up because, I think, transmigration was promising to him personally. He had, after all, been uncommonly lucky: a little refinement of the soul towards the end and up he would go. That, he once explained to me, was why he had given up meat and hard liquor once he was past sixty. I wish I could hope that Sam was right in expecting to come back to earth for another life. If he could, I doubt whether it would be so rarefied a life as he had aimed for, but it would certainly be several degrees more enjoyable than the one he left, which would make it much better than most.

Meanwhile, perhaps because he carried into the beginning of my old age something belonging to younger days, he is still alive in my head, and I am glad of it. Dear Sam. □

ON MONDAY LAST WEEK

Chimamanda Ngozi Adichie

K amara moved closer to the bathroom mirror, turning from side to side, examining the folded lumps of her belly. She closed her eyes and imagined her belly flat as a book cover and then she imagined Tracy touching it with those paint-stained fingers. She opened her eyes. Josh was standing by the bathroom door when she came out. Tracy's seven-year-old son; he had his mother's round nose.

'Pee-pee or a poopy?' he asked.

'Pee-pee.' She walked into the kitchen and packed up the books scattered on the table, where they had been practising all afternoon for his Read-a-Thon competition. The grey venetian blinds cast strips of shadow over the counter.

'Have you finished your juiced spinach?' she asked.

'Yes.' He was watching her steadily. He knew—he had to know—that the only reason she went into the bathroom each time she handed him the glass of green juice was to give him a chance to pour it away as she had done since the first day he tasted it and made a face and said, 'Ugh. I hate this.'

'Your dad says you have to drink it every day before dinner,' Kamara said. She paused, added, 'It's only half a glass. It would take a minute to pour it away,' and went to the bathroom. That was all. When she came out the glass was empty, as it was now, placed beside the sink.

'I'll cook your dinner so you will be all set for Zany Brainy when your dad comes back, okay?' she asked. American expressions like 'all set' still felt clunky in her mouth but she used them for Josh.

'Okay,' he said.

'Do you want a fish fillet or chicken with your rice pilaf?'

'Chicken.'

She opened the refrigerator. The top shelf was stacked with plastic bottles of juiced organic spinach. Cans of herbal tea had filled that space two weeks ago, when Neil was reading *Herbal Drinks for Children*. Before that, soy beverages cluttered the shelf. Before that, protein shakes for growing bones. The juiced spinach would go soon, Kamara knew, because when she arrived this afternoon the first thing she noticed was that *A Complete Guide to Juicing Vegetables for Children* was no longer on the counter; Neil must have put it in the drawer over the weekend.

Kamara brought out a packet of organic chicken strips. 'Why don't you lie down for a bit and watch a tape, Josh?' she said. He liked to sit in the kitchen and watch her cook but he looked so tired. The four other Read-a-Thon finalists were probably as tired as he was, their mouths aching from rolling long, unfamiliar words on their tongues, their bodies tense with the thought of the competition tomorrow. Kamara watched him slot in a *Rugrats* tape and lie down on the couch. He was small for six, a slight child with olive skin and thick curls. Half-caste was what they had called children like him back in Nigeria; *half-caste* meant light-skinned good looks, trips abroad to visit white grandparents, and Kamara had always resented the glamour of half-castes. But in America, half-caste was a bad word. Kamara learned this when she first called about the babysitting job advertised in the *City Paper*: generous pay, close to transportation, car not required. Neil had sounded surprised that she was Nigerian.

'You speak such good English,' he said, and it annoyed her, his surprise, his assumption that English was somehow his personal property. And because of this, although Tobechi had told her not to mention her education, she told Neil that she had a master's degree, that she had recently arrived in America to join her husband and wanted to earn a little money babysitting while waiting for her green card application to be processed so she could get a proper work permit. 'Well, I need somebody who can commit until the end of Josh's school term,' Neil said.

'No problem,' Kamara said hastily. She really should not have said that she had a master's degree.

'Maybe you could teach Josh a Nigerian language? He already has French lessons twice a week after school. He goes to an advanced programme at Temple Beth Hillel, where they have entrance exams for four year olds. He's very quiet, very sweet, a great kid, but I'm concerned that there aren't any biracial kids like him at school or in the neighbourhood.'

'Biracial?' Kamara asked.

Neil's cough was delicate. 'My wife is African-American and I'm white, Jewish.'

'Oh, he's a half-caste.'

There was a pause and Neil's voice came back, thicker. 'Please don't say that word.'

His tone made Kamara say 'sorry', although she was not sure

what she was apologizing for. The tone, too, made her certain that she had lost her opportunity for the job and so she was surprised when he gave her the address and asked if they could meet the following day. He was tall and long-jawed. There was a smooth, almost soothing quality to his speech that she supposed came from his being a lawyer. He interviewed her in the kitchen, leaning against the counter, asking about her references and her life in Nigeria, telling her that Josh was being raised to know both his Jewish and African-American backgrounds, all the while smoothing the silver sticker on the phone that said NO TO GUNS. Kamara wondered where the child's mother was. Perhaps Neil had killed her and stuffed her in a trunk; Kamara had spent the past months watching Court TV and had learned how crazy these Americans were. But the longer she listened to Neil talk, the more certain she was that he could not kill an ant. She sensed a fragility in him, a collection of anxieties. He told her that he was worried that Josh was having a hard time being different from the other children in his school, that Josh might be unhappy, that Josh didn't see enough of him, that Josh was an only child, that Josh would have issues about childhood when he was older, that Josh would be depressed. Halfway through, Kamara wanted to cut him short and ask, 'Why are you worrying about things that have not happened?' She didn't, though, because she was not sure she had the job. And when he did offer her the job—after school until 6.30, twelve dollars an hour paid in cash—she still said nothing because all he seemed to need, desperately need, was her listening and it did not take much to listen.

Neil told her that his discipline method was reason-based. He would never smack Josh because he did not believe in abuse as discipline. 'If you make Josh see why a particular behaviour is wrong, he'll stop it,' Neil said.

Smacking is discipline, Kamara wanted to say, and abuse is a different thing; abuse was the sort of thing Americans she heard about on the news did, putting out cigarettes on their children's skin. But she said what Tobechi had asked her to say—'I feel the same way about smacking. And of course I will only use the discipline method you approve of.'

'Josh has a healthy diet. We do very little high fructose corn syrup and trans fat. I'll write it all out for you.'

'Okay.' She was not sure what the things he had mentioned were. Before she left, she asked, 'What of his mother?'

'Tracy is an artist. She spends a lot of time in the basement for now. She's working on a big thing, a commission. She has a deadline...' His voice trailed off.

'Oh.' Kamara looked at him, puzzled, wondering if there was something distinctly American she was supposed to understand from what he had said, something to explain why the boy's mother was not there.

'Josh isn't allowed in the basement for now, so you can't go down there either. Call me if there are any problems. I have the numbers up on the fridge. Tracy doesn't come up until the evenings. Scooters delivers soup and a sandwich to her every day and she's pretty self-sufficient down there.' Neil paused. 'You have to make sure you don't bother her for anything whatsoever.'

'I have not come here to bother anybody,' Kamara said, a little coldly, because he suddenly seemed to be speaking to her as people spoke to housegirls back in Nigeria. She should not have allowed Tobechi to persuade her into taking this common job of wiping the buttocks of a stranger's child; she should not have listened when he told her that these rich white people on the Main Line did not know what to do with their money. But even as she walked to the train station nursing her scratched dignity, she knew that she had not really needed to be persuaded. She wanted the job, any job; she wanted a reason to leave the apartment every day.

And now three months had passed. Three months of babysitting Josh. Three months of listening to Neil's worries, of carrying out Neil's anxiety-driven instructions, of growing a pitying affection for Neil. Three months of not seeing Tracy. At first Kamara was curious about this woman with long dreadlocks and skin the colour of peanut butter who was barefoot in the wedding photo on the shelf in the den. Kamara wondered if and when Tracy left the basement. Sometimes she heard sounds from down there, a door slamming shut or a brief burst of loud music. She wondered whether Tracy ever saw her child. When she tried to get Josh to talk about his mother, he said, 'Mummy's very busy with her work. She'll get mad if we bother her.' Because he kept his face carefully neutral, she held back from asking him more. She helped him with homework and played cards with him and watched videos with him and told him about the crickets she used to catch as a child and basked in the attentive pleasure with which he listened to her. Tracy's existence became inconsequential, a background reality like the wheezing on the phone line when she called her mother in Nigeria. Until the Monday of last week. Josh was in the bathroom and Kamara was sitting at the kitchen table looking through his homework when she heard a sound behind her. She turned, thinking it was Josh. But Tracy appeared, lithe in leggings and a tight sweater, smiling, squinting, pushing away long dreadlocks from her face with paint-stained fingers. It was a strange moment. Their eyes held and suddenly Kamara wanted to lose weight and wear make-up again. *A fellow woman who has the same thing that you have? Tufia! What kind of foolishness is that?* her friend Chinwe would say if she ever told her. Kamara had been saying this to herself, too, since the Monday of last week. She said this as she stopped eating fried plantains and braided her hair in the Senegalese place in West Philly and began to sift through piles of mascara in the beauty-supply store. Saying it changed nothing because what had happened in the kitchen that afternoon was a flowering of extravagant hope, because what now propelled her life was the thought that Tracy would come upstairs again.

Kamara placed the chicken strips in the oven. Neil added three dollars an hour for the days when he did not come home on time and she cooked Josh's dinner. It amused her, how 'cooking dinner' was made to sound like difficult work when it was really a sanitized string of actions: opening cartons and bags and placing things in the oven and microwave. Neil should have seen the kerosene stove she had used back home with its thick gusts of smoke. The oven beeped. She arranged the chicken strips around the small mound of rice on Josh's plate.

'Josh,' she called. 'Dinner is ready. Would you like ice cream for dessert?'

'Yes.' Josh grinned and she thought about the curve of his lips being exactly like Tracy's. She hit her toe against the edge of the counter and yelped. She had begun to bump into things too often since the Monday of last week.

'Are you okay?' Josh asked.

She rubbed her toe. 'I'm fine.'

'Wait, Kamara.' Josh kneeled down on the floor and kissed her foot. 'There. That'll make it go away.'

She looked down at his little head lowered before her, his hair in helpless curls, and she wanted to hug him very close. 'Thank you, Josh.'

The phone rang. She knew it was Neil.

'Hi, Kamara, is everything okay?'

'Everything is fine.'

'How's Josh? Is he scared about tomorrow? Is he nervous?'

'He's fine. We just finished the practice.'

'Great.' A pause. 'Can I say a quick hi?'

'He's in the bathroom.' Kamara lowered her voice, watching Josh turn off the VCR in the den.

'Okay. I'll see you soon. I just literally pushed my last client out of the office.' He laughed shortly.

'Okay then.' Kamara was about to place the phone down when she realized that Neil was still there.

'Kamara?'

'Yes.'

'I'm a little concerned about tomorrow. I'm not sure how healthy that kind of competition is at his age.'

Kamara ran the tap and rinsed away the last streaks of dark green liquid. 'He'll be fine.'

'I hope going to Zany Brainy takes his mind off the competition for a little while.'

'He'll be fine,' Kamara repeated.

'Would you like to come to Zany Brainy? I'll drop you off at home afterwards.'

Kamara said she would rather go home. She didn't know why she had lied about Josh being in the bathroom; it had slipped out so easily. Before, she would have chatted with Neil and probably gone along with them to Zany Brainy. But she didn't feel like that get-along relationship with Neil any more. She was still holding the phone; it had started to buzz noisily. Neil recently placed a new sticker on the cradle: PROTECT OUR ANGELS. He had brought it back the same day he called, frantic, because he had just seen a photo of a child molester who had recently moved to their neighbourhood and who looked exactly like the UPS delivery man. *Where is Josh? Where is Josh?* Neil asked, as if Josh would have been anywhere else but somewhere in the house. Kamara hung up feeling sorry for him. She had come to understand that American parenting was a juggling of anxieties. It came with having too much food. A sated belly gave Americans time to worry that their child would have a rare disease that they had just read about, made them think they had the right to protect their child from the things that were part of life: disappointment and want and failure. A sated belly gave Americans the luxury of praising themselves for being good parents, as if caring for one's child were the exception rather than the rule. It used to amuse Kamara, watching women on television talk about how much they loved their children, what sacrifices they made for them. Now, it annoyed her. Now that her periods insisted on coming month after month, she resented those manicured women with their effortlessly conceived babies and their breezy expressions like 'healthy parenting'.

She put the phone down and tugged at the black sticker to see how easily it would come off. When Neil interviewed her for the job, the NO TO GUNS sticker had been silver and it was the first thing she told Tobechi about, how strange it was to watch Neil smooth it over and over again, as if in a ritual. But Tobechi was not interested in the sticker. He asked her about the house, details she could not possibly know. Was it a colonial? How old was it? And all the while his eyes were shining with watery dreams. 'We will live in a house like that one day in Ardmore, too, or another place on the Main Line,' he said.

She said nothing because it was not where they lived that mattered to her, it was what they had become.

They met in university in Nsukka, both of them in their final year, he in engineering and she in political science. He was quiet, bookish, smallish, the kind of boy parents said had 'bright prospects'. But what drew her was the way he looked at her with awed eyes that made her like herself. After a month, she moved into his room in the Boys' Quarters on a tree-lined avenue of the campus and they went everywhere together, climbing on the same *okada*, she lodged between him and the motorcyclist. They took bucket baths together in the bathroom with slimy walls. They cooked on his little stove outside. His friends began to call him 'woman wrapper' and he smiled, as if they did not know what they were missing. The wedding, shortly after they completed their National Youth Service, was hurried because an uncle had just offered to help Tobechi get an American visa by including his name in a group going on business. America was about hard work, they both knew, and one would make it if one was prepared to work hard. Two years and Tobechi would get a green card and send for her. But two years passed, then four, and she was in Enugu teaching in a secondary school and doing a part-time master's programme and attending the christenings of friends' children, while Tobechi was driving a taxi in Philadelphia for a Nigerian man who cheated all his drivers because none of them had papers. Another year passed. Her aunties' whisperings became louder and louder. What is that boy waiting for? If he cannot organize his papers he should let us know, because a woman's time passes quickly! When Tobechi called, she heard the strain in his voice. He could not send as much money as he wanted to because he had finally managed to find a black American woman to do a green-card marriage but she was giving trouble, asking for more money, threatening to report him to immigration, to not turn up for the green-card interview. Kamara consoled him. She held on to hope. Once, only once, she gave in to the principal of the secondary school, who promoted her to a level-2 salary after she lay on a hotel-room bed while he panted above her. And then the day finally came: Tobechi called to say his green card was on the table in front of him and that it was not even green.

Kamara would always remember the air-conditioned staleness of Philadelphia airport. She was still holding her passport in her hand, slightly folded on the page that had the visitors visa with Tobechi's name as sponsor, when she came out at Arrivals and there he was, lighter-skinned, chubby, laughing. It had been six years. They clung to each other. In the car, he told her that his divorce from the Black American woman was already done, that they would marry in an American court and he would file for her green card. Back in his apartment, he took off his shoes and she looked at his toes, dark against the milk-coloured linoleum of the kitchen floor, and noticed that they had sprouted hair. She did not remember his toes with hair. She stared at him as he spoke, his Igbo interspersed with English that had an ungainly American accent: *Amah go* for *I will go.* He had not spoken like that on the phone. Or had he and she had not noticed? Was it simply that seeing him was different and that it was the Tobechi of university that she had expected to find? He excavated memories and aired them, rejoiced in them: do you remember the night we bought *suya* in the rain? She remembered. She remembered that they had eaten the grilled meat wet and that it had been so peppery their noses ran. She remembered everything they had done together. She remembered, too, how their relationship had been filled with an effortless ease. Now, even their silences were awkward. She told herself that it would get better, that they had been apart a long time. In bed, she felt nothing except the rubbery friction of skin against skin. He had never been so eager, so theatrical, in the past; it was as if he wanted to impress himself. Most worrying of all was that he had begun to talk and in that false accent that made her want to slap his face. *I wanna fuck you. I'm gonna fuck you.* She closed her eyes and longed to become pregnant because if that did not shake her out of her dismay at least it would give her something to care about. The first weekend he took her out to see Philadelphia, they walked up and down Old City until she was exhausted and he asked her to sit on a bench and wait while he went and bought her some pretzels, so she could try an American snack. And as he walked back towards her in his slightly-baggy jeans and a T-shirt, the sun behind him, she thought for a moment that he was somebody she did not know at all. The second weekend, they went to a courthouse to exchange vows in front of an impatient-looking woman. Now, they were married in America. He had filed for her green card. She would go to nursing school when it came through because Americans did not care for foreign degrees and there was little she could do with her Masters in Local Government Administration anyway.

Most of all, nurses made good money. While she waited for a work permit, she paced the apartment and watched TV. She ate everything in the fridge, even spoonfuls of margarine when there was no bread. Her clothes pinched her waist and armpits, and so she took to walking around with only her *abada* wrapper tied loosely around her and knotted under her arm. She was finally with Tobechi in America, finally with her good kind man, and the feeling was that of flatness. When she talked to her mother on the phone, she said everything was fine. 'We will hear the patter of little feet soon,' her mother said, and she said, '*Ise!*' to show that she seconded the blessing. It was only Chinwe she felt she could really talk to. Chinwe was the friend who had never told her she was foolish to wait for Tobechi, and if she told Chinwe how she did not like her bed but did not want to get up from it in the morning, Chinwe would understand her bewilderment. She called Chinwe and Chinwe began to cry after the first hello and *kedu*. Another woman was pregnant for Chinwe's husband and he was going to pay her bride price because Chinwe had two daughters and the woman came from a family of many sons. Kamara pacified Chinwe and then hung up without saying a word about her new life; she could not complain about not having shoes when the person she was talking to had no legs.

Tobechi was now a manager at Burger King and he came back from work every day, smiling and bearing a little gift: the latest *Essence* magazine, Maltina from the African store, a chocolate bar. She was not sure if he pretended not to notice the greyness that clouded her days, the fact that hard things had slipped in between them, or if he really did not notice. Either way, his hopefulness saddened her. When he said, as he often did, that the wait would not be much longer before she started school, she wondered why he could not see that it had little to do with school. On the Monday of last week, though, he *had* noticed the change in her.

'You're bright today, Kam,' he said as he hugged her. He sounded happy that she was bright. She was both thrilled and sorry, for having this knowledge she could not share with him, for suddenly believing again in ways that had nothing to do with him. She could not tell him how Tracy had come upstairs to the kitchen and how surprised she had been, because she had given up wondering what kind of mother this was.

'Hi, Kamara,' Tracy said, coming towards her. 'I'm Tracy.' Her voice was deep and her body was curvy and her sweater and hands were paint-stained.

'Oh, hello,' Kamara said, smiling. 'Nice to finally meet you, Tracy.'

Kamara held out a hand but Tracy came close and touched her chin. 'Did you ever wear braces?'

'Braces?'

'Yes.'

'No, no.'

'You have the most beautiful teeth.'

Tracy's hand was still on her chin, slightly tilting her head up, and

Kamara felt, first, like an adored little girl and then like a bride. She smiled again. She felt extremely aware of her body, of Tracy's eyes, of the space between them being so small, so very small.

'Have you ever been an artist's model?' Tracy asked.

'No...no.'

Josh came into the kitchen and rushed to Tracy, his face lit up. 'Mummy!' Tracy hugged him and kissed him and ruffled his hair.

'Have you finished your work, Mummy?' He clung to her hand.

'Not yet, honey.' She seemed to be familiar with the kitchen. Kamara had expected that she would not know where the glasses were kept, how to operate the water filter. 'I'm stuck, so I thought I'd come upstairs for a bit.' She was smoothing Josh's hair. She turned to Kamara. 'It's stuck right here in my throat, you know?'

'Yes,' Kamara said, although she did not know. Tracy was looking right into her eyes in a way that made Kamara's tongue feel inordinately heavy.

'Neil says you have a master's degree,' Tracy said.

'Yes.'

'That's wonderful. I hated college and couldn't wait to graduate!' She laughed. Kamara laughed. Josh laughed. Tracy rifled through the mail on the table, picked up one envelope and tore it open and placed it back. Kamara and Josh watched her in silence. Then she turned. 'Okay, I guess I better get back to work. See you guys later.'

'Why don't you show Josh what you're working on?' Kamara asked, because she could not bear the thought of Tracy leaving.

Tracy seemed taken aback by the suggestion for a moment, then she looked down at Josh. 'Want to see it, buddy?'

'Yeah!'

In the basement, the wide painting leaned against the wall.

'It's pretty,' Josh said. 'Right, Kamara?'

It looked like haphazard splashes of bright paint to her. 'Yes. It's nice.'

She was more curious about the basement itself, where Tracy practically lived, the crumpled couch and cluttered tables and coffee-stained cups. Tracy was playing with Josh and Josh was laughing. Tracy turned to her. 'Sorry it's such a mess in here.'

'No, it's fine.' She wanted to offer to clean up for Tracy, anything to remain here.

'Neil says you've only just moved here? I'd love to hear about Nigeria. I was in Ghana a couple of years ago.'

'Oh.' Kamara sucked in her belly. 'Did you like Ghana?'

'Very much. The motherland informs all of my work.' Tracy was tickling Josh but her eyes were steady on Kamara. 'Are you Yoruba?'

'No. Igbo.'

'What does Kamara mean? Am I saying it right? Ka-mara?'

'Yes. It's from Kamarachizuoroanyi: May God's Grace be Sufficient for Us.'

'It's beautiful, it's like music. Kamara, Kamara, Kamara.'

Kamara imagined Tracy saying that again, this time in her ear, in a whisper. *Kamara, Kamara, Kamara*, she would say while their bodies swayed to the music of her name. Josh was running and Tracy ran after him; they came close to Kamara. Tracy stopped. 'Do you like this job, Kamara?'

'Yes.' Kamara was surprised. 'Josh is a very good boy.'

Tracy nodded. She reached out and, again, lightly touched Kamara's face. Her eyes gleamed in the light from the halogen lamps. She smelled of paint.

'Would you take your clothes off for me?' she asked in a tone as soft as a breath, so soft Kamara was not sure she had heard correctly. 'I'd paint you. But it wouldn't look much like you.'

'Oh. I don't know,' Kamara said.

'Think about it,' Tracy said, before she turned to Josh and told him she had to get back to work.

'Time for your juiced spinach, Josh,' Kamara said, and went upstairs with Josh, wishing she had said something bolder, wishing Tracy would come upstairs again. That night she dreamed that Neil drowned in the bathtub; instead of water, it was green juiced spinach that Neil spluttered in until he was silent.

Neil had only just begun letting Josh have chocolate sprinkles again, after a new book claimed his sugar-free sweetener was carcinogenic, and so Josh was eating his dessert of sugar-free organic vanilla ice cream dotted with chocolate sprinkles when the garage door opened. Neil was wearing a sleek dark suit. He placed his leather bag down on the counter, said hi to Kamara and then swooped down on Josh. 'Hello, bud!'

'Hi, Daddy.' Josh kissed him and laughed when Neil nuzzled his neck.

'How did your reading practice with Kamara go?'

'Good.'

'Are you nervous, bud? You'll do great, I bet you'll win. But it doesn't matter if you don't because you're still a winner for Daddy. Are you all set for Zany Brainy? It should be fun. Chum the Cheeseball's first visit!'

'Yes.' Josh pushed his plate aside and started to look through his school bag.

'I'll look at your school stuff later,' Neil said.

'I'm looking for my shoelaces. I took them off in the playground.' Josh brought out a piece of paper from his bag. His dirt-encrusted shoelaces were tangled on it and he pulled the laces apart. 'Oh, look! Remember the special family Shabbat cards my class was working on, Dad?'

'Is that it?'

'Yes!' Josh held the crayon-coloured paper up, moving it this way and that. In his precociously well-formed hand were the words: *Kamara, I'm glad we are family, Shabbat Shalom.*

'I forgot to give it to you last Friday, Kamara. So I'll have to wait till tomorrow to give it to you, okay?' Josh said.

'Okay, Josh,' Kamara said. She was rinsing out his plate for the dishwasher.

Neil took the card from Josh. 'You know, Josh,' he said, giving the card back, 'it's very sweet of you to give this to Kamara but Kamara is your nanny and your friend, and this was for family.'

'Miss Leah said I could.'

Neil looked at Kamara, as if seeking support, but Kamara looked away and focused on opening the dishwasher.

'Can we go, Dad?' Josh asked.

'Sure.'

Before they left, Kamara said, 'Good luck tomorrow, Josh.'

Kamara watched them drive off in Neil's Jaguar. Her feet itched to go down the stairs, to knock on Tracy's door and offer something: coffee, a glass of water, a sandwich, herself. In the bathroom, she patted her newly braided hair, touched up her lipgloss and mascara and started down the stairs that led to the basement. She stopped many times and went back. Finally, she rushed down the stairs and knocked on the door. She knocked again and again.

Tracy opened it. 'I thought you'd gone,' she said. She was wearing a faded T-shirt and paint-streaked jeans.

'No.' Kamara felt awkward. *Why haven't you come up since the Monday of last week? Why have your eyes not lit up at seeing me?* 'Neil and Josh just left for Zany Brainy. I'm keeping my fingers crossed for Josh tomorrow.'

'Yes.' Tracy sounded vague. There was something about her that Kamara feared was an irritated impatience.

'I'm sure Josh will win,' Kamara said.

'He just might.'

Tracy seemed to be moving back, as if about to shut the door.

'Do you need anything?' Kamara asked.

Slowly, Tracy smiled. She moved closer to Kamara, too close, her face against Kamara's. 'You *will* take your clothes off for me,' she said.

'Yes.' Kamara kept her belly sucked in until Tracy said, 'Good. But not today. Today isn't a good day,' and disappeared into the room.

Even before Kamara looked at Josh the next afternoon, she knew he hadn't won. He was sitting in front of a plate of cookies, drinking a glass of milk. Neil was standing beside him. A pretty blonde woman wearing ill-fitting jeans was standing in front of the fridge, looking at the photographs of Josh posted on it.

'Hi, Kamara. We just got back,' Neil said. 'Josh was fantastic. He really deserved to win. He was clearly the kid who had worked the hardest.'

Kamara ruffled Josh's hair. 'Hello, Joshy.'

'Hi, Kamara,' Josh said, and stuffed a cookie into his mouth.

'This is Maren,' Neil said. 'She's Josh's French teacher.'

The woman said hi and shook Kamara's hand and then went into the den. The sides of her face were stained with blush and her lips were a cheery red and she was nothing like Kamara imagined a French teacher would be.

'The Read-a-Thon ate into their lesson time so I thought they might have it here and Maren was sweet enough to say yes. It's okay, Kamara?' Neil asked.

'Of course.' She liked Neil for making her feel that she mattered.

She liked the way the blinds sliced up the sunlight coming into the kitchen. She liked that the French teacher was here because when the lesson started, she would go down and ask Tracy if it was the right time to take off her clothes. She was wearing her new lacy bra.

'I'm worried,' Neil said. 'I think I'm consoling him with a sugar overload. He's had two lollipops. Plus we stopped at Baskin-Robbins.' Neil was whispering although Josh could hear. It was the same unnecessarily hushed tone that Neil had used to tell her about the books he'd donated to Josh's Pre-K class at Temple Beth Hillel, books about Ethiopian Jews complete with pictures of people with skin the colour of burnished earth but Josh said the teacher had never read them to the class. Kamara remembered the way Neil had grasped her hand gratefully after she'd said, 'Josh will be fine,' as if all Neil needed was to have somebody say that.

Now, Kamara said, 'He'll get over it.'

Neil nodded slowly. 'I don't know.'

She reached out and squeezed Neil's hand. She felt filled with a generosity of spirit.

'Thanks, Kamara.' Neil paused. 'I better go. I have clients lined up and I'll be late today. Is it okay if you make dinner?'

'Of course.' Kamara smiled again.

Then they heard the footsteps coming up from the basement. Kamara's excitement brought a dull throbbing to her temples. Tracy appeared in her leggings and her paint-stained shirt. She hugged and kissed Josh. 'Hey, you are my winner, buddy, my special winner.'

Kamara was pleased that she did not kiss Neil, that they behaved like brother and sister.

'Hey, Kamara,' Tracy said, and Kamara told herself that the reason Tracy seemed normal, not absolutely delighted to see her, was because she did not want Neil to know.

Tracy opened the fridge and took an apple. 'I'm so stuck. So stuck,' she said.

'It'll be fine,' Neil murmured, and then, raising his voice so that Maren, in the den, would hear, he added, 'You haven't met Maren, have you?'

Neil introduced them. Maren extended her hand and Tracy took it.

'Are you wearing contacts?' Tracy asked.

'Contacts? No.'

'You have the most unusual eyes. Violet.' Tracy's eyes were steady on Maren's face.

'Oh, thank you!' Maren giggled nervously.

'They really are violet. Real violet.'

'Oh...yes, I think so.' More giggles.

'Have you ever been an artist's model?'

'Oh no...'

Maren was gushing, staring at Tracy. Neil was looking on with an indulgent smile and Kamara realized that he had seen this many times before; so many times that he knew how meaningless it all was. She sat down next to Josh and took a cookie from his plate.   □

GRANTA

IDA AND LOUISE

Louise Carpenter

Ida and Louise Cook with tickets to the opera, 1926

1.

Money has overtaken and refurbished Morella Road, Wandsworth, just as it has overtaken many other ordinary streets in London. There is nothing exceptional about the architecture. The houses of Morella Road are bay-windowed Victorian terraces, fundamentally plain but with plasterwork and little spires added to give a French Gothic touch. London has a thousand brick-built streets like this and for most of the twentieth century they symbolized respectable middle-class living. Now such a house might cost close to £2 million—'now' being early 2007, when London house prices were rising on average at £7,000 to £11,000 a month. Audis, Mercedes and BMWs are parked in the street and the front doors are painted in the kinds of shades that suggest the householder has made a prolonged study of the colour charts. Among this evidence of wealth and fashion, it isn't easy to imagine how things once were: how the woodwork would have been sober dark green or black, how brokers' clerks and civil servants in bowler hats would have walked down the path each morning towards the railway station or the tram stop and come home again to plates of boiled root vegetables and cheap cuts of meat. An era of monochrome virtues: plain food, careful accounting, social deference, suppressed emotions, good manners—when nobody wanted to excite the interest of their neighbours, when it was best not to be extraordinary.

The sisters Ida and Louise Cook lived at number 24 Morella Road for more than sixty years of the twentieth century, from shortly after the First World War ended until the very last years of the Cold War. In many ways—though not all—they defy the generalizations of social history: they were extraordinary. One morning in March this year I took a train to Wandsworth, walked to where they had lived and looked up at the window of the highest room—the second floor, under the eaves—which had for several decades been Ida's study. So much romancing and typing had happened in this small workshop of make-believe. It was here that Ida had sat in front of her manual typewriter and clattered out her letters to opera singers, her magazine pieces, her romantic novels, and her and her sister's autobiography. But what I thought of when I looked up at the window was something else that had been composed there: an unpublished manuscript by Ida called 'Some Psychic Experiences', written in the 1960s, when Ida and Louise had fallen under the influence of a spiritualist, Leslie Flint. Flint, a former cemetery gardener and occasional gravedigger, had become a celebrity medium by specializing in a method known as 'direct voice'. Through seances held in Flint's large and gloomy drawing room in Paddington, many voices had come to the sisters, mostly those of the old opera stars who were their lifetime obsession; but only one had ever made them cry. When the sisters came back from that particular seance, Ida climbed up the stairs to her study and wrote up her account:

> I suppose the most moving—and the most utterly unexpected—of all was one day when several people had already spoken and suddenly, out of the air, very clearly and distinctly though with a marked German accent, a woman's voice said, 'You may think it very strange that I should come and speak to you because you do not know me. But there are many people here you do not know who love you very much.'
>
> Surprised and touched, we thanked her, and she went on, 'My name is Anna. I was—killed—in Dachau.'
>
> 'Were you, dear?' we whispered.
>
> Then she hurried on, 'But I have long ago put behind me all that terrible time.' She went on to say that she had heard how we had tried to help some of her people, and now she wanted to thank us—which she did, in the simplest and most moving terms. At the end she evidently found it a little difficult to hold the line, because she finished, 'Well—I don't know—I meant to say so many important things but—I love you. Auf wiedersehn.'
>
> Understandably, Louise and I—and Leslie too—were reduced to tears.

A voice from the Holocaust (though the sisters never knew those events by that term), relayed to two elderly English spinsters by the suspicious means of a gravedigger turned communicator-with-the-World-Beyond in a London room with the curtains drawn. To disbelieve it gets us nowhere. The point is that the Cook sisters did believe it. They were moved. In lives which swung dizzyingly between the purest fantasy and the utterly real they had every reason to be.

My interest in the Cook sisters began after a friend gave me a copy of Ida's long out of print memoir, *We Followed Our Stars*, published in 1950, which among other things tells the story of how she and Louise, plain and anonymous in their tatty cardigans and Woolworth glass beads, became among the most effective British transporters of Jews out of Germany between 1937 and the outbreak of war. During those years the sisters made numerous quick trips to Nazi Germany, avoiding the suspicion of German border officials by taking flights from Croydon and returning via Holland and ship to Harwich. It isn't clear how many Jews they saved—the record speaks of 'twenty-nine cases', but many cases were families rather than individuals so the number may have fifty, sixty, or more.

This considerable humane achievement takes up just over a quarter of a book that is mainly devoted to chronicling their love of opera, or to be more exact their star-struck worship of its singing stars. They had such small interest in what might be called the 'real', these two women best characterized by their sisterly devotion, their belief in the spirit world, and their long escape into the confectionery of the operatic stage and the romantic 'woman's' novel. Why and how did they become involved in the dangerous and expensive business of rescuing several dozen of Hitler's potential victims? This was the question the sisters had managed to avoid answering with any degree of satisfying honesty or self-knowledge throughout their lives. 'I don't care for all this modern emphasis on hidden motives,' Ida Cook told a reporter for the American magazine *McCall's* in 1966. 'There's altogether too much of this psychoanalysis. After all, what you are is what you do, isn't it?'

2.

Louise Cook, christened Mary Louise after her mother, was born on June 19, 1901, in the coal mining and shipbuilding town of Sunderland. Three years later, on August 24, 1904, Ida arrived. According to their mother's later account, when Ida appeared her father had cried, 'Good Lord, isn't she ugly!', proving that powers of observation are not always blunted by paternal devotion. But the three-year-old Louise thought the infant heaven itself. She clung to her as if she were her own, and when their nurse insisted on taking the child out for some air, Louise threw herself at the foot of the stairs in hysterics, fearing her sister lost forever. Their mother was a practical woman full of common sense. She soon began to instil these values in her four children—the sisters had two younger brothers, Jim and Bill. Kisses and cuddles were rare, but so were floods of tears and sulks. The one fanciful aspect to Mrs Cook's character was her belief in ghosts and spirits, a preoccupation which, as we have seen, she would pass on to her daughters. Their father, James Cook, was a hard-working officer for Customs and Excise. When he married Mary Brown, he and she found in each other all they needed and aspired to no more.

When Ida was two and Louise was five, the family moved to the London suburb of Barnes, near Wandsworth, and then in 1912 back north to Alnwick in Northumberland, where the girls were enrolled in The Duchess School, founded by the Duchess of Northumberland a hundred years before and housed in Alnwick Castle's old dower house. It was an enchanting place for girls like Ida and Louise, whose gazes were then directed firmly at all that had gone before rather than all that was to come. The dynamic of Ida and Louise's relationship was formed during these years. Ida was the more gregarious child, Louise the more reflective and discerning, the less emotional, the natural intellectual. Louise, the family joked, liked nothing more than settling into an armchair with Dante's *Inferno* or her Latin grammar, while Ida was inclined to entertain the room with her chatter. Train a telescope on them and the temptation is to think of Ida as the leader of the two, but the truth of their relationship is that neither could act without recourse to the other. By the time they became young women, they were essentially two halves of a whole. Looking only to each other and the goodness of their parents—at teatime Mr Cook liked to give his children lectures on morality—they continued to exist in the kind of domestic emotional security that infants feel, or are ideally supposed to feel, in the presence of their mother. As a result, they provided each other with a confidence that ruled out self-doubt. 'Two girls can often do what one on her own cannot,' was how Ida put it in *We Followed Our Stars*.

Their looks may have reinforced their mutual protectiveness. By 1919, when the family moved back to London and the house in Morella Road, it was clear that neither would be a beauty. Each had a high forehead and a large nose and lips. Ida had one or two teeth protruding at odd angles, heavy eyes brows and hair frizzed about her ears. Louise was always the prettier of the two, although false teeth eventually brought Ida some improvement. In London, they needed to work. Louise went into the Civil Service as a clerical assistant in the Board of Education, earning £2 6s a week (top marks in Latin in the entrance exams) and Ida followed her a year or two later as a copy typist. They were now independent young metropolitan women in an age which was breaking free from an older morality, and yet they craved none of its excitements. Young men were of course in short supply, thanks to the slaughter of the First World War, but the sisters didn't even make an effort in that direction. They didn't dance the charleston, they didn't drink or smoke. Instead they came home every night to their twin-bedded room in Morella Road, perfectly content in their own company.

Other than the routine sounds of conversation and household chores—the filling of baths, the crackling of bacon—the house existed in perfect unmusical silence. There was no radio, no gramophone, no piano. Ida and Louise had had no musical education and harboured no musical ambition: they neither sang nor played. So when, one day in 1923, the melody of 'Un bel di vedremo' from Puccini's *Madame Butterfly*, sung by the coloratura soprano Amelita Galli-Curci, flooded their bedroom it was an entirely new and profound sensory experience. This was Louise's doing. One afternoon at the Board of Education she had wandered into a music lecture given by the Welsh composer and organist Sir Walford Davies and came home that night 'slightly dazed'. Enlisting Ida to her enthusiasm, she spent a recent bonus by putting down a deposit on a £23 hand-cranked gramophone and the ten classical records that went with it: music by Bach and Gluck as well as the voice of Galli-Curci.

Soon after, while Ida was away as a bridesmaid at a northern wedding, Louise went into the gallery at the Royal Opera House, Covent Garden, to hear *Madame Butterfly*. She went back with Ida to hear for the first time *Tosca*, *La Traviata* and *Rigoletto*, always from the gallery's cheapest seats. They began to see prima donnas as heroines—people to love and live for—and marked their places in the Covent Garden queue by hiring collapsible stools from people then called 'the stool men', which were placed outside the theatre during the day while they typed away steadily in Whitehall.

They stood patiently outside stage doors, hoping for a glimpse, an autograph or (they had a small camera by then) a picture.

One episode that reveals a spirit that was to serve them well in the future was the extent to which they took their devotion to the voice of Galli-Curci. Having heard her perform a platform concert in the Albert Hall—her first British appearance—and learning the crushing news that she sang in opera only in New York, Ida became determined that within the next five years they should travel there to hear her. Would Louise come? 'Rather!' she cried. They wrote to Galli-Curci outlining their plans and she replied by return of post: 'If you ever succeed in coming to America you shall have tickets for everything I sing.' Calculating that they needed £100 for the entire trip, they then spent two years of penury during which they ate only brown rolls, bought no new clothes or sweets, and never once took a bus if they could walk. If ever they were overwhelmed by hunger, they would study a Rand McNally guide to New York to remind them of their goal: 'We knew what we wanted and we held on to our purpose,' Ida wrote in a magazine produced by and for civil servants called *Red Tape*. 'Fortunately, we have always realized the futility of grumbling enviously about someone else's salary—it only makes you overlook what can be done with your own.'

In December 1926, they sailed third class on the *Berengaria* and rented a room in a hotel in Washington Square West, where, on arrival, they unpacked their trunks and laid out their opera outfits: scarlet for Louise, pink and silver for Ida, opera cloaks for both, all of which Ida had run up from patterns published in *Mab's Fashions*, a magazine read mostly by typists and edited by Miss Florence Taft. They then put on their smart little moleskin hats and went to the offices of Galli-Curci's agent to pick up their free tickets. The next night, they went to the Met for the first time to hear Galli-Curci sing *La Traviata*. 'We were two of the best-dressed people in the Opera House!!!' Ida writes in a letter home. 'People quite goggled at our cloaks... other people had diamonds and bare backs and all that sort of thing, but, with all due modesty, our get-ups looked so pretty and young and colourful—besides, they had the Mab's touch!!!'

During the encore, Galli-Curci picked them out in the audience and waved, a gesture they interpreted as 'truly romantic'. An invitation to her Fifth Avenue apartment followed, with a Cadillac to pick them up. Their letters home to their parents ('Mop' and 'Pop') are filled with a childish euphoria: 'Oh Rapture! Rapture! Rapture! [Galli-Curci] is more than we expected.' 'Isn't she a little duck?' they asked Mop in a later letter, by which time they had

Ida and Louise off to America, 1926

become the Italian soprano's new best friends. In her Fifth Avenue apartment, they curled up on her library sofa for chats about 'anything from Mozart's chamber music to reincarnation'.

For Ida and Louise, this first trip to New York revealed many things: that there was life beyond Morella Road and the Civil Service; that their profound faith in their own will was justified; that sublime music could belong to them just as much as it did to the ladies they had seen at the Met, bare-backed and adorned in diamonds; and that through their devotion to this high art, they could pursue and befriend their 'stars'. In 1929, they fell heavily for the American soprano Rosa Ponselle on her debut at Covent Garden singing *Norma*. Ponselle had started her career as a vaudeville act with her sister, singing between films in cinemas, until at Caruso's suggestion the Met hired her for the role of Leonora in Verdi's *La Forza del Destino*. The beauty of her voice became a talisman for them, the embodiment of all that was good about life. 'It's Ponselle weather today,' they'd say when it was sunny; in bleaker times they would comfort each other with the thought that there was 'always Rosa'.

The third serious contender for their affections was the Austrian conductor Clemens Krauss, director of the Vienna Staatsoper until he moved to the Berlin Staatsoper in 1935—a move which led to his appearance before a de-Nazification committee after the war. They saw him first in 1934, when he conducted his wife, the Romanian soprano Viorica Ursuleac, in Richard Strauss's new opera *Arabella* at Covent Garden. Then that summer they followed him to Salzburg. Dollfuss, the Austrian Chancellor, had just been murdered and Jews were leaving Germany in increasing numbers, but Ida and Louise had no intention of missing the festival. A letter home from Ida:

> I rather gather that the English newspapers are still being very alarming, but it's all my eye really... Occasionally about twenty-five soldiers stroll along in the sun grinning a bit sheepishly and not keeping very good time, but that is the sum total of the military manoeuvres here!

Krauss was much more interesting. 'He's the most perfect poseur I've ever seen and gets away with it so marvellously that you can only gasp with amused admiration,' Ida wrote home in August 1934.

Before he does do any slipping away, he strikes a match and leans forward to light a cigar with every bit of his disgustingly good looks marvellously illuminated. The match is permitted to burn itself out—and then (and only then) off he goes in the car amidst the gasps of gallery rapture. It's quite perfect.

Letters, some of them twelve pages long, are given over to Krauss and Ursuleac's relationship, and are signed off 'Yours in a state of fizzle'. They sent red roses to Ursuleac's dressing room and one afternoon they followed the couple 'with a skill…of which Sherlock himself might have approved' back to their hotel on the outskirts of town. Later that year they stalked him in Amsterdam, where the beginnings of an unlikely friendship with his wife were forged after they were invited to her dressing room. 'I think she doesn't quite know what to make of us,' Ida wrote home. 'She thinks we're darlings evidently ("intelligent women!") but beyond that she's a bit at sea!'

Like Galli-Curci, Ursuleac became smitten with the two sisters, impressed by their scholarly knowledge of her art and touched by their adoration. Throughout the remainder of the week, Ida and Louise began attending her dress rehearsals, where they noticed for the first time that they had a female rival, a distinguished-looking old lady whom they had seen once or twice with the couple in Salzburg. As their Dutch trip neared its end, the old lady was introduced to them backstage as Frau Mitia Mayer-Lismann, the official lecturer of the Salzburg Festival against whom, they remembered, they had been initially prejudiced on account of her double-barrelled name. That night, having obtained permission to see Ursuleac on to her train, Ida and Louise found Frau Mayer-Lismann on the platform. Ursuleac took them by the arm. Would they please, please look after Frau Mayer-Lismann when she came on a short trip to London? They promised they would. 'Now you will be all right,' the soprano assured Frau Mayer-Lismann.

'We remembered that scene again and again in the years that followed,' Ida recalled in We Followed Our Stars, 'for, though we did not know it then, our first refugee had been commanded to our care.'

Back in London, Ida and Louise took the Mayer-Lismanns sightseeing. In Westminster Abbey, Frau Mayer-Lismann asked the sisters if it were a Protestant or Catholic church. The same question arose in St Paul's. 'Are you a Protestant?' Ida asked her. 'I? I am Jewish,' the old lady told them. 'Didn't you know?' They did not, nor, until then, what it had come to mean. Gradually, over the week, the Mayer-Lismanns explained the consequences of Hitler's rule. Ida writes of their growing awareness in *We Followed Our Stars*:

> We began to see things more clearly and to see them, to our lasting benefit, through the eyes of an ordinary devoted family like ourselves. This was one of the most heaven-sent things that ever happened to us. By the time the full horror of what was happening in Germany, and later in Austria, reached the newspapers, the whole thing had become almost too fantastic for the ordinary mind to take in. It took a war to make people understand what was happening in peace time, and to tell the truth, very many never understood it. But our understanding of the problem grew quite naturally... To us, the case of the Mayer-Lismanns was curious and shocking, but not incredible. We were shocked, but we did what I suppose most people would have done. We asked, 'Where did they hope to go? What had they to offer in the work markets of the world? and, finally, what could we do to help?' It was all what I can only describe as un-urgent to us in those days.

By the sisters' own admission, once the Mayer-Lismanns had returned to Germany, concern over their 'affairs' was eclipsed by the opera season.

3.

By now, Ida was no longer a civil servant. Ever since the 1926 trip to see Galli-Curci, she had kept in touch with Miss Taft at *Mab's Fashions*, supplying the occasional article on such subjects as country life in Northumberland and 'at home' with Galli-Curci in the Catskills. Ida did not take herself seriously as a writer: writing was a way to help to fund the sisters' operatic trips in Europe. Then, in 1932, Miss Taft offered Ida a job as a sub-editor. Ida refused ('I'm in the Civil Service,' she protested, 'and so are my father and my sister. There's the pension...') but Miss Taft persisted and eventually Ida made the short journey from the law courts, where she had been working as a typist, to the office of *Mab's Fashions* in Fleet Street.

There she began to write short stories as well as edit. In 1935 the sisters were flat broke—'our appetite for foreign travel was beginning to grow alarmingly'—so when Miss Taft suggested that Ida attempt a serial for *Mab's*, Ida agreed, her mind running only on the high fees commanded by the most successful writers.

Miss Taft requested 'something strong'. Ida wrote three chapters. Miss Taft read them and changed her mind. She wanted 'sweet' instead. Ida fought her ground and won. The completed serial, *Wife to Christopher*, had a violent marital rape and was anything but sweet. Christopher, the hero, is tricked into marrying Vicki by her beauty. The rape is presented as the 'collection' of her debt to him: 'I'm going to collect what you sold, Vicki,' he tells her. 'And I'm not at all sure that it won't be rather sweet doing it.'

Christopher showers kisses on Vicki's angry, bruised mouth as the whiteness of her skin shows through the lace of her nightdress; he swings her off her feet, knocking the lamp over so that there is darkness; and then...she wakes up in 'sweet ecstasy', with the realization that 'if he came with something of the terror of an avenger, he came with the glory of a lover, too'.

'The terror of an avenger'? 'The glory of a lover'? Where was Ida getting this stuff? From the opera, perhaps? From her own sublimated desires? But Miss Taft knew exactly where to place such a book. She got in touch with Mr Charles Boon, the joint partner of the publishing house Mills & Boon. The imprint, then as now, was a byword for romantic fiction, so much so that the words 'Mills & Boon' came to recommend books to readers rather than the names of their individual authors. Less well known is their indirect role in financing the small operation that saved a few dozen people from death in the camps of Germany and Poland.

Boon, 'the original wideboy' according to one of his descendants, founded the company in 1908 with Gerald Mills, the son of prosperous Midlands glass-factory owners. Early authors visiting its gentlemanly offices near Fitzroy Square included P. G. Wodehouse, E. F. Benson, Jack London and Hugh Walpole. Its original success was built largely on Jack London's backlist and a series of textbooks penned by retired schoolmasters. In the Twenties, it was almost bankrupt before Boon took firm control and concentrated the list on what became known through their distinctive branding as 'the books in brown'. These

Louise Carpenter

hardback romances were a particular favourite of commercial lending libraries and corner shops. In Boon's view, their success depended on each novelist following a 'format' while at the same time writing with absolute sincerity. The heroes needed to be at least 5 feet 9 inches tall, physically strong and moody. Heroines should never have sex outside or before marriage, or, if they did, required to be punished in some way. Strong, even violent bedroom scenes were permitted to enhance a book's 'passion', but only if those involved were married.

Boon read Ida's manuscript, found it a perfect fit for his formula and bought it immediately. Ida got £40 for *Wife of Christopher* with royalties running at ten per cent thereafter. The book was a success and a few months later, in November 1936, Boon asked her to provide three longer novels of around 70,000 words each, with advances rising from £50 to £100. The following February, she signed a third contract, this time for four novels. Ida, writing under the name Mary Burchell, was about to become among the most lucrative and prolific of the Mills & Boon stable of novelists (another nineteen of them, all young women, published their first Mills & Boon novels that same year). Including her first, Ida wrote 129 novels over the next fifty years, many of them in her study at Morella Road, above the bedroom where she and Louise slept chastely each night. 'I am I think by nature a tale-spinner, and passionately interested in people,' she said later by way of explaining her success. 'The thing that I found I was capable of doing was romancing—rather strongly for my period.'

The money was good. By the late 1930s Ida was earning close to £1,000 a year from her books, about four or five times a typist's salary in the Civil Service, and she gave up her job at *Mab's*. But her unexpected good fortune did nothing to change the dynamic between her and Louise. Ida had been clear from the start that her money was *their* money and so they would regularly stroll around London 'discussing the extraordinary phenomenon' as if it were a heaven-sent miracle rather than the product of days and nights at the typewriter. They spent thousands in their imagination: cars; fur coats; trips to Europe; trips to America; Louise's possible retirement from the Civil Service. Then, at the moment of temptation, they found themselves thrown on a different course. 'Fortunately (oh how fortunately!),' Ida wrote in *We Followed Our Stars*, 'before I had any chance to alter my way of living...the full horror of what was happening in Europe finally, and for all time, came home to us.'

The sisters had kept in touch with Frau Mayer-Lismann, who was planning to leave Frankfurt for good. Only now did they start to understand the implications of the Nuremberg Laws as well as the practical difficulties and official obstinacy that German Jews faced when they sought refuge abroad. Britain saw itself mainly as a country of transit for Jewish refugees, and as a result most entrants needed to have prospects of re-emigration. (The United States, by contrast, admitted perhaps three times as many. By 1945, only 60,000 Jewish immigrants from the pre-war years remained in Britain.) Admission to Britain became tighter still when Austria was annexed in March 1938 and a complicated visa procedure clogged up government systems and led to dangerous delays.

The restrictions, as Ida and Louise learned them, were these. A refugee child could be brought over provided a British citizen would adopt her until the age of eighteen. A woman could enter on a domestic permit provided there was enough evidence that she had a job and that job had been advertised. Men between eighteen and sixty were accepted only if they had documentary proof that they were going on to another destination. In most cases, this meant proof of a quota number in the queue waiting to go to America, with the wait stretching from six months to two years. Such cases were accepted into Britain only if a British citizen would assume financial responsibility for them, from the moment they landed in Britain until they reached the final country of adoption. A searching guarantee was required and for men over sixty it had to be for life. The Refugee Committee dealt only in cases where the paperwork was complete.

By now, Ida's income from her romances was showing a steady rise. She became 'intoxicated' by the sight of her money and 'the terrible, moving and overwhelming thought—I could save life with it.'

4.

Would Ida and Louise have begun their refugee work had they not loved opera and its performers? I doubt it. Opera mattered to them above everything, and in the beginning they were responding directly to requests for help from people they so dearly admired, in particular Krauss, Ursuleac and Mitia Mayer-Lismann. Ida's income meant they could provide financial guarantees. Their willingness to help bound

top, Ida and Louise with Maria Callas, 1954;
left, Louise and Ezio Pinzo at the Salzburg Festival, 1934;
right, with Amelita Galli-Curci, 1934.

them closely to the Krausses and their world in a way that was more profound and rewarding—and equal—than as fans hobnobbing with them backstage. To say that a closer relationship with Krauss and Ursuleac may even have been an important incentive to their work doesn't diminish their achievement. As Ida wrote, Krauss and Ursuleac 'sugared that ghastly pill—with both their matchless performances and their dear friendship'.

And so it was, in the beginning, that the Mayer-Lismanns and Krauss and Ursuleac supplied them with the names of Jewish friends, mostly musical and intellectual, who wanted to leave Germany. A routine emerged. Because Louise still worked at the Civil Service, travel was largely confined to weekends. Every two or three months, she would cover her typewriter on a Friday evening and hurry from Whitehall to Croydon airport, where Ida would be waiting. They would be in Cologne by 9.30 p.m. and then catch the Munich train, alighting at Frankfurt. On Saturday they would meet their contacts and make arrangements. On Sunday they would take the train to the Hook of Holland and catch the overnight ferry to Harwich—a different route home to avoid the frontier police becoming too familiar with them. On Monday both would be back typing at their respective desks.

Their first case for which they had obtained the necessary financial guarantee and relevant paperwork was Mitia's daughter, Else, a seventeen-year-old music student. She later recalled (to the Recorded Vocal Arts Society in 1987) the moment she saw Ida and Louise get off the train:

> It was very exciting to meet them at the Bahnhoff in Frankfurt... my dollish hat was nothing in comparison with the hats of the Cook girls... the entrance of the Cook girls into our lives was revolutionary, because we never ever, ever realized or knew that anybody like Ida and Louise existed. They were so unique...they were never depressed...[their] attitude to life has been something which is an enrichment...it was an extraordinary experience.

Else Mayer-Lismann was the first refugee to make use of a flat in Dolphin Square, on the Embankment, which Ida had recently taken on to serve as 'a clearing house' for those they brought over to Britain. It was relatively modest, only big enough for one family at a time, but the windows were of a good proportion and it was filled with light. And with Ida and Louise still continuing to live at Morella Road with their parents, it provided an excellent headquarters and temporary accommodation (Ida and Louise would keep it until Ida's death).

Word began to spread in Jewish communities of the sisters' willingness to help, and their circle of contacts widened to include people in Berlin and Munich as well as Frankfurt. Hundreds of letters from strangers begging for help began arriving at the British Refugee Headquarters addressed simply to 'Ida and Louise'. The sisters felt an increasing sense of urgency to do their duty, and subterfuge and cunning now began to play a part in their trips. They learned, for example, that in order to persuade others—friends and family, and towards the end, strangers—to provide a financial guarantee they had to convince them that they wouldn't necessarily end up spending the money. Refugees couldn't leave Germany with their money or possessions. On the other hand, they could convert some of their cash into exportable goods, which the sisters could then carry across the border without alerting too much suspicion. Jewellery, especially diamonds and pearls, was one obvious export—tiny things which in Britain could be easily converted back to cash. Faced with Ida and Louise's resolute ordinariness, which customs official would imagine that the pearls and diamond brooches fastened to their chain-store, glass-buttoned jumpers were anything other than paste? (The only jewels they could not accept were diamond earrings; neither sister had pierced ears.) They left their own wristwatches behind and returned with the best Swiss models on their wrists. A cleverer dodge came with the fur trade. In the winter months they would travel out with labels from fashionable London stores, tucked safely in the bottom of their handbags, and relabel and then wear the German furs that their contacts had given them for export.

As for their cover, Ida and Louise had from the beginning decided that they would pose—though posing required no effort—as two eccentric opera lovers who were prepared to travel all over Germany for their art. Still, the frequency of their trips began to attract attention at the immigration post at Cologne aerodrome. At first they had been waved through, but now they met unfriendly questioning. A better cover was needed and here their hero, Clemens Krauss, stepped into the breach.

The sisters' relationship with Krauss during this time is an interesting one to contemplate. What did they make of him? In Blythe House, the archive of the V&A, which encompasses the Theatre Museum, there exist nineteen boxes of material spanning the course of the sisters' lives. Most of it comprises opera and theatre programmes, photographs of stars and letters, but it also includes cuttings they kept from newspapers published in March 1935, just before Krauss transferred from the Vienna Staatsoper to succeed Furtwängler in Berlin. They suggest that Ida and Louise should certainly have understood that Krauss's move laid him open to the charge of Nazi sympathies. One report clipped and kept by the sisters, headlined FIGHT IN VIENNA OPERA HOUSE, writes of 'the scene of unusual demonstration' during a performance of Verdi's *Falstaff*. As Krauss approached the conductor's rostrum he was met with loud cries of 'Shame!' and hisses from Austrian government supporters, while other sections of the opera house—the Nazis—cheered him on. By the interval, police with truncheons were breaking up a fight. In another story, published the following day, it was reported that Krauss had pulled out of the performance that evening, as had his friend, the leading tenor, Herr Franz Volker, and that a Tchaikovsky opera had to be hastily substituted for the 'Egyptian Heles'. Three days later, he was installed in the Berlin Opera House.

It was two years before he could prove conclusively to the sisters that he was not a Nazi. In 1937, hearing of Ida and Louise's worry about the border guards, and by now having got himself out of Berlin and transferred to Munich, he offered to use his position and influence at the Munich State Opera to ease their reception at the border. Whenever they needed a trip 'covered', he told them, he would supply them with details of all opera performances and their casts lists so that they might improve their credentials at immigration control. Whenever possible, he added, Ida and Louise could also choose the programme. That way, in fulfilling their mission, they could be rewarded with one of their favourite operas. 'Sometimes we thought we could not bear to go back yet again into that hateful, diseased German atmosphere,' Ida wrote in *We Followed Our Stars*. 'And for that extra bit of courage and determination which took us back time after time, Clemens Krauss and...Ursuleac must take full credit.' Following Krauss's death in 1954, Ida wrote:

[The decision to transfer from Vienna to Berlin] was wrong, of course—tactically, and perhaps humanly too. But, although his enemies would have us forget the fact, Berlin at the time was still an open capital city, like any other European city, for the purposes of political, social or artistic matters. I think I can say now after twenty years of close friendship with him...that Krauss bitterly regretted that decision very soon after it was taken. But to retrace the step was impossible and, in making what he could of a situation which revolted him, he threw himself, with single-mindedness characteristic of him, into serving the art he loved, even in the midst of horror... it was only with his active and unfailing help that we managed to bring twenty-nine people out of Hitler's Germany.

To show they had nothing to hide, they began to stay in the finest hotels precisely because they were packed with high-ranking Nazis. 'We knew them all—Louise and I,' Ida writes in *We Followed Our Stars*:

Goering, Goebbels, Himmler, Streicher, Ribbentrop (who once gave Louise 'the glad eye' across the breakfast room at the Vier Jahreszeiten in Munich). We even knew Hitler from the back... If you stood and gazed at them admiringly as they went through the lobby, no one thought you were anything but another couple of admiring fools.

The contrasts and adventure in their lives are almost too novelistic. They arrive, say, in Berlin after a shaky plane journey from Croydon. They reach a house and there, in front of an anxious Jewish family, pick up a couple of furs, rip out their labels and replace them with those brought from London. Later, befurred, they stride into the foyer of the Adlon, Goebbels and Himmler in the crowd. The next day they interview would-be Jewish refugees before heading off for a night at the opera—one which, if performed under Krauss, might have been scheduled entirely for their benefit. They return the next day by train and steamer. On Monday morning, Louise goes straight to her Civil Service desk. Ida makes her way to the bank vaults to deposit a diamond or two. Amazing; but it wasn't Ida's kind of novel. Hers would always favour love over unhappiness, often expressed in grand gestures or fluttering hands, and complicated by emotional indecision rather than any of the real inconveniences of life, but resolved—always—with a happy ending. ('As Mary stepped out on to the terrace she saw that he was standing there in the moonlight, like a figure on a stage, and he held out his arms to her. Without even pausing to think what she was doing or what this might imply, she ran straight into his arms. And as he held her and kissed her she made only a fugitive clutch at her vanishing common sense'—*Unbidden Melody*, 1973.)

What happened to Ida and what she invented for money (which allowed things to happen to her and to others): those were separate compartments. In *We Followed Our Stars*, she writes:

> I marvel now when I think of how we lived in a state of high drama part of the time, and continued our normal lives during the rest of the time. I wrote novels and Louise worked at the office. We had holidays. We had our recurring opera seasons. We had our family interests and our hobbies, particularly our gramophone records, which were a great consolation to us between opera seasons.

Louise learned German and in Frankfurt the sisters began to work with a German agent, Frau Jack, a Roman Catholic who had assumed responsibility for collating lists of potential families to be interviewed by them in a room in her house in Arndtstrasse. The sisters, the families saw, possessed the power and the funds, thanks to Ida's income from Mills & Boon and contributions from friends and family, to offer them a way out. 'We weren't playing God,' Ida told *McCall's* in 1966:

> It was more like gambling at Monte Carlo. I still shudder when I think about it. The Jew who had a practical skill—an electrician or an engineer—sometimes made it ahead of the intellectual. The one who had converted all his material assets into diamonds or what-have-you and was able to demonstrate to his English guarantor that he would not become a dependent on him had it over the man and his wife who were still clinging—as though furniture were a part of life itself—to their bedsteads and family portraits.

On November 10 and 11, 1938, Hitler gave the order that throughout Germany, Austria and Czechoslovakia all Jewish males were to be rounded up and sent to concentration camps. Certain age

groups were released but only on condition that they signed an
undertaking to be out of the country within eight weeks, taking little
money and only a tiny proportion of their goods. A month later Mitia
Mayer-Lismann, now safe in Britain, handed Ida and Louise a list of
names and addresses with the words 'God bless you and help you'
scribbled in violet ink along the top. Among the names was that of
Lisa Basch, an aspiring twenty-five-year-old photographer whose
industrialist father had been taken to Dachau (he was later released
on the condition that he left Germany immediately).

Louise couldn't leave her job on this occasion, so Ida went alone
to the Basch family home, a large Gothic mansion in Offenbach near
Frankfurt. Its contents were in ruins: the SS had stormed through the
house when they arrested Herr Basch, ripping paintings, breaking
mirrors, shattering every piece of china, and tearing out the keys of
the grand piano. The remnants of the Basch family remained; two
sons were already in the United States and a daughter and son-in-
law getting ready to follow. Basch and his wife were waiting to leave
for France, where a business associate had provided a guarantee. That
left Lisa as the only Basch with no exit, the only one without a
guarantee. Ida interviewed her that day and later raised a guarantee.
Lisa eventually left Germany in April 1939 for England via Paris.

That was not their last case, but by the spring of 1939 they were
no longer so stolid in the face of fear and desperation. Days spent
at Frau Jack's were long and traumatic; the sisters hated the fact that
they could not help all whom they saw. They would go back to their
hotel room to hold each other and sob. Late on August 24, 1939,
Ida's thirty-fifth birthday, the telephone rang at Morella Road. It was
Frau Jack: 'Ida, there is one more. A young man and his wife. Is it
possible? They have only one more week.' It wasn't possible. The
war came ten days later.

5.

Who remembers them? I found Jim Cook, Ida and Louise's surviving
brother, living alone in a small bungalow in a cul-de-sac in Epsom,
Surrey. He was in his nineties, frail, and not long out of convalescence
in a nursing home. He led me to the front bedroom facing on to the
small patch of lawn. 'Everything comes down to the last one,' he said,
and we looked around a room that smelled fusty from lack of use.

It housed what he'd inherited of his sisters' legacy, mostly records of their old operatic favourites such as Ponselle, the photographs and programmes having been boxed up and shipped to Blythe House years before. I asked him to describe his sisters' characters and he replied, 'My sisters did not have the normal likes and dislikes. They had very strong views about many things—they thought it was a great pity, for example, when women began wearing trousers, and they would often take against singers.' He paused. 'They wanted the world to be the way they wanted it to be, and if it wasn't, they'd invent it.'

He pointed to an old suitcase, which he had somehow managed to lift on to one of the beds. It was now open and revealed two large piles of paperwork. 'Things filter down,' he said, before shuffling out and leaving me alone. I began to unpack it. It smelled peculiar, heavier than the room. I saw among the tenancy agreements and wills and the odd contract from Mills & Boon a few newspaper clippings: *New York Times*, Wednesday March 24, 1965: SISTERS HAILED FOR RESCUING JEWS — 2 BRITISH SPINSTERS THANKED BY ISRAEL FOR SLIPPING 29 OUT OF NAZI GERMANY. EXPLOITS OUT OF JAMES BOND, read another headline, above the text: 'They were just naïve, warm-hearted women and they got away with it. They just didn't look the type.'

We had sandwiches for lunch, which we ate in the sitting room using trays on our knees. I asked Jim if he thought his sisters had ever understood the reality of what they were doing in Germany. My hunch was that they had known exactly. Ida and Louise might have looked like rather ineffectual spinsters, but as early as 1926, when they had got themselves to New York, they had understood entirely the power of their own will. 'My sisters had no real desire to talk about what they had done, no desire at all,' Jim said. 'It's often what the English don't want to talk about...' I thought he was going to say 'that matters' but he didn't finish the sentence. Then he added, 'My sisters were very Anglo-Saxon.'

I'd found Ida's address book in the suitcase. It contained an intriguing collection of names, including many that I recognized from *We Followed Our Stars* as people they had rescued. Jim was sure they were all dead, but I thought it possible that some might be still alive. He let me borrow the address book and at home I began slowly working through it, phoning the British numbers first. None of them worked. When I came to Lisa Basch of 640 W153rd Street, New

York, I dialled the number expecting the same disappointing tone of number unobtainable. But the number rang and somebody picked up. The voice was female, shaky and East Coast, but there was no mistaking the fact that it had come of age in Germany.

6.

Ida and Louise felt something similar just after the war when they 'found' Rosa Ponselle. The Second World War had the opposite effect on the sisters to that of its impact in most of the population of Europe. Tension and excitement were drained from their lives. 'The horizons had shrunk to the limits of ordinary life,' Ida wrote. The war robbed them of six years' worth of adventure and opera and created in Ida a temporary creative block, untimely given that the conflict had created a stronger demand for romance than ever before. Worse, they were separated for the first time, considered by both to be a harsher fate than bombing. Louise moved with her office to Wales for two unbearable years, while Ida remained in London, working as a full-time warden in a Bermondsey air-raid shelter. During the rare weekends they spent together, they would repeat as a mantra, 'There's always Rosa,' and, after the war, they found there was.

Their post-war quest to find Rosa Ponselle was their attempt to capture the romance of the past. Although they had never managed to befriend her, she had become a kind of challenging symbol—like an unattained peak—by which they lived. Then Ida wrote a letter addressed simply to 'Rosa Ponselle, Baltimore, USA'. It found its destination and by January 4, 1947, twenty years to the day since they had first walked along Fifth Avenue on their way to hear Galli-Curci, they returned to America, this time to visit their heroine Ponselle, who had retired from the Met's stage in 1937 after singing there for nearly twenty years, a career that established her among the century's greatest singers. They themselves began to be moderately well known. They joined the Adoption Committee for Aid to Displaced Persons (later renamed Lifeline), with a special interest in non-German refugees in Germany, who numbered many Poles brought there for slave labour. They raised funds for daily supplies of fresh milk to children under six and for the treatment of tuberculosis sufferers, travelling backwards and forwards to a camp in Bavaria, getting to know their 'cases' just as they had done until September 1939.

Spiritually, at least, they ensured that their life continued to be about change, never acceptance. 'There is never a complete answer to anything that stems from man's inhumanity to man,' Ida wrote in *We Followed Our Stars*, 'so one always goes on to another facet, though of course as one gets older, it has to be a slightly less active part that one plays.'

With this new connection to human suffering—something Ida had identified, perversely, as lacking for her during the war—her romantic fiction became prolific once more. By 1949, she had published forty-one novels and was featuring strongly in Mills & Boon advertising campaigns: '406,473 copies of Mary Burchell's books have been sold... on average each book is lent 100 times at 3d a time.'

That same year she also found the time to write *We Followed Our Stars*, which was published by Hamish Hamilton in 1950. Set against the backdrop of Ida's increasing fame as Mary Burchell, the book attracted press and broadcast interest. The sisters told their story on a BBC radio show (*A Tale of Two Sisters*) and then in 1956 Ida, 'known to millions as Mary Burchell', was lured into a television studio and made the subject of an early edition of *This is Your Life*. Among the guests waiting to come on stage and shake Ida's hand were Miss Taft, Viorica Ursuleac, Frau Jack and a few refugees the producers had managed to track down who were still living in Britain, among them Walter Stiefel, the last of their refugees to be got out of Berlin. 'My mother and my father and I myself owe our lives to you...' came Stiefel's voice as he waited, invisible to the audience, behind a screen. 'It is impossible for any of us to express adequately our gratitude.'

The ultimate honour came in 1965, when the Yad Vashem Holocaust Memorial Authority in Jerusalem bestowed on them the honour of 'Righteous Among the Nations', an accolade which at the time made them two of only four Britons to be listed alongside Oscar Schindler and others who had saved or sheltered Jews in the face of Nazi persecution. On March 23, they collected their certificate from the Israeli ambassador in London and the following day their photograph appeared in the *New York Times*—a picture of two women who, with their wash-and-set hair and school-mistressy skirt-suits (never trousers), were beginning to betray their roots in a different age; both regretted, for instance, the demise of the hat.

Tastes in romantic fiction changed but 'Mary Burchell' spurned demands for more sex and still wanted her 'girls' to check their hats in the mirror as they left home in the morning. Mills & Boon, aware of her dying readership, now sought to cast her in the role of a figurehead, a grande dame of romantic fiction who could inspire a younger generation (a role helped by her position as President of the Romantic Novelists' Association). As for Louise, she carried on her humble work for the Civil Service and in her spare time sometimes translated libretti for the operas of Richard Strauss.

But opera was not what it was. In 1948 Galli-Curci, who had stopped performing in 1930, told *Time* magazine, 'Music is an art. It's not a yelling business, or a ballyhoo business. It was an art the way we used to do it. Today I'm afraid it's different... The times are hysterical and yell-y.' It was an attitude the sisters shared. Occasionally, theatrical divas such as Maria Callas would emerge to remind Ida and Louise of their earlier adulation of Galli-Curci and Ponselle, but from the 1960s onwards the quality of emerging operatic talent largely disappointed them. Still, their 'gramophone parties', which had begun in the Thirties, continued in the flat at Dolphin Square and attracted an eccentric mixture of guests. Callas might be there: according to Ida, 'a star if ever there was one...the top of the voice was thrilling, the rest not completely in focus'. Or Tito Gobbi: Ida ghosted his autobiography. Or Ponselle, who would participate by a prearranged telephone call, or the English soprano Eva Turner. But among them might be a couple of spinster friends from Essex, Ida's editor at Mills & Boon, her publisher Alan Boon (son of Charles), some office colleagues of Louise. Ida played the leading hostess at these evenings—Louise preferred to sit in a chair rather than circulate—and by then her reputation had established her as a figure of respect and, to some extent, awe: think of Margaret Dumont with the Marx Brothers. The sisters were now regular visitors to New York. After the Yad Vashem award they became minor celebrities on the Upper East Side, where lunches and teas were held in their honour and to raise money for the State of Israel Bonds. And it was around this time that Ida—always mindful of the need to keep the money rolling in—signed up with The Maurice Frost Lecture Agency. Her calling card read 'Ida Cook: Writer; Lecturer; Traveller'. She offered a 'menu' of talks: 'How I Became a Writer;

Round the World in a Month; 'This is Your Life'; Two Against Hitler; People I Have Met; So You Want to be a Writer; Opera and Opera Stars (which can be illustrated with gramophone records for Music Clubs, if the time available is at least one and a half hours)'.

These talks could be seen as Ida's way of reliving her past, but only that past that was inside her as her memory and imagination. Might the past not also have a present? Might it not somehow go on existing externally—somewhere? If so, could it be contacted? Ida and Louise began their first serious experiments with spiritualism by enlisting a well-known clairvoyant, Estelle Roberts, and her spirit guide, Red Cloud, and paying them to come to Morella Road to run a weekly 'Home Circle' comprising the sisters and four of their friends. During these meetings, they would sit in a circle in the dark and pray for protection, guidance and instruction on how to be of service to their fellow men and women. After that came the singing of hymns or, if they were trying for physical phenomena, the playing of tape-recorded music—they found strong musical vibrations helped. A tin megaphone on a wooden box was placed in the centre of their circle, which they reported would often move in time to the music. They would regularly hear a tapping sound on the wooden box, as if a conductor—Krauss perhaps, who died in 1954—were rat-tatting his baton. Often, gramophone records would fly out of glass-fronted cabinets on to the floor, particularly a recording of the aria in Gluck's *Orfeo ed Euridice* in which Amor tells Orpheus that he can bring his wife back from the Underworld.

Back in 1923, the sisters had boasted that following their musical awakening they had managed to 'convert' three or four of the typists in their office. And so it was now, with their new obsession with spiritualism. They enlisted Tito Gobbi to their seances and Krauss's widow, Ursuleac, and even Alan Boon. Who were they searching for? Krauss would be the biggest catch. (A week after he died, Louise reported sighting him in their dining room and the following Sunday, during a recital at the Albert Hall, Ida said she spied him sitting on the platform, one ankle crossed over the other knee, which made Louise cry.) But there was also their youngest brother, Bill, who died in a motorway crash in 1967, and their father and mother, who died in 1959 and 1961 (twenty years after their death, Morella Road was still crowded with their possessions).

Louise Carpenter

In 1969, they switched from Estelle Roberts to Leslie Flint after seeing an advertisement in *Physic News*. His methods were more extreme, his results more startling. He specialized in 'trance mediumship' and 'direct voice', a process during which spirits either speak through the voice box of the medium or give out some form of 'ectoplasm' which enables a voice box to be built in the air. Flint had made a business of his skill. There was his autobiography, *Voices in the Dark*, his international lectures and his celebrity following (after his death in 1994, an educational trust was established). 'I think I can safely say I am the most tested medium this country has ever produced,' he once said. 'I have been boxed up, tied up, sealed up, gagged, bound and held, and still the voices have come to speak their eternal message.' Tapes of them cost £4.99 each: Charlotte Brontë reflecting on the influence of creative people 'on earth'; Maurice Chevalier on his confusion and frustration at passing on; Winston Churchill on science and space travel; Mahatma Gandhi on truth and religion, and Oscar Wilde, who began by saying 'my name caused me a lot of trouble'.

The sisters' first two sessions with Flint drew a blank. At the third, their brother Bill came to them, whispering 'Obah, Obah', his childhood nickname for Louise. Many opera stars followed. Ida and Louise went on visiting Leslie Flint for almost twenty years at some considerable cost. There are, after all, legions of the dead.

7.

Who remembers them? In September, 2006, I flew to New York to meet the voice I'd heard on the telephone: Miss Lisa Basch, now aged ninety-four, found by Ida at Offenbach near Frankfurt and rescued by the sisters in April 1939. I wonder now if I should have gone, if I should have spared the distress that remembering caused her. But on the phone she seemed happy enough, if a little surprised that I'd found her. We spoke many times before our meeting, mostly when a new thought or idea occurred to Miss Basch and she picked up the telephone to tell me about it. I didn't mind. Sometimes she would throw in an intriguing titbit, such as 'Ida was not all she seemed!' or 'There was a dark side which not many people knew about' or 'Ida had a love affair with [the bass] Ezio Pinza.' She warned me that she might be dead by the time I arrived.

Miss Basch said we couldn't meet at her apartment—it was too small, nobody went there—so instead we arranged to meet around the corner from Columbia University in the apartment of my friend, who is a professor of English there. This delighted Miss Basch since she'd worked herself in the university library from 1942 to 1964 and still lived just a few blocks away in Harlem, in a flat that Ida had found for her more than fifty years before, and where she had lived happily alone with just the *New York Times*—'my best boyfriend'—for company.

I wanted to send a cab for her, but she had insisted on the subway. I opened the door to find a tiny, birdlike woman dressed entirely in shades of purple and lilac. She wore an old-fashioned hat, which she was quick to tell me covered up the horrid wig underneath. She was almost blind through macular degeneration and as a result had thick, haphazardly applied make-up. She grabbed my arm and peered up at my face. 'So young! So young!' she cried. 'Look at you. I want to cry!'

We sat down opposite one another and I noticed her purple trousers had two glass butterflies fluttering over a thigh and a shin. She had fallen, she explained. One butterfly covered the hole, the other an ink spot. 'I am very thrifty,' she said. 'My pants cost me a dollar.' And then immediately she told me of her pre-war sexual crush on Clemens Krauss. It was as if Ida and Louise were speaking from the grave. 'I followed his first wife as a young woman. I wanted a little bit of him,' she said. 'Such beautiful lips. When Ida found this out during my interview with her in Frankfurt, she said to me, "You are my girl!" She knew she would help me then.'

This was Miss Basch's story. She was born in 1912 to a family of Viennese intellectuals who had settled in Germany. Her father, the industrialist, was handsome and successful, adored by women, including his daughter, for whom he remained the most important person in her life. He had taken the governess as his mistress, but Frau Basch turned a blind eye. She complained only about the fact that she looked like a charwoman in photographs and that the veins snaking through her hands made jewellery look unsightly. In the years leading up to the war, Mitia Mayer-Lismann had come regularly to Sunday tea or musical soirées in the Baschs' large, oak-panelled library, which their servants would fill with chairs and refreshments while Lisa and her sister would stick pillows up their blouses—'Mitia had a lot of bosom'—and imitate her high voice.

Lisa Basch,1936

'I hear you have this wonderful English lady visit you and she is helping Jewish people get out of Germany and I am all alone now,' Miss Basch told her in 1938, which was when Mitia scribbled down her name in violet ink. Photographs from that time show Miss Basch as a tall, handsome young woman with an athletic, almost boyish build. 'My bedroom was okay and my mother's bedroom was okay, but there was no china to drink from,' she said of the scene Ida found when she arrived. 'I remember asking a neighbour across the street to bring me at least two cups that we could drink coffee from. But then the gas was taken away because one Jewish family had committed suicide in the gas range... we had to buy little bricks of coal.'

When her memory failed, which it sometimes did, Miss Basch would rummage through the shopping bag she'd brought with her, which was never far from her feet. She produced letters and pictures of herself, her parents and her old house. A lot of the time, my questions seemed to go unheard. Miss Basch had very little to say about Louise, and as for Ida, she seemed caught between deep admiration and a mild form of liberal superiority. 'Ida was racist, you know,' she said. 'She didn't like sitting next to negroes on buses.' (In fact, in Ida and Louise's letters home from New York in 1927, I saw that they spoke of the negro bellboys at the hotel with a tone of fascination. It was not racism exactly, but nor was it Miss Basch's educated liberalism.) On the other hand, Ida had been like a mother to her. 'She saved me from the gas chamber,' she said. 'Through her saving me I was never exposed to that later time when those people who couldn't get out became victims... I don't know how we thanked them really. Not sufficiently. Ida once said to me, "You don't owe us anything"... I remember I bought her a pretty bag for the greatness of it all. We didn't have much money afterwards, and that little bit was for daily living. And we had no jewellery. There was only one ring or two and one golden wristwatch that had to be turned in to the Nazis. My mother never wanted jewellery. I have blue veins just like her.'

She stretched out her hands and I bent forward to be nearer to her. 'Don't look at my fingernails,' she cried. 'I can no longer see them. I have to get a pedicure and a manicure! But look, read this letter! Read it.'

It was dated March 26, 1965, nearly thirty years after they first met (they kept in touch until Ida's death), and recounted an extraordinary meal the sisters had enjoyed with Marlene Dietrich, whom they had met through Jinette Spenier, the *directrice* of the fashion house Balmain: 'Darling Basch family,' I read to her, recognizing Ida's hand:

> how sweet of you all to write... we...had the amusing experiencing of meeting Marlene Dietrich... At first one thought 'Oh, she is rather faded by now. Poor Pet.' But as she ate an enormous meal, looking thin as a sprat, meanwhile, lucky thing, and talked and talked, it was as though a light slowly came up inside her and suddenly you thought 'Why, it is the fabulous Dietrich,' and I see why. She is a terrific one for holding the floor and although I don't expect you to believe me, even I couldn't get a word in edgeways.

Miss Basch chuckled as I read this bit and it dawned on me that she was entirely unsentimental about the oddity of Ida and Louise's lives. 'But these spirits who spoke to them!' she said at one point. 'It worries me that anybody can be so odd and strange... I kept my mouth shut. I had no words. I thought it ridiculous, absolutely ridiculous. Only a psychiatrist could perhaps understand it.'

'I was always driving them anywhere they wanted,' she told me of her friendship with them when they visited New York. 'I was like a chauffeur. I was completely at their service. Wherever they had to go, whomever they wanted to visit, I drove them there. Ida always said to me, "You don't have to repay anything," but I wanted to. I was so grateful. I loved her really, and if it hadn't been for her...' She paused. 'The Jewish business occupied Ida very much and she loved to have me round as a representative of what she had done. I guess people got sick and tired of seeing me... and I always presented her with the best chocolate candy, truffles with chocolate cream inside...'

I tried to picture clever Miss Basch strolling about the Upper East Side with Ida and Louise after the war, biting her tongue as they went on about the spirits they'd recently raised. Or piling them into the back of her Chevy for the long drive to Maryland to see Rosa Ponselle. It seemed the unlikeliest friendship. Ida and Louise were staunch and illiberal conservatives—Ida once said of pre-marital sex, 'what you mean is fornication. If you don't know the word, look it up in the Bible—and the penalties'—while Miss Basch had spent her adult life under the intellectual sway of leftist academics. She had also fallen in love. 'I wasn't a lesbian, nothing of that kind of thing,' she said, perhaps sensing that I had wondered. 'I had lots of boyfriends, gee whiz...' Men had been real for Miss Basch and they had not been the dark heroes Ida had conjured. As she told me about them all—the music critic in Prague; the married man in Capri; the ski instructor with whom her mother had warned she'd have nothing to talk about when the snow melted; the car mechanic who looked like Robert Redford but who turned out to be gay—the gulf between her and the sisters seemed wider than the Atlantic.

Also she had been for eight years an alcoholic. She knocked back bottles of sherry, port and wine, making herself sick, forgetting where she had parked the Chevy. Once she missed a date with the sisters, who were visiting New York on an opera trip, because she was at home vomiting. She told them the truth. They had been rather disgusted at the loss of control, and had not wanted to discuss it further—frightened, perhaps, by the unhappiness and confusion it hinted at. 'I think I made a mess of my life,' she said suddenly. 'I consider myself a Greek tragedy. I didn't live the life I should have done. I didn't travel, see more of the world. All I can do is regret. I look at travelogues, I go to travel offices and look at the countries on paper, only I know photographically some of these travelogues and illustrations are wrong because the sky isn't as blue and the lake isn't as blue and the Danube isn't as blue.'

We can book a trip for you tomorrow, I told her. She shook her head. 'I don't know where I would even want to go,' she said. She repeated the sentence three times. After she left, I was hit by the overwhelmingly sad but obvious thought that Ida and Louise's act of salvation in 1939 had not guaranteed happiness thereafter. Life had happened instead, in Miss Basch's case a complicated tangle of love affairs, alcohol and regrets.

We met again the next day. I had a question that went back to something Jim Cook had told me. Did she think Ida and Louise avoided confronting aspects of life that didn't fit with their own vision of how it should be? The question gave her an opening to tell me what had been on her mind all night. She had been up since 7.45 a.m. trying to make sense of it, she said, trying to remember the sequence of events properly. 'What happened to me when I left Germany,' she said, 'I don't know if I could have ever told Ida that. They asked me questions in

Cologne and then they examined me vaginally. The German frontier people, they said they were looking for diamonds and pearls in my vagina, and whether I was exporting them. I kept thinking to myself after they led me into a little room and were examining me, "Had I said I was visiting Ida? Had she said she was coming to see me at any point? Had she had to give my name to them?" In hindsight, I suppose they just kept tracks. I can't prove anything but I'd never heard of another woman being examined like that.'

Had she told the sisters this? Miss Basch began to cry. 'I never cry, I never cry,' she said. 'I don't think I could have told anybody... Did I wear already pants or just a skirt? What can a woman put in her vagina? People who have had children have wider vaginas but I was a single woman.'

As I tried to understand what she was saying, she said, 'You are making my brain very painful to think about these things, like fingers intertwined. I am embarrassed I am not a better help to you. Why am I so confused and upset?'

We decided we should go for a walk and for some lunch and she quickly perked up again. She was back on fighting form in the diner. She insisted on washing her cutlery in clean water brought to the table. 'I know what they do back in those kitchens,' she said. She ate well, which pleased me. Afterwards, we strolled around the block and she pointed to a building. 'I bumped straight into Eisenhower there,' she said. 'His face was pink just like a salmon!'

8.

Three days before Christmas 1986, Ida died of cancer in Parkside Hospital, Wimbledon, and was later cremated at Putney Vale. Only a year before she had negotiated a generous arrangement with her publisher, Alan Boon, which helped secure Louise's old age. But would Louise cope without Ida? She decided to sell Morella Road and move into another flat in Dolphin Square—not the one which Ida had used for their parties and latterly as a place to write. She missed her sister very much and felt her presence in the early hours of each morning. In May 1987, she sought the obvious solution and went to see Leslie Flint. A tape recording still exists of that seance.

Ida: 'I love you, I'm very close, I shall never be far...' [there is some crackling and whispering] 'I am just waiting for the time eventually when you join us but you have got a little longer to go yet, I'm afraid...'

Louise: 'O darling! O darling, is that you? O darling...'

Ida: 'I love you. I want you to be happy. I want you to be patient with yourself. You have to take things as they come. I'll come again! I'll come again.'

Louise: 'Oh, it's wonderful! It's wonderful!'

Ida then came to her with a question about the sale of Morella Road: 'What about the attic?...You haven't got everything out.'

Louise, falteringly: 'Most things are out... I thought it had been cleared. Perhaps not quite.'

Ida: 'No, not quite everything... Have you made up your mind what you are going to do or perhaps it is too early?'

Louise: 'Oh yes, it is difficult to look through them. I don't often go to the house, you see.'

As well as Ida's fiction, the second-floor attic rooms of Morella Road had stored a box of correspondence from before the war. The letters, sometimes with photographs, were from the many families who asked for their help. They were not neatly filed and had not been looked at since 1939; some of them were reminders of all those families the sisters had not been able to save. 'They are packed away,' Ida explained in We Followed Our Stars, 'because, tragic though they are, I cannot bring myself to destroy those pages out of history.'

Louise threw the contents of the box on to a fire soon after. Every best-selling book that Ida ever wrote also disappeared, either given away to charity or burned, so that by the time their brother Jim handed over the keys to the new owners there seemed to be very little left to tell their story. Nobody can be sure of the reasons why. A long life of private jealousy? The torment of grief? More likely that the death of one sister amounted in the survivor's mind to the death of two.

Louise finally died on March 27, 1991, in Westminster Hospital, from septicaemia. They were in one sense or other together again. In 1966 Ida had told McCall's magazine: 'Many women of our generation made the choice of dignified spinsterhood rather than marry someone uncongenial. Perhaps Louise and I felt a bit regretful, but I don't remember that we suffered.'

They had lived for art. ☐

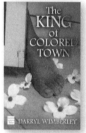

SCAN
Helen Simpson

Helen Simpson

She was deep in London clay, a hundred feet underground, the train having paused for a rest just short of Baker Street. In the darkness outside was visible the enfolding curve of the tunnel and also, at a distance, a gleam of yellow, a worm with lampy eyes making its way in another direction altogether. There came into her mind wartime images of burrows and shelters, the leaf-encircled entrance to a green lane; landlocked landscapes with no sky or sea, no people bar the odd melancholy dreamer like her reflection in the window. The urge to hide was what powered so many children's books of that time, escaping into wardrobes or living under the floorboards; the hobbit in his cosy bunker; midnight gardens silvered with nostalgia, clocks transfixed so that time stood still. Since last week's diagnosis she had herself fallen out of time.

Perhaps this was what it was like, being born, the claustrophobic tunnel; you were being squeezed by the passage walls themselves, you were being pressed on centimetre by centimetre, with no inkling of the future but that far gleam of light. What about before you were born, though; before you were conceived? Well, you can't remember it so it can't have been too bad, she told herself; presumably it will be the same after you've died. The trouble with this idea was, before you've been born you've not been you; but once you've been alive you definitely *have* been you; and the idea of the extinction of the you that has definitely existed is quite different from the idea of your non-existence before you did exist. Why were they stuck here? Had the train broken down?

She peered through the window and was able to make out thick cables running along the walls of the tunnel, regions of ribbed felty dust. When you're dead, surely you don't know you're dead. That would be too horrible. That would be a contradiction in terms. No, it would be like when you passed out; there was no memory of *that* afterwards.

She'd started collapsing, blacking out, which was why she was now on her way for another test. 'Let's take a look inside that head of yours.' They wanted to see whether it had spread.

Now when she woke up in the morning the old unconscious happiness only lasted a few seconds before she remembered and thought, 'I wish this hadn't happened.' But it had. There was an Anglo-Saxon word that meant 'terror in the morning'. *Morgencolla,* that was it: *morgencolla*. You'd wake just as it was getting light, and see death coming up the river, the men with axes poised to leap out of their longboats and set fire to your home and disembowel you.

There came a whir, a whirring grumble, then a tense high-pitched hum and a rhythmic chunk-a-chunk vibration. Come on, she thought, come on or I'll be late. She glanced at her watch. There was a lurch, then nothing; another lurch, and they were inching towards the platform. It's all right, she thought once the doors had opened, it's all right, I'm not late yet, and she hurried with the others along tiled tunnels and up flights of sliding stairs.

Outside, on Baker Street, there were three lanes of traffic under a veil of fine-needled rain. A tall beaky sad-faced boy in deerstalker and tweed cape from fifteen decades ago stood handing out leaflets to a general lack of interest. She took one and glanced at the sketch of Sherlock Holmes peering through his magnifying glass, the great detective on the trail of Moriarty. Past the shops selling bears in beefeater outfits she hurried, past the tourists struggling with maps and collapsible umbrellas, then turned right at a church courtyard where cherry trees were loaded with sodden blossom, foolishly pink against the downcast sky. Another short cut and she was into the windy wastes of Harley Street with its heavy one-way traffic. She checked the number of the place where she was to have this scan, and saw how near it was. She wouldn't be late after all. A family dressed in full-length black stood weeping on its steps, their robes flapping in the wind. She averted her eyes and made her way inside.

Here, everybody was brightly lit, neutral and flat-faced. Thirty-four. Single. No children. Journalist. Yes, her employers provided private health insurance. MasterCard. The girl didn't look up once.

She paused at the mouth of the waiting room as if it were the entrance to the cave of suffering. Instinctively she knew about what went on in there, the long waits, disappointments, apparent improvements and the ugly reversals. She grabbed a magazine from the central table and stared at it. How to get the body you always wanted.

So it was her fault, then, what had happened. She hadn't been trying hard enough. In the absence of trouble she had imagined herself to be well, but now it seemed health was something that must be worked at; it must be courted with blueberries and pedometers and other expensive tokens of love. You had to be constantly on the qui vive for signs of betrayal or you were a fool. I thought I *was* my body, or at least friends with it, she observed; but obviously not. 'No truly happy person grows a teratoma,' said the reiki healer she had consulted in her initial alarm. 'Have you allowed yourself to be angry in your life?' *Angry?*

It was tempting to turn the blame inwards, but it wouldn't do. 'Am I responsible for the filth in the air I breathe?' she railed silently. 'Is the arrival of electrosmog my fault? My workplace is now an official Wi-Fi hotspot where we're all gently microwaving our internal organs, Bluetoothed radiation nibbling away at the blood–brain barrier. Maybe *that's* why I'm here, that bit further along the electromagnetic corridor, waiting for an exposure of my insides, and the promise of gamma rays next week.' She was allowing herself to be angry now, certainly.

In the mirror of the changing cubicle her flesh looked denatured beneath the shadowless halogen light. Remove all jewellery. Once naked she realized she was still wearing her watch, and unstrapped it. She was outside time now, along with the sick and the dead.

Last of all she shed her earrings, the starfish studs he had bought her in Brighton. Mr X was how he was known at work—her new mystery man. She placed them carefully in one of her shoes. It was a definite farewell. She hadn't known him long enough to claim his company on such an unlooked-for journey. 'This has all been very sudden,' she murmured, which was what you used to say when someone asked you to marry them. It wasn't just him, she hadn't told anybody yet; she needed to get used to the idea.

He might have enjoyed this unseemly hospital gown under other circumstances, open at the back, inadequately secured with tapes. Never mind seeing her with no clothes on; she was about to be seen with no flesh on. The medical gaze was nothing if not penetrating.

They were after pictures of the inside of her imploding head. She lay down in the white gown on the motorized bed and inch by inch was drawn inside. The inexorable gliding pomposity of it reminded her of something, but she couldn't immediately think of what.

What was it? she wondered as she lay stiff and still in the viewless tunnel. Oh, of course, she thought as it came to her, it was the coffin's slow glide to curtains hiding the fire. This noise was very loud, the same as the walloping grumble and whine of the underground this morning but magnified tenfold. Someone had used the phrase 'in case of claustrophobia' when they were explaining about the process and now she realized why: the tunnel wall was six inches above her forehead.

So there would be twenty minutes of this, and she was still in the first. Her mind began leaping around all over the place. Keep calm. Think of something else. She'd been ignoring his texts and emails and the flashing answerphone. She felt pulled towards him but she must push him away; she couldn't face him but she wanted him. In her dream last night she'd been immune to traffic jams, high on a velvety camel swaying down St Martin's Lane. It would be good if all this *was* just a dream, if in a little while she might wake up out of it, and stretch, and shrug it off.

It wouldn't work, she wouldn't be able to play at being a corpse for another eighteen minutes if she didn't get a grip. Time was getting stuck again, like the train in the tunnel. Time equals distance over speed. Time was supposed to slow down as it approached a black hole; the gravitational pull was so strong there that even light couldn't escape. A black hole was a star which had collapsed in on itself. She would have to harness her mind, put blinkers on, for the duration; otherwise she'd moan and groan and spoil the scan. Think of some careful time-consuming process, spin it out. Risotto, that would do.

She took an onion, hard and sound in its papery brown coat, and slit off its tight coat, sliced it in half. This loud grinding and thumping was like being deep in the bowels of a ship, down in the engine room with the men in boilersuits.

Narrowing her eyes against the tear-producing fumes, she cut the onion halves into fine layered crescents, then turned each half and diced the slices into lozenges. Think it through, she told herself, if you really can't stop thinking about what's happening. Magnetism is measured in gauss and tesla. Concentrate. Remember how it works. A fridge magnet has a pull of about 100 gauss, or 0.01 tesla. This machine has a magnetic field of one tesla, or 10,000 gauss.

Once she could smell the oil heating she used the blade of the knife to send her diced onion over the edge of the chopping board and into the pan. There was a small sizzle and she turned the flame down. People would look uncomfortable or upset and say, anything they could do, and treat her like a trip to the dentist.

So when the onions were soft and see-through, she'd add the rice.

Flesh itself had become see-through thanks to the X-ray, whose discovery at the turn of the last century had whipped the press into a state of lubricious excitement. Not only could you see up her skirt, leered the papers, but with this machine you could now see *all the way*.

Push the enamelled grains round with a wooden spoon, oiling them all over, introducing them to the onions. So here she was lying in a powerful magnetic field and next they would unloose a flood of high-frequency radio waves on to the scene. At this, all the water in her body—about seventy per cent of her—would rise up. The hydrogen nuclei within her myriad water molecules would respond in a dance, aligning themselves into patterns which a computer would transform into images of whatever monster it was that was crouching in there.

Add some stock, then wait until it's absorbed; add some more and stir again. The tesla is the unit of magnetic flux density. The becquerel is the unit for measuring radioactivity. Death is a black camel that lies down at every door. Watch it, it mustn't catch.

Surely it must be nearly over now. The noise was getting louder. Don't be tempted to rush it. The noise changed, the motorized bed started to move backwards, and she opened her eyes. She thought, 'My luck has run out.'

'All right there, are you?' said the nurse as she came out of the tunnel.

'Fine,' she smiled, breathing again, yawning, rubbing her face with her hands to revive the blood flow. She couldn't wait to get away from the machinery and the credit-card swipe, the stale swagged grandeur of the reception area.

Walking columns of water, she thought as she hurried down Weymouth Street. Even thought could be photographed now, the synaptic spark in a rat's brain like a jag of lightning. What happens to thought, though, when the meat goes off?

She didn't have to go into work until after lunch and it was still only eleven-fifty. A sub at work who had needed chemotherapy last year had described how she'd followed each session with a blast of retail therapy. Cheer herself up with a new lipgloss? Hardly. She bared her teeth, then dialled his number on her mobile and waited, grimacing; heard the start of his voice message and cut the call straight off.

Behind the railings of the central garden in Manchester Square stood several large soot-eating plane trees just in leaf, bluebells brightening their roots. Where had her health gone? She went up to the railing spikes and took in some deep breaths, smelling the wet hawthorn on the other side. There she had been, taking it for granted, its good behaviour and innocence; next thing she knew it was all over the place, it was in hysterics, threatening to leave her. Then it had packed its bags and walked out, slamming the door behind it.

Somewhere round here was an art collection, tucked away above the scrum of Oxford Street. 'I'm sick of thinking about myself,' she muttered. 'I don't want to think about me.' Here it was, at the top of the square, this red brick mansion—the Wallace Collection. She walked up to the swing doors. It was free.

Along the centre of the entrance hall reared a marble staircase, winged snake-necked griffins biting its banisters. She went and stood over by the fireplace to one side of it. The clock on the mantelpiece was ticking in her ear. She checked the time it told against her watch, and it was right: twelve o'clock.

There came a silvery chiming from the room opposite, and distant carillons from other rooms too, the sound of midday chimes and striking mechanisms. I don't want to obey these rules, she thought, that everything's always going to be over and everyone must die.

She crossed into a room dominated by a massive free-standing chronometer on top of which lounged old Father Time, winged and bearded, and a baby holding a scythe. The clock itself, not content with mean time alone, also showed solar time, the passage of the sun through the zodiac, the age and phases of the moon, the date, the day of the week and the time at any place in the northern hemisphere. It was a skeleton clock: through the glass side panels you could see its elaborate working parts, the spring which must be wound once a month and the pendulum maintaining the regular beat.

This room was full of china in glass cabinets, soft-paste Sèvres porcelain bulb pots and tea services in sea green, salmon pink and lapis blue. She took a laminated information sheet from the box by the door and started to read about cailloute and vermicule gilding, relishing the terminology of an unfamiliar technique where none of it remotely involved medical procedures. Cailloute meant pebble-like and vermicule was worm-tunnel. After the initial biscuit-firing came the glazing process; then the paste was fired again and painted with cherubs or marine scenes or triple wreaths of foliage and flowers tied

with ribbon. Last of all came the gilding. Honey and powdered gold
had been brushed on to these vase brims and teacup handles three
centuries ago, then fired, then burnished with a dog's tooth to
increase the shine. A dog's tooth!

When they put art on a hospital wall it was to do with the need
not to be reduced to a lump of gristle and malfunctioning cells. Here
was Catherine the Great's ice-cream cooler with a ground of bleu
céleste. But a garage doesn't worry that it smells of oil and petrol;
why *shouldn't* a hospital smell of surgery? They had not all been sent
to the guillotine as might have been expected; the Sèvres factory had
carried on making porcelain but with revolutionary symbols, Phrygian
bonnets and tricolore flags instead of cherubs and roses.

She walked into a large gallery room and here he was again, in this
little painting at eye level, the greybeard with his grizzled wings. At his
feet was an infant holding up an hourglass. Time was just another
name for death, she got the point. He was sitting to one side playing
a lyre, providing the music for four beautiful heavy-limbed dancers who
moved hand in hand in a ring and faced outwards, fearless as children.

There are the facts of life, she thought, the predictable traps and
horrors. What struck her now though was the irrelevance and
centrality of emotion in human life and how the facts happened
anyway, whatever you chose to feel about them.

Turning off into another room she was caught by tender greens
and blues and glimpses of amorous outdoor parties. *Le Petit Parc*,
she read, *La Fête Galante*. A girl in loose lustring looked away, the
nape of her neck exposed to outdoor kisses, while her companions
lounged and whispered in each other's ears, waiting for the lover who
stood tuning his lute. In the mid-distance a man looked out to sea
through a telescope.

Homesickness for the recent past brought savage nausea.
Garlands of fade-free flowers these paintings promised; musical
fountains and trees in perpetual leaf. She wanted to climb up over
the edges of their frames, and clawed at the air. Her legs dissolved.

'Oh, I'm still here,' she said, or tried to say, some minutes later. 'I
thought I was in a tunnel.' Her view of things was from a different
angle. Just then the scene above her whirled away as something else
bulged inside her head, and burst. □

CLYDESIDE

Martin Parr

Text by Ian Jack

Ian Jack

The towns of Port Glasgow, Greenock and Gourock stretch along eight or nine miles of the Clyde's southern bank, just before the river turns south at an abrupt ninety degrees from its east–west axis and becomes an estuary, the Firth of Clyde. The towns run one into another; there are no fields between. And they are often wet: in a rainy country, Greenock's rainfall statistics are among the highest. Behind the towns, steep hills rise, the north face of the Renfrewshire moors. In front, there is a view across the broad tidal river to the mountains which mark the beginning of the Highlands. It would be impossible to live here and be unaware of what nineteenth-century writers called 'nature's grandeur'; but equally impossible to live here and not know the social effects of heroin, tobacco, alcohol, and the sugar and fats which give the former industrial working class of the west of Scotland one of the world's least healthy diets.

When I travel through them, which I do five or six times a year, I sometimes wonder what a stranger would make of these towns. They have many ordinary aspects of modern life: fast-food chains, supermarkets, car parks, a dual carriageway, complicated roundabouts. But these clearly replace something—there are acres of wasteland and the towns have a provisional appearance, as though they were stuck between two ways of living: old Scottish town and New Jersey suburb. What went on here, once? A few remaining cranes give the clue. Until thirty years ago, the empty ground beside the river was filled with shipyards—Ferguson's, Hamilton's, Lithgow's, Scott's, the Greenock Dockyard Company—and behind them the factories that made the things ships need—ropes, marine engines, torpedoes, winches, cabin furniture. Only one small yard, Ferguson's, precariously remains to build and repair coastal ferries. Its factory gate opens opposite a plain, tall building, early Victorian, now being converted into flats. This was the offices of the Gourock Ropeworks, where my cousin Margaret worked as a comptometer operator, a modern-sounding job when she left school in 1959.

Greenock and Port Glasgow are among the world's earliest settlements to be born of the industrial revolution and imperial shipping. Before their incarnation as shipbuilding towns they were ports, facing west to Britain's American and West Indian colonies and landing and processing their exports of sugar and tobacco (and so slavery accounts for some of their eighteenth-century prosperity). At that time, the Clyde upstream to Glasgow was shallow and hard to navigate: a dozen miles of shoals and fords that no seagoing sailing vessel could easily penetrate. But then the river was narrowed, deepened and dredged (five million tons of mud came out of it in the course of the nineteenth century) and Glasgow's docks captured most of Scotland's Atlantic, African and Indian trade. 'The Clyde made Glasgow and Glasgow made the Clyde' was the saying, but it wasn't such good news for the ports downstream, which in Port Glasgow's case had been created purely to serve the needs of its namesake.

The craft of building ships began before this temporary slump in trade—the Scott family built their first fishing boat at Greenock in 1711, which meant that when Scott's (eventually Scott-Lithgow's) yard closed in the 1980s it was the end of a 275-year-old tradition. But it was the coming of the steamship in the early nineteenth century that gave the towns their dynamism and physical shape: the rows of tenements stacked on the hills (because the valuable flat ground was taken up with quays and slipways), the town hall with its 245-foot tower, the rival railway companies and their stations, the daily newspaper and the football club (the Greenock *Evening Telegraph* and Greenock Morton FC, both of which somehow still survive). James Watt, whose improvements to the steam engine made this new kind of society possible, was born in Greenock in 1736. The *Comet*, Europe's first commercial steamboat, came out of John Wood's yard in Port Glasgow in 1812. By the end of the nineteenth century Greenock was the sixth largest town in Scotland. More than 80,000 people lived there. The figure now is about half that number, with an especially steep decline since the 1960s.

As a child, I often came to Port Glasgow to stay with my cousins, my uncle and my aunt, who lived in a second-floor tenement flat just across the railway line from Lithgow's shipyard. The stuttering of rivets being driven home, the banging of hammers, the creak of swivelling cranes—all were constant and unremarkable noises from Monday to Saturday mornings. Uncle Lindsay worked in the drawing office at Kincaid's marine engine works—light duties compared to his original work as a fitter, because he had a weak heart and would stop to catch his breath in the street and on the stairs. On Saturdays he might take us by bus or train the few miles to Gourock, half suburb and half holiday resort, where industry was left behind, the houses

Ian Jack

were larger and cleaner, and the light came sparkling off the sea. His hobby was photography. He had a camera with extending bellows and did his printing in a blacked-out bathroom. Thinking of his pictures now, I remember portraits of my cousins at the piano, dramatic clouds over the Holy Loch, fireworks on Coronation night, and the silhouetted pattern of dozens of shipyard cranes at sunset. Beauty was what he was after; unlike Martin Parr, he would never have dreamed of recording everyday townscapes or moments in ordinary lives, partly because the ordinary then felt so permanent and as an insider he was part of its plain facts.

It wasn't permanent, of course. In these photographs by Martin Parr only remnants of that age survive: a disused sugar warehouse, an empty dock, a drunk on the pavement, a street of Victorian tenements. A lot once came out of Greenock—inventors, comedians, writers and artists as well as ships—but now it lies among the eddies of the modern current and thinks itself lucky to have a new call centre or a drive-in McDonald's. The economic world, moving on restlessly, has treated it unkindly.

Historical memory may not be a blessing in such situations. Things are as they are; to dwell on how they were is to feel sad and impotent. When I last drove through Greenock (a week ago at the time of this writing) I noticed that a vast new Tesco superstore was being built on the very spot in Port Glasgow where Henry Bell's *Comet* was built in 1812, and where hundreds of ships were launched in the 150 years thereafter. A full-scale replica of the old *Comet* lies just behind the new store; I went to its naming ceremony in 1962, when Clyde shipbuilding was celebrating its past in the context of a continuing future. The juxtaposition of Tesco and ship was striking. Once Greenock produced, now it consumes. There is no halfway house. Everybody wonders how it's done. □

ABSURDISTAN

Gary Shteyngart

- Voted one of the best ten books of 2006 by the *New York Times*

- Shteyngart is one of the writers included in *Granta 97: Best of Young American Novelists*

978 1 86207 972 4   £10.99
www.granta.com

GRANTA BOOKS

CRICKET FIGHTING
Hugh Raffles

A Chinese fighting cricket

1.

On the way to the cricket fight, Mr Wu slipped us a piece of paper. It looked like a shopping list. 'More numbers,' said Michael, my translator. He read:

THREE REVERSALS
EIGHT FEARS
FIVE FATAL FLAWS
SEVEN TABOOS
FIVE UNTRUTHS

It was Mr Wu's answer to a question I'd asked him earlier that day in the private banquet room upstairs at the Luxurious Garden Restaurant in Minhang, an enormous industrial suburb in south-west Shanghai. Ask him anything you want, Michael said. But when I told Mr Wu that I didn't understand the Three Reversals, he looked straight though me without a smile.

Michael, a Shanghai college student, had signed on to work with me as a translator but had quickly become my fully-fledged collaborator. Together we were learning about cricket fighting, a centuries-old pastime that seemed to be undergoing a revival. We followed crickets all over the city and found ourselves in places new to both of us as we met traders, trainers, gamblers, event sponsors, entomologists, all kinds of experts. By the time we sat down to eat in the Luxurious Garden, we already knew two of the Reversals and wanted only to confirm the third. But like so many other people we met in Shanghai, Mr Wu wanted us to know how much deeper the world of Chinese cricket fighting was than we, or even he, could ever hope to understand.

2.

We first met Mr Wu in the back room of a factory social club full of men playing card games. He had jagged stitches in his palm and winced when we shook hands. He was a little nervous: although cricket fighting is legal, gambling is not, and recent crackdowns in the city have even led to executions. Nonetheless Mr Wu was willing to help and promised to take us to a serious cricket fight. A few nights later he led us to a warren of run-down apartments blocks, through an open front door and into a brightly lit side-room just big enough for a TV, a fish-tank, and a gold plastic love-seat.

Mr Wu was close with the father of Boss Xun, the sponsor of the cricket casino we were going to. Boss Xun not only provided the premises, he handled the local police, guaranteed a referee to arbitrate the fighting and the cash, and made available a secure and well-organized public house in which the animals were deposited before the fight. For all this, he and his partner, Boss Yang, took five per cent of the winnings. Mr Wu was a cricket lover of the first order and, we would find out, a gifted judge of cricket form, but he was only a small gambler and not a full member of this underworld, and this, he later explained apologetically, was why he was nervous.

Boss Xun, however, was relaxed and welcoming. He wore track pants, a T-shirt, plastic flip-flops and a gold chain; his grey hair was close-cropped and his nails carefully manicured. 'Please feel at home,' he said. But Mr Wu was chain-smoking and on edge. I remembered the instructions he'd given us in the cab: no smoking during the fight, no alcohol, no eating, no cologne, no scent of any kind, no talking, no noise of any kind. 'We will be like the air,' Michael assured him. But it was hard to be unobtrusive. Boss Xun insisted on seating us at the head of the long, narrow table next to the referee, with the best possible view of the crickets and directly opposite the only door. The casino was basic—a bare whitewashed room—and its simplicity was a measure of transparency. As the gamblers entered, they could take in everything, the room and its occupants, at a glance. A few nights earlier Michael and I had watched a TV exposé of a cricket gambling den complete with hidden cameras and pixellated interviewees, so we expected a darkened cellar full of shadowy dealings. But Boss Yang and Boss Xun's casino was lit by an antiseptic fluorescent strip that threw its glare into every corner, and their table was covered by a white cloth on which sterile implements were laid out on either side of the clear plastic arena.

This was a secure zone—the windows were stuffed with thick cushions to keep noises in and noses out—but it was also a place of entertainment. Boss Xun worked the room with self-contained charisma. The referee called the bets with finesse, moving everything along swiftly, and managing friction with boisterous humour, despite the large amounts of money flying across the table.

'Who will call first?' he began, addressing the two trainers, one on either side of him. Their motions were slow and deliberate. They pulled on white cotton gloves supplied by the house, lifted the lids from the pots to examine their animals, stirred them with long straws of yard grass, and delicately transferred them to opposite sides of the arena. One of the trainers was clumsier than the other; he faltered as he eased his fighter out of the transfer case, nervous in the knowledge that most of the bets are placed before the animals are even visible, that many people wager on the trainers more than on the insects. As the crickets emerged under the lights, everyone leaned in, eager for that moment when the animal's spirit, power and discipline would be revealed.

For several minutes, the bets mounted on one animal, then the next, stopping only when the second pile of cash in front of the referee had grown to equal the first. Men with fistfuls of 100-yuan notes clamoured to have their bets acknowledged by the referee or, once the house bets closed, called odds to entice others with whom they might make side bets. The referee's voice boomed above the rest, building up the crickets and the stakes. Some men offered a loud commentary on the animals and the wagers. Others simply watched.

And then at the instant the referee directed the trainers to prepare their crickets the room fell silent. The two trainers began again to gently stroke their animals (back legs, abdomen, jaws) with the yard grass. The crickets didn't move. If you were close enough, you could see the beating of their hearts. The referee called, 'Open the floodgate!' and lifted the panel that divided the arena. The silence intensified. It was obvious that these animals were far more combative than any Michael and I had seen before. A sudden assault, a dart, a lunge at an opponent's jaw or leg, and the room emitted a sharp, involuntary gasp.

This was a typical gambling house in the industrial zone, Mr Wu told us later as everyone poured out of the building into the empty streets of the housing estate. Downtown the sponsors rent hotel suites and hand-pick their high-rolling punters, and at those places the minimum bet is 10,000 yuan—a low but not unusual annual wage in Shanghai—and total stakes can exceed a million. Tonight in Minhang, though, the referee opened the bidding with modest encouragements: 'Bet what you like, we're all friends here, even 100 is fine tonight.' Still, at one point during the evening, as the stakes climbed over 30,000 yuan, a gambler who had travelled here from Nanjing showed his hand for the first time and, with no change of expression, almost, it seemed,

Hugh Raffles

absent-mindedly, tossed a bankroll of 6,000 yuan into the middle of the table. He watched impassively as the referee delegated an observer to count and recount the cash until the gate was lifted in the arena and the crickets aggressively locked jaws, wrestling, and flipping each other over, again and again, in a blur of bodies. And then—as if abruptly losing interest—the animals disengaged, walking away into opposite corners and refusing their trainers' attempts to entice them back into the fray. Even the referee's effort to stimulate them by eliciting singing from the two crickets kept for this purpose in pots beside the arena had no effect. It was a draw, a rare outcome that provoked a contemptuous clucking from Mr Wu, who stage-whispered to us that really good crickets fight to exhaustion, that though athletic and well-matched these animals were poorly trained.

If the crickets appear to tire, if they hang back or if one turns away, the referee lowers the gate to separate the fighters, resets the sixty-second timer, and invites the trainers to tend to their insects. Like corner men at a boxing match, the trainers try to restore their charges' fighting spirit but often one cricket simply slumps, his opponent puffs up and sings, and the referee calls an end to the fight. Then, all at once, the cash again begins to fly in the casino—large notes out to the winners, five per cent in small bills coming back to the referee.

The winning cricket is returned carefully to his pot, ready for the journey home or back into the public house to prepare for another fight. The loser, no matter how valiant, or how physically unscathed, has finished his career. The referee collects him in a net and drops him into a large plastic bucket behind the table, for release 'into nature', everyone told me. It was okay, Michael added, I shouldn't worry, the animal would be all right, the curse on anyone who harms a defeated cricket guaranteed it.

3.

In Linnaean terms the fighting crickets kept in Shanghai are mostly *Velarifictorus micado*, a black or dark brown species that grows to 13–18 mm long and is highly territorial and aggressive in the wild, or, in smaller numbers, the equally bellicose *V. aspersus*. They appear in early August, at *Li qiu*, the division in the lunar calendar that marks the start of autumn and the moment when crickets in eastern China undergo their seventh and final moult. The crickets are now mature and sexually active, and males are able to sing and, as their colour darkens and they grow stronger, ready to fight. *Li qiu* is also the signal for tens of thousands of cricket lovers, from Shanghai, Hangzhou, Nanjing, Tianjin and Beijing, to head for railway stations. They pack the trains to Shandong province, which has established itself over the past twenty years as the source of the finest fighting crickets. People told us that the travellers to Shandong usually bet more than 100 yuan on a fight. Small-time gamblers like Mr Wu are more likely to wait for the cricket markets in Shangahi to fill with insects from the provinces.

As the fighting season approaches its height in November the line of pots creeps further along the table and the contests stretch deeper into the night. But that evening of our first visit to Boss Xun's casino was in late September and there were just a handful of fights. After they were over Boss Xun asked if we wanted to visit the public house.

The public house is designed to counter some of the more underhand tactics said to be popular among cricket trainers. The most sensational of these is doping, especially with ecstasy. Although a tripped-out cricket is likely to be a winning cricket, the drug's real target is the opposition: crickets are acutely sensitive to stimulants. They rapidly detect when their adversary is chemically enhanced and they respond by turning tail, so forfeiting the contest.

Every cricket slated for Boss Xun's casino spends at least five days undergoing detox in his public house. Part maximum security zone, part clinic, it was a four-room apartment stripped and retooled. Three rooms had multiply-padlocked steel gates, the fourth was a social space equipped with couch, chairs, TV and PlayStation, its whitewashed walls decorated with colour close-ups—glamour shots—of crickets. Nobody drank or smoked. Two of the gated rooms were bolted storage areas lined with shelves on which I made out stacks of cricket pots. The third was unlocked and, like the casino, brightly lit. Boss Xun led us inside and I saw a long table and a row of men—owners and trainers there to care for their insects—each tending to a pot. Two assistants, men I recognized from the casino, were stationed across the table. One of them fetched the labelled pots from a cabinet behind him while the other closely observed the visitors. But what made the scene momentarily disorienting was that the men lined up at the table, silently intent on their crickets, were dressed identically in white surgical gowns and matching white masks.

Hugh Raffles

Bio-security is everything. It is well known that trainers dip their yard grass in solutions of ginseng and other substances, which, like smelling salts in a boxing corner, can revive even the most battered fighter; they try to contaminate the food and water of their competitors' animals; they try to engulf them in poisonous gas. They'll even insert tiny knives in their yard grass and put poison on their fingertips hoping to get close enough to the opposition.

Nonetheless, the public house isn't foolproof. One chink in the armour is when the insects first enter. This is when they're fed and then weighed on an electronic scale. This weight is recorded on the side of the pot, along with the date and owner's name, and it then becomes the basis on which insects are allocated to fighting pairs. Great care is taken to match crickets as precisely as possible. Weights are recorded in *zhen*, a Shanghainese cricket-specific measure now used nationally for this purpose. One *zhen* is around a fifth of a gram, and there should be no more than 0.2 *zhen* between paired fighters. Trainers have become adept at manipulating their insects' weight. In the past, they would subject the animals to an extended sauna to extract liquid just before the weigh-in. Nowadays, it's more common to use dehydration drugs, impossible to detect and, by all accounts, with few ill-effects. Once fed, weighed and admitted, the animal has at least five days under the care of the public house staff and his visiting trainer to recover his strength, and, if all goes to plan, he'll ultimately fight below his weight—imagine Mike Tyson versus Sugar Ray Leonard...

4.

The speed of urban growth and transformation in Shanghai is stunning. In less than one generation, the fields that gave the crickets a home have all but gone. Now, dense ranks of giant apartment buildings, elongated boxes with baroque and neo-classical flourishes, stretch pink and grey in every direction, past the ends of the newly built metro lines, past even the ends of the suburban bus routes. The spectacular neon waterfront of Pudong, the symbol of Shanghai's drive to seize the future, is only ten years old but already under revision. I marvelled at the brash bravery of the Pearl Oriental Tower, a multi-coloured rocket-ship that dominates the dazzling skyline, and thought how impossible it would be to build something so bold yet whimsical in New York.

Michael and his college-age friends laughed. 'We're a bit tired of it, actually,' Michael said. But they also know nostalgia. Only ten years ago, in what seems like another world, they helped fathers and uncles collect and raise crickets in their neighbourhoods. They moved in and out of each other's homes and alleyways, sharing a daily life that the high-rise apartments have now banished. Downtown, remnants of that life are visible in pockets not yet rebuilt or thematized. Sometimes, though, residents are merely waiting, surrounded by their neighbours' rubble, holding out against forced relocation to distant suburbs as the government clears more housing in time for the city to host Expo 2010.

Eighteen kilometres from the city centre and a crowded fifteen-minute bus ride from the huge metro terminus at Xinzhuang, the township of Qibao is a different kind of neighbourhood. An official heritage attraction, a stroll through a past violently disavowed for its feudalism during the Cultural Revolution but now embraced as a part of national culture, Qibao is newly elegant with canals and bridges; its narrow pedestrianized streets are lined with reconstructed Ming- and Qing- dynasty buildings. There are storefronts selling all kinds of snack foods, teas and craft goods to Shanghainese and other visitors, a temple with Han, Tang, and Ming dynasty architectural features, a weaving workshop, an ancient tea-house, a famous wine distillery and—in a house built specifically for the sport by the great Qing emperor Qianlong—Shanghai's only museum dedicated to fighting crickets.

All these crickets were collected here in Qibao, said Master Fang, the museum's director. He stood behind a table laden with hundreds of grey clay pots, each containing one fighting male and, in some cases, its female sex partner. Qibao's crickets were famous throughout East Asia, a product of the township's rich soils, he told us. But since the fields here were sold off in 2000, crickets have been harder to find. Master Fang's two white-uniformed assistants filled the insects' miniature water bowls from pipettes and we humans all drank pleasantly astringent tea made from his recipe of seven medicinal herbs. Master Fang was an animated storyteller and Michael and I were drawn to him immediately. 'Master Fang is a cricket master,' confided his assistant, Ms Zhao. 'He has forty years' experience. There is no one more able to instruct you about crickets.'

Everyone at the museum was caught up in preparations for the Qibao Golden Autumn Cricket Festival. The three-week event includes a series of exhibition matches and a championship, with all fights broadcast on closed-circuit TV. The goal is to promote cricket fighting as a popular activity distinct from the gambling with which it is now so firmly associated, to remind people of its historical and cultural origins, and to extend its appeal beyond the demographic in which it now seems caught: men in their forties and above.

Twenty years ago, before the construction of the new Shanghai gobbled up the landscape, when city neighbourhoods were still patchworks of fields and houses, people lived more intimately with animal life. Many found companionship in cicadas or other musical insects that they kept in bamboo cages and slim pocket boxes, and young people, not just the middle-aged, fought crickets. They learned how to judge a likely champion and train the fighters to their fullest potential and how to use the pencil-thin brushes made of yard grass or mouse whisker to stimulate the insects' jaws and provoke them to combat. They also learned the Three Rudiments around which every cricket manual is structured: judging, training and fighting.

Cricket fighting is experiencing a revival in China. Even as it loses out to computer games and Japanese manga with the young, it is thriving among older generations. Yet, it's an insecure return that few aficionados are celebrating. For even as the cricket markets flourish and the gambling dens proliferate, much of this enthusiasm is accompanied by a sense that this is another feature of daily life which, like so much else, is already as good as gone.

Master Fang pulled a cricket pot from the shelf behind him and ran his finger over the text etched on its surface. In a strong voice, he began recite, drawing out the tones in the dramatic cadences of classical oratory. These are the Five Virtues, he announced, five human qualities found in the best fighting crickets, five virtues that crickets and humans share.

The First Virtue: 'When it is time to sing, he will sing. This is trustworthiness.'

The Second Virtue: 'On meeting an enemy, he will not hesitate to fight. This is courage.'

The Third Virtue: 'Even seriously wounded, he will not surrender. This is loyalty.'

The Fourth Virtue: 'When defeated he will not sing. He knows shame.'

The Fifth Virtue: 'When he becomes cold, he will return to his home. He is wise and recognizes the facts of the situation.'

On their tiny backs crickets carry the weight of the past. The loyalty of the Third Virtue, for example, is no ordinary loyalty; it is the loyalty one feels for the emperor, the willingness to lay down one's life, and not to shirk one's ultimate duty. These are not simply ancient virtues, they are points on a moral compass. As anyone will tell you, these crickets are warriors; the champions among them are generals.

The passage on Master Fang's pot is taken from the thirteenth-century *Book of Crickets*, the earliest surviving manual for cricket lovers and perhaps the world's first book of entomology. Its author, Jia Sidao (1213–75), is still remembered as imperial China's 'cricket minister', the sensual chief minister in the dying days of the Southern Song dynasty, so absorbed in the pleasures of his crickets that he allowed his neglected state to tumble into rack, ruin and domination by the invading Mongols.

Jia Sidao was the first to document the complex system by which cricket lovers classify their animals. He identified and ranked four body colours: first yellow, then red, black and finally white. The authoritative xishuai.com cricket lovers' website now adds purple and green. Each colour corresponds to a broad category of behaviour. However, most of the cricket experts I met in Shanghai describe only three colours: yellow, green and purple. Yellow crickets are said to be the most aggressive, but not necessarily the best fighters, because green insects, although quieter, are more strategic and—according to the annual illustrated list of cricket champions—include a greater number of Generals.

Below these gross distinctions is a further set of divisions into individual 'personalities', whose total number is often put at seventy-two. Trainers use a system based on physical variables and complex clusters of characteristics. Length, shape and colour of the insect's legs, abdomen and wings are all systematically parsed, as is the shape of the head—current manuals might include seven or more possibilities—and differences in number, shape, colour and width of the 'fight-lines' that run front-to-back across the crown. Experts also consider the energy of the antennae, the shape and colour of the animal's 'eyebrows' (which should be 'opposite' in colour to the antennae), the shape, colour, translucence and strength of the jaws, the shape and size of the neck plate, the shape and resting angle of the forewings, the sharpness of the tail-tips, the hair on the abdomen, the width of the thorax and face, the thickness of the feet, the animal's overall posture. The insect's 'skin' must be 'dry', that is, it must reflect light from inside itself, not from its surface; it must also be delicate, like a baby's. The cricket's walk must be swift and easy; it should not have a rolling gait. In general, strength is more important than size. The jaws are decisive.

Judging a cricket's quality requires deep knowledge. Nonetheless, judging is only one of the three rudiments of cricket knowledge, and for Master Fang, it is less important than training.

Master Fang told us that the trainer's task is to build on the cricket's pre-existing natural virtues to develop its fighting spirit. This indispensable quality is revealed only at the moment the insect enters the arena. Though a cricket might look like a champion in all respects, it can still turn out to lack spirit in competition. This, Master Fang insisted, has less to do with the individual cricket's character than with its care. It is the task of the trainer to build up the cricket's strength with foods appropriate to its stage of growth and individual needs, to respond to its sicknesses, develop its physical skills, cultivate its virtues, overcome its natural aversion to light and habituate it to new surroundings. A cricket knows when it is loved and cared for and it responds with loyalty, courage, obedience and the signs of quiet contentment.

Master Fang removed the lid from one of his pots, took his yard-grass straw and barked orders at the cricket as if at a soldier ('This way! That way! This way! That way!') and the insect, to Michael's and my real astonishment, responded unhesitatingly, turning left, right, left, right, a routine of exercises that Master Fang explained increased the fighter's flexibility, made him limber and elastic, and showed that man and insect understand each other through the language of command as well as beyond it.

5.

A few days later, Michael took me to Wanshang, the largest flower, bird, beast, and insect market in Shanghai. The main hall was filled with traders—mostly women—recently arrived in Shanghai from Shandong and other provinces of eastern China. They sat in rows with their crickets laid out neatly in small pots before them. Around the edges of the hall, permanent stalls were occupied by Shanghainese dealers, also newly returned from buying crickets in the rural districts, their clay pots arrayed on tables, the insects' origin chalked up on a blackboard behind them.

Michael showed me the same pattern at cricket markets throughout the city. At Anguo Road, in the grim shadow of Tilanqiao, Shanghai's largest jail, Shanghainese sellers sit at tables while traders from the provinces squat on stools in their own distinct areas, their pots laid out on the ground.

Even though the provincial traders at these markets don't plan to stay in Shanghai and even though they are likely to be relatively prosperous in their home districts, once in the city they are migrants, subject to harassment, discrimination and expulsion. Nonetheless, most expect to do well. By minimizing their outgoings, travelling with relatives, going home infrequently, carrying as much stock as possible when they return, and sleeping in cheap hotels close to the market, they can make considerably more in the three months of the cricket season than in the entire rest of the year.

Shanghainese traders don't sell female crickets. Females don't fight or sing and are valued only for the sexual services they provide to males. It's the provincial traders who deal in these, selling them in bulk, stuffed into bamboo sections in lots of three or ten, depending on their size (bigger is better) and colouring (a white abdomen is best). Females are cheap, and, at first glance, it seems as if these traders only sell cheap animals, female and male.

The signs in front of the provincial traders said ten yuan for each male, sometimes two for fifteen. The buyers filed past their pots, browsing the rows with an air of detachment, occasionally lifting the lids to peer inside, taking the grass brush, stimulating the insect's jaws, perhaps shining a flashlight to gauge the colour and translucence of its body, trying to judge not only its physical qualities but its fighting spirit. Despite their studied indifference, they were often drawn in, quickly finding themselves bargaining for an insect priced anywhere between thirty and 2,000 yuan. Only children, novices like me, the elderly, the truly petty gamblers who play crickets for fun, and bargain hunters who believe their eye is sharper than the seller's, would buy the cheap crickets, it seems.

But how do you judge an insect's spirit without seeing it fight? Groups of men crowd around the Shanghainese stalls. Eventually, someone moved aside to share the view: two crickets locking jaws inside their table-top arena. The stallholders tended to the animals like trainers at a real fight. But they were seated in chairs, pots piled around them, and as the match progressed they delivered relentless patter like auctioneers, talking up the winner and attempting to raise its price.

This is a risky sales strategy. No one buys a loser, so the defeated are quickly tossed into a plastic bucket. And if, as often happens, the winner isn't sold either, he has to fight again and may be beaten or injured. The seller relies on his ability to inflate the winner's price enough to compensate for the losses. But the woman from Shanghai who eagerly waved us over as she spooned tiny portions of rice into doll's-house-sized trays, told us that the Shanghainese insisted on watching the crickets fight before they'd put their money down; that they liked to shift the risk to the seller.

'Provincial traders don't dare fight their crickets,' the woman said. She was lively and straightforward and generous, too, inviting us to share her lunch and giving me a souvenir cricket pot, disappointed I wouldn't take the insect as well. She expounded on her neighbours, traders from Shandong province. 'They sell their crickets as brand new to fighting,' she said, so casually it almost slipped past, and it was only thanks to Michael's quickness that I discovered she was telling us that crickets circulate throughout the market, unconstrained by social division; they pass not only from trader to buyer but also from trader to trader, from Shanghainese to Shandongese, and from Shandongese to Shanghainese. And, as they travel through these crowded spaces, they gain and even recover value; they're born again: losers become ingénues, cheap crickets become contenders.

For a few weeks, the crickets are everywhere. On working-class street corners, groups of men cram themselves around an arena, watching the battles unfold. In the newspapers, it's high culture and lowlife, elite sponsorship and police raids. The crickets bring the gambling houses to life. They light up the stores that sell the elaborate implements every cricket trainer needs: tiny food and water dishes; wooden transfer cases; 'marriage boxes'; grass and whisker brushes made of duck down; tiny long-handled metal trowels and other cleaning implements; pipettes; scales (weighted and electronic); technical manuals; specialized foods and medicines; and, of course, cricket pots in enormous variety, some old (and often fake), some new, most of clay but some of porcelain, some to commemorate special cricket events, some large, some small, some with inscriptions, mottoes or stories, some with intricate images, some (perhaps the most beautiful of all) plain.

6.

Dr Li Shijun of Jiao Tong University invited us to his home. A few journalists, some cricket experts, and a university colleague or two would also be there. We must be sure to show up as planned.

I was keen to meet Dr Li. I'd seen him interviewed on a TV programme included on a DVD I'd picked up at one of Shanghai's many cricket markets. The reporter was enthusiastic about the professor's campaign to promote cricket fighting as a high-culture activity free of gambling, a project in line with state policy. 'Gambling,' she said in the final voiceover, 'has ruined the reputation of cricket fighting. Cricket fighting is like Beijing Opera, it is the quintessence of our country. Many foreigners regard it as the most typically oriental element of our culture. We should lead it to a healthy road.' Just a few days before I arrived in Shanghai, Dr Li had again featured prominently in the media: this time in a newspaper article on a gambling-free tournament he had staged downtown. The newspaper journalist identified Dr Li as the 'Cricket Professor'. The TV reporter called him the 'Venerable Cricket Master'.

Dr Li's apartment was tucked away in a corner of a low-rise housing complex close to the university campus. He was a charming host, warm and welcoming, a youthful sixty-four-year-old with a mane of silver hair. Several people were already there when we arrived and he swiftly corralled us into his office, all the while pointing out the prizes from his lifelong passion: the cricket-themed paintings, poems and calligraphy created by himself and his friends that enlivened the walls and bookcases, the large collection of southern cricket pots that formed the focus of one of his four published books on cricket-related matters.

Dr Li grew up in Shanghai and, like other men of his generation, his fascination with crickets was sparked and nurtured by an older brother. He described passing the large (now long-gone) cricket market at Chenghuangmiao every day on his way to school in the late 1940s; he remembered using his pocket money to buy crickets and the circle of 'insect friends' that grew around him—boys his own age and the adults who would stop to play with them.

At the end of his book *Fifty Don'ts of Cricket Collecting* (don't buy a cricket with rounded wings, don't buy a cricket with just one antenna, don't buy a cricket that is half-male, half-female, etc.), Dr Li remarks that it's no mystery that society looks down on cricket fighting; whereas at the university he teaches in a suit and tie, at the insect market, surrounded by 'low-level people', he has to wear a T-shirt, shorts and slippers like everyone else. The lack of cultivation—evident in the smoking, cursing and spitting all around him—was not simply a personal matter: 'If you want others to treat you with respect you must first act decently,' he insisted. It wasn't just a question of deportment either. For Dr Li, there is a crisis of civility in Chinese society and cricket fighting is part of the solution. With its ancient traditions and scholarly demands, cricket-fighting is a rare practice, closer to tai chi than mahjong. But it is a practice debased by gambling.

Campaigns against gambling have been a feature of the People's Republic since 1949. But despite periodically aggressive policing and especially since the post-Mao reforms, the Party has had little success in controlling its expansion. Unlike the failed attempt to outlaw mahjong during the 1980s, the assault on crickets has been indirect and, in this respect, has paralleled policy during the Ming and Qing dynasties, when imperial prohibitions ran up against the emerging professional network of urban cricket houses, but legislation continued to target gambling rather than crickets.

Dr Li told us about his scheme to promote development in Henan province by helping local farmers enter the Shanghai cricket market in competition with traders from Shandong, Anhui and elsewhere. He was spending significant sums of his own money on this project and investing a great deal of his considerable energy, even travelling to the countryside to donate equipment and teach villagers how to distinguish between different insect species. The village he was working with was on the same latitude as Shandong and he had every reason to expect its crickets to be as strong. The pilot project had produced promising results. It was now only a question of convincing the buying public.

He led us into a large sitting room in which he had laid out a variety of pots and implements. Selecting two pots, he carried them over to a low coffee table positioned in front of a couch. He transferred the crickets into an arena on the table and invited me to sit beside him. He put a yard-grass straw in my hand and, as people often did, encouraged me to stimulate the insects' jaws. I was clumsy with the brush and always felt as if I was tormenting the insect, who, more often than not, simply stood still and suffered my attentions. But I was jiggling my wrist as best I could when I looked up to find that all the other people present, with the exception of Dr Li, who continued to stare intently at the crickets as if he and I were alone in the room, had produced digital cameras, and were lined up in formation, snapping away at close range like paparazzi at a premiere. And now Dr Li turned creative director, instructing me how to position the grass, how to hold my head, what to look at, how to sit...

A few days later an article appeared in the *Shanghai Evening Post* under the headline ANTHROPOLOGIST STUDYING HUMAN–INSECT RELATIONS, U.S. PROFESSOR WANTS TO PUBLISH A BOOK FOR CRICKETS. Its author was Li Jing, a smart young reporter I had met at Dr Li's house. Li Jing subtly traced Dr Li's erudition. She noted his eager recourse to the yellowing books on his shelves and his willingness to take me as his acolyte as well as his friend ('Questions flew out of his mouth like bullets,' she wrote of my reaction to the crickets). In offering me guidance, Dr Li was *chuandao jie huo*, a Confucian term for the teacher's task of passing on the knowledge of the ancient sages and resolving its interpretive difficulties. She let her readers know that his pro-cricket, anti-gambling campaign was a matter of culture, that it reached out from the whirlpool of the present to a higher ground that was both an available safe haven of the past and an anchor for the future. The photo caption, adapting a well-known saying, read, 'United by their love of crickets, these two strangers immediately became friends.'

7.

Centuries before anyone thought of placing crickets in pots and provoking them to fight each other, their evocative singing and their presence in the home gave them a special place in Chinese life. In this poem from the *Shijing* (*The Book of Songs*), an anthology

Hugh Raffles

compiled around 3,000 years ago, the cricket seeks out human company and finds its way into the heart of the household:

It is in the wild in the seventh month,
Under the eaves in the eighth month,
In the house in the ninth month,
and under my bed in the tenth month.

There is a long history of cricket friends—people who become friends through crickets and crickets who become friends with people. Jia Sidao recommends trainers chew sesame seeds before feeding them to their insects, just as mothers sometimes do before feeding them to their babies. But crickets are friends, not babies. And this is something that cricket lovers (unlike some pet lovers) are unlikely to forget. Because, as well as the Five Virtues, they have the Three Reversals.

If the Five Virtues show the similarity between crickets and people, the Three Reversals recognize the differences.

The First Reversal: 'A defeated cricket will not protest the outcome of a fight; he will simply leave the arena without complaint.'

The Second Reversal: 'A cricket requires sex before a fight and performs better for the stimulation it provides; rather than having an enervating effect on athletic performance (as, according to this reversal, it does in men), among crickets, pre-game sex promotes physical prowess, mental focus and fighting spirit.'

The Third Reversal: 'Crickets have sex with the female on the male's back'—a position functionally impossible for people (without complicated equipment). Moreover, as the entomologist L. W. Simmons points out in what we might think of as a decisive commentary on Reversal Three: 'Since the female must actively mount a courting male there is little if any opportunity for forced matings by males.'

The last time I saw Boss Xun, he invited me to travel with him the following year to Shandong. We would spend two weeks there collecting crickets, he said. He knew everyone and had excellent relations with the local authorities. His offer tugged at me strongly— to be around cricket friends, human and insect, once more. Michael was enthusiastic, too. Perhaps, he said, we could spend the entire season with the crickets. That, we agreed, would really be something to come back for. □

GRANTA

THE LAST OF
THE SMOKERS
Jackie Kay

' All my ex-lovers were lovely people: if I can believe that I can give up smoking,' she said. 'Yeah, right,' I said, wheezing and laughing. It was past midnight, Saturday night, well, Sunday morning. We were having one of those wild smoking nights. Debbie Murray was practically the only pal left in the whole wide world that still smoked and the one person who could still make me cry with laughter. She pulled two cigarettes out of the pack, tapped them both gently, affectionately on the pack—the way a mother pats a baby's bottom—lit them both at once and handed me one. I took it, smiling. It was kind of a romantic friendship.

'I'm serious,' she said, 'dead serious. I've tried every other possible way. Tried the patches, tried the inhalers. In pubs, I'd try and hide the fact that I was sucking that stupid thing, like a five year old hiding a dummy. Did I tell you I even tried hypnosis?'

'No way!' I said, and laughed so much I brought on a fit of conspiratorial coughing. 'You numpty. What was that like?'

'Mental. And it set me back one hundred and fifty quid which I didn't have,' she said, blowing smoke in my face.

'Which you still don't have,' I said, a little irritated. I'd lent Debbie 300 smackers last October, which she still hadn't paid back. The idea that she'd burned 150 quid on a charlatan hypnotist took the biscuit.

'It was odd. He had a very posh voice and he was trying to frighten me to death. *Your toes are feeling exceptionally heavy. Your legs are very, very heavy. Relax. Think about how filthy your lungs must be...* He'd asked for the names of the people I love best in the world. I'd asked if any of them could be dead already and he'd said No, no, no and at that moment I was wondering why not—I mean does he think the dead have no hold over the living? If anything the dead have more hold over the living!' Debbie said. 'True enough,' I said. It was going to be a long night.

'Did you fall into a total trance then?' I asked. I poured us both a glug of extra wine. 'One more for the road,' I said gamely, knowing that we weren't on a wee country road any more, with badgers hiding behind hedges; no, we were on a big fucking three-lane motorway, midnight juggernauts hurtling down. Debbie inhaled deeply. 'A bit, but just as I was going under I asked him if he had ever sent himself to sleep while hypnotizing someone. He had a lovely voice really. Yes, he said, once, when he was trying to help a petite woman get over her massive panic attacks. He woke to her shaking him roughly back and forth. She was in a total state. That sort of kyboshed it.'

'How long did it work for?'

'Ten days.'

'I hope you went for your money back,' I said with all the authority of my forty-three-year-old self.

'Nah!' Debbie said.

'Why not?' I said, the irritation rising. (Isn't it strange how you can love friends and they can also be horribly maddening?)

'He said it had a ninety-nine-per-cent success rate. I was ashamed. I didn't want to be the one per cent.'

'Neither did anybody else, probably. What a con. What a rip-off.'

Debbie shrugged her shoulders. She was one of those types that seemed to revel in being ripped off. There was always something grander than money on her mind.

'Anyway, that's all a distraction, Claire,' she said. 'Giving up smoking is a question of belief. If I can substitute one belief for another, right, I might get there. It's not so much that smoking is my crutch. It's that I've got to make giving it up my church! Need to stop being a martyr, stop seeing it as some sort of sacrifice, right?'

'You're a slaverer,' I said. 'You're a blether of hell.'

'Last time I was at an airport I went into the smoking room, which was right next to the praying room. Then I went into the praying room and prayed I would give up smoking, because the smoking room was enough to put you off for life. Smokers don't actually like other people's smoke. It's nasty.'

I inhaled deeply and blew out. I didn't really want Debbie to give up smoking. Nearly everybody I know has given up smoking; even the ones that you would think could never have pulled it off—the thirty-a-day-for-thirty-years diehards. I recited the litany of unexpected names, old friends and lovers who had crossed the border successfully into the non-smoking terrain: Isabel Aird, Adjoa Andoh, Suzanne Batty, Ann Marie Murphy, Pat Milligan, Femi Okafor, Ian Jack, Kathryn Perry, Catherine Marcangeli, Brendan Griggs. The list went depressingly on and on. I was starting to feel more and more like I belonged to a tiny band of weirdly devoted people, and every time I ran into a smoker, even a stranger-smoker, I'd light her cigarette gratefully. We were the grateful-not-yet-deads. Perhaps we should all have a special haircut to identify us—The Last of the Smokers, the last of the Big Pretenders. Debbie got up and put on some John Martyn. I only ever listened to him when I was with Debbie Murray. We blew perfect smoke rings to *Solid Air*. She tried to sing along, but John Martyn is hard to sing along to. You just sound wrecked.

'You're not very good at picking lovers. You've been with some real lou-lous,' I said. I could hear my voice was starting to slur.

'Lou-lous? Christ, where did that come from?'

'Nutters then, bampots and weirdoes!'

'No, they were all lovely! All my ex-lovers were absolutely lovely!' Debbie repeated like a mantra. John Martyn was singing 'May you never lay your head down without a hand to hold', and 'May you never make your bed out in the cold.' Debbie sang along to that bit, quite fiercely. 'The only person in my life who has lasted is you,' Debbie said at the end of the song sadly. 'Maybe friends are the big loves of your life. Maybe we get it all wrong, focusing on lovers like we do.'

'We ask too much of lovers,' I agreed.

'Like hell we do! We don't ask *enough*!' Debbie said. She had reached the point where she might start to turn.

'I think we should get to bed. It's late. It's one in the morning.'

'We've got to sort this out,' Debbie said. 'This is important. If we sort this out right now, tonight, by tomorrow we could be non-smokers. Think of it! We could be free! Think how wonderful it would be to say *I don't smoke*. What a beautiful fucking sentence!'

'We'll never be non-smokers,' I said. 'The most we can hope for is being ex-smokers. It never even occurred to the non-smoker to smoke. They just don't get it.'

'Don't be smart!' Debbie said, and went to light up two again at the same time. 'You're all right,' I said. 'I don't want one right now.' I felt a moment's lovely superiority. Debbie looked fazed, then dazed, then lit up regardless, trying to look debonair. Joni was singing now.

'So that's the secret,' Debbie said, leaning forward excitedly. 'Ex-lovers and ex-smokers. We have to do a switch.'

'You've lost me,' I said.

'Concentrate!' she said. 'I'm on to something!' She swallowed the last swirl of wine. 'Open another bottle to go with this! This is electrifying!'

'No, it's too late to open another bottle,' I said.

I was starting to wonder about her theory actually. It's impossible for me to become someone who has never smoked. It is impossible for me to become someone who has never loved. I will not ever become a non-lover. I have accumulated exes. These days I read the zodiacs of three major exes to see if they are having any luck. The full moon this Wednesday forecasts major changes for all my ex-lovers. I gave in and opened a screw top called 'Laid Back Ruby' to help me work out Debbie Murray's Fantastically Complicated Way to Give up Smoking.

I am lover-less at the moment; so is Debbie. We've both been like that for two years. If one of us gets a lover the other will find it tricky, but not as tricky maybe as if one of us gives up smoking. We've been smoking together for nearly thirty years. I remember our first Sobranie. Our pal Gillian Baxter's parents gave us one each on New Year. Her mother held open a beautiful Black Russian box. I picked a pink sobrani; Debbie picked a blue. We both had an advocaat and lemonade. We were fourteen, sophisticated, cool, already inhaling. That New Year Debbie sang along to Gilbert O'Sullivan singing 'Claire'. She liked that there was a song with my name in it. I remember smoking our first Consulate and Debbie saying, it's no worse really than sucking a Polo mint; then she blew a smoke ring the size of a Polo mint hole.

If she gives up and I don't, I'll regard it as a huge betrayal, worse even than her stealing a girlfriend. Debbie's last bloke was a moron. Then she had a girl, Lucky; well, she called her Lucky because she gambled all the time, but actually she was very unlucky and she blew all Debbie's savings. She never really liked any of my lovers when I think about it. Maybe she was jealous. Trying to think about them as lovely people is a real challenge. I am not deluded!

I've lived through two lesbian dictatorships: one of them even had a tiny moustache. For some reason, I've always been drawn to people stronger than me, to obsessive types. The first of the lesbian dictators had a big thing about cats. In fact, she first fell for me because one of her Refuge cats sat on my lap. 'That's very unusual,' she said, her eyes widening with excitement. 'Mrs MacDonald is usually very, very fussy about who she sits on.' 'Is that right?' I said. I wished her cats weren't called such stupid names. 'Yes, I've no idea what happened to her before she came to me, but somebody abused her. You can tell an animal's past.' Then she leaned towards me and kissed me on the lips. It took me aback. When I did that thing, you know, replaying what had happened to try and give some pleasure, that line about the animal past always stuck and stopped me going further. It was as irritating as static.

She was called Caroline, the Cat Woman, and she was very beautiful really. She had a haughty intelligence that you could detect around her cheekbones that was quite cat-like. She was enigmatic, never gave much away. I never met any of her family and she never spoke of them at all. She enjoyed listening to me talking about my family. She loved my imitations of my mother and father. Her face would grow furry with pleasure. She even kept a cat journal. The last straw for me was when we came back from Florence. 'Mrs MacDonald is sulking because we've been away,' Caroline wrote in the journal. 'Not even Michelangelo's *David* was worth it. I've put Mrs MacDonald back months, just as she was starting to trust me. That's it—no more holidays!' I read that with growing alarm.

'Smoking is my first erotic memory when I think about it,' Debbie was saying. We were so drunk by now that we were more or less talking or thinking to ourselves. We'd returned to the state of the quintessential smoker, a luxurious state of aloneness. I took my fag out and stood at the back door and smoked under the sizzling, smoky stars. I would miss the starry-smoke the most. What is the point in having a gorgeous night sky without a cigarette to go with it? Just thinking about stopping was making me feel nostalgic. I went back in. Debbie was stuck on the same sentence again. 'Yes,' she was saying, as Joni sang. 'Yes, smoking is erotic.' She stubbed her fag out. The ashtray was overflowing. It was filthy actually. Filthy, dirty. How any of us could do it was beyond me. Every time I managed to give up, I stared with horror at those that still smoked. How can they do it, how can they, I'd think, in the twenty-first century, knowing all that we know? I'd stare at the woman puffing away waiting for a bus, at the widower with his widower's shopping in one hand and his fag in the other, at the clutch of teenage girls inhaling and exhaling nonchalantly, and I'd think, you're crazy, crazy, crazy, you're going to die! Picture the oxygen tent! And then three weeks or nine months or one year later, I'd be back with them again. Unbelievable, un-fucking believable! Apart from anything else, it looks deeply weird, smoking, like something human beings were never supposed to do. Unnatural, all that smoke coming out the nose and the mouth.

'Do you remember your first kiss?' Debbie said, 'your first long snog? I remember mine. It was under a desk. Kenny Davies stuck his tongue in my mouth and then slid his lips across like two wee grass snakes or something. It wasn't very pleasant.'

'Yuck,' I said.

'Slippy, slithery, sneaky. See. That's another similarity between smoking and sex. The first time both stink. The first fag is a nauseating experience, right? It gives you the boke. I remember Margaret Millar forcing me to inhale so I could be one of the gang. It was horrible. Really-really-really. Not nice. Not pleasant. I remember thinking, there's no way I'm ever going to get addicted to this. They said, don't start or you'll get addicted, but I smoked on and off, and off and on, and I'd say to myself, I'm not addicted, right?'

Debbie was looking traumatized now. The thought of giving up completely was doing her head in. I know. It was like facing the abyss, the well of loneliness. No companion there. What was there? It was like a big dark void or something. I poured us both another glass of wine. My watch said three a.m. 'You still thinking we should give up tonight?' I said. 'What about tomorrow? Tonight's not the best night.'

'Don't play games with me!' Debbie said, snarling in my face. 'It will always win. You can't bargain. It will always get you. The only way is to make them lovely people. What did they give me—the ex-lovers. The buzz? They gave me a hit, an excitement, right, and I thought I couldn't sleep without them, right, and that I would get terrible mood swings if I gave them up, and that I wasn't capable of being sociable on my own.'

'Are you talking about lovers or cigarettes?' I asked.

'Same difference. Actually the cigarettes, they understood me better than the lovers. A cigarette is an enigmatic lover who understands all your intricate complexities without you having to say a single word or have a word said back,' Debbie said. She was one of those people that could actually sound quite pompous drunk. It was lovable really.

'I see,' I said. Well, I did.

I was back on my own again thinking about the lover that came after Caroline, the Cat Woman. She was another right warmer. Fiona. She was very judgemental and had absolutely no sense of humour. But she was a mixture because she was sentimental too. On the day we met the juke box was playing that song—who sang it?—she's got Bette Davis eyes. A smoky voice, remember? It was romantic. She smoked back in those smoking days. But then she suddenly and violently changed, joining the vicious band of ex-smokers who believe that smoking is evil like a new wacky religion. I remember the day she gave up; she said, very snootily, 'Once you decide, it's easy. You just have to choose your moment. Actually,' she said, even more snootily, *'the moment chooses you!'* That day she took the curtains to the dry-cleaners and hired one of those shampoo-the-carpet jobs. She sniffed the air. She painted the living-room walls magnolia. Fresh start, she said. You too. I pretended to give up, but any opportunity I got I sneaked a fag and then sucked extra strong mints all the way home. I'd get in, run up the stairs, wash my hands, spray perfume all over, until one time she caught the hint of something on my breath and said that she couldn't trust me any more. If I was going behind her back to smoke in secret, I could just as easily have an affair. She asked me to choose, the fags or her. I chose the fags, packed my bags and I was out of there in a week. No love lost really. I fell upon my pack of cigarettes and upped my daily intake.

'It's all about desire,' Debbie was saying as I rummaged in the cupboard for something else to drink. I found an old bottle of tequila. Well, the sun was rising. We'd moved on to Neil Young now. He was singing in his heartbreaking beautiful voice, 'I've seen the needle and the damage done, a little part of it in everyone, but every junkie's like a setting sun.' One last nip for the road, I said warningly. I tried to visualize a Junction 7 exit on our motorway. 'Yep,' she said. She was nearly passing out now anyway. 'Did you ever desire me?' 'No, don't be daft,' I said shocked and a bit wary. 'Why not?' she said, genuinely curious. 'Why not when you are a lesbian.'

'You're my mate,' I said. 'And you're like my sister. It would be like incest or something.'

Debbie smiled. This answer seemed to please her. 'Well, I never desired you either. I desired to smoke. I desired my cigarettes. For them, I had too much desire,' she said grandly, putting on an Edith Piaf accent. 'There was a while when I craved a lover,' I said, 'but that's gone now. Don't even feel a pang of regret. Well rid. That's what I think. I got well rid.'

'That's not the right attitude,' Debbie said, sounding suddenly sober. She could do this: suddenly turn sober. It was very fucking freaky. Like somebody going BOO! 'The correct attitude is to find a way to make them lovely in your memory. Give them the nostalgia!' she said triumphantly, like she had suddenly found the key. 'Give them the nostalgia!' she repeated, her voice deepening. 'GIVE THEM THE NOSTALGIA!' she said, this time sounding very crude.

'I'll tell you what, Debs,' I said. 'If all I've got to do at the end of this head-fuck night from hell is give up smoking, it's going to be quite easy. My ex-lovers had nice things about them, yes. The Cat Woman loved her cats. She was nice to her friends. She got upset at tsunamis and disasters. She gave money to charity. She donated her blood regularly. She visited a lonely old neighbour every Sunday afternoon and took her a little cake, an Eccles cake.'

'Really?' Debbie swung around and stared at me, definitely stone cold sober now. 'You never told me any of this. How come you never told me any of this?'

'It was more fun slagging her off, like it was more fun smoking,' I said, putting out my last doubt ever, squashing it into the ashtray with a new, fresh determinedness.

Debbie lit up again. God, she must have smoked twenty-five, at least! The room was thick with fug. I opened the window. 'Let it out,' I said. 'Tomorrow, I'm going to take the curtains to the cleaners.' 'You what?' Debbie said. She looked disappointed in me, like she wasn't expecting to be taken seriously. 'I'm through with smoking,' I said flashily. 'Smoking is so last year.'

'I hate it when people use the word *so* like that,' Debbie said morosely.

'Smoking is common,' I said, ignoring this. 'We've got to get out before we're the last ones left on the planet who smoke. Let's join the other gang. They're the cool ones now.'

Debbie cupped her hands around her fag. She looked so lonely. I felt sorry for her, but I had my health to consider. I had my lungs to think about, my blood circulation. 'Listen,' Debbie said, taking a deep drag, miffed. 'This was my idea.'

'I know,' I said, 'but it's going to be a tough one for you, because your ex-lovers were psychopaths. Mine were all quite nice people really.'

'You think that because it was you that left them. None of them left you,' Debbie said, lighting up yet another filthy cigarette.

'True, true,' I said evenly.

'I'm always the one that's left,' Debbie said, and suddenly shocked me by bawling her eyes out. 'Put the fag out,' I said, 'and come and look at the sun coming up. It is bright red.' We stood outside my back door, linking arms looking at the red eye of the rising sun for a long, long time. Debbie didn't light up. Maybe Debbie would never light up. Maybe we would both become very boring, fat people. 'I think we're going to become boring people,' Debbie said with that uncanny ability to speak my inside thought aloud. 'Shut up, baby,' I said in my best *Double Indemnity* voice. 'Let's get some shut-eye. It's late.' The morning clouds were swirling about in the sky like wee puffs of smoke.

☐

DEAR OLD DAD
Paul Theroux

Paul Theroux (second from left) with his father and brothers, 1953

My father—whom I loved, and who loved me—never read a word I wrote or, if he did, never mentioned the fact. It was like an embarrassing secret we shared, of a creepy proclivity I had, something that we couldn't discuss without awkwardness. And what was odd was that from 1967 until his death in 1995, I published more than thirty books and hundreds of essays and magazine pieces. He would have had to go out of his way to avoid reading them, actually to step over them, since many were in his house. It was not that he didn't read. He enjoyed history, especially local history—of Boston, New England and his ancestral province of Quebec. The Lewis and Clark expedition fascinated him to the point where he would declaim the hardships the team faced, with the stout-hearted Sacagawea, the bad weather, the plagues of wasps. ('They were taw-mented!' he would cry, in his characteristic way.) He read the newspaper every day, he read his Holy Missal the way a Muslim reads the Holy Qur'an—and his missal had the thickened and thumbed look of a Wahhabi's Qur'an. He read Usher's dense and very dry *History of the Town of Medford*, he read about whaling and could tell you what flensing was, and the composition of baleen; the Gloucester fishermen, the Civil War, the Battle of Lexington, the works of Edward Rowe Snow, all of that, but no work of mine.

At first I was bewildered, then relieved, and finally I was indifferent. My father did not read novels—anyone's novels, at least not modern ones. And I had not become a writer to please my parents, only myself. A writer is rarely able to do both, and I know that, far from wishing to please them, I wrote as an act of rebellion.

Edmund Wilson's mother said she'd never read a word of his. D. H. Lawrence's father mocked his son's writing and called it a kind of slacking. Joyce's wife famously jeered at his verbal ingenuity. At the end of his memoir *Family Romance*, John Lanchester comments, 'Once my mother wasn't able to read my novels, I began writing them.' These reactions do not shock me.

My father satirized himself as 'dear old Dad', when he felt especially put upon. 'And who'll end up doing it?'—cleaning the garage, shovelling the walk, washing the car—'Dear old Dad.' That's how I thought of him—beloved. But when I look at his sketchy history I'm not sure I understand him, or know what his life was like. His was a life with no documents—no long letters, hardly any letters at all, no serious diaries, no affidavits, not even a will, nothing written down. A birth certificate, a death certificate, nothing in between. This is a critical lack—dealing in suppositions is like dealing with a mythical character, mostly guesswork. My father was not a joiner. He did not have many friends, and no close friends, so there are no witnesses outside the family. Except for the last years of his life, when he was ailing, he didn't drink. Even then, in pain, it was merely a measure of Wild Turkey. He didn't smoke. He seldom went out at night, except to church or choir practice or the Holy Name Society, always in his terms 'The Holy Name'. He was quietly amiable, with no strong opinions, and generally uncritical. His genial nature made him, I now see, impenetrable, almost impossible to know. Assemble all the evidence, scraps of paper, snapshots, scribbled postcards, and what do I have? Just bones, or less, bone fragments. Mr Bones, he called himself, at the minstrel show in which he appeared.

He was born just under a hundred years ago. I clearly remember that he was sixty-five—the age I am now—when I set out to write *The Great Railway Bazaar*. My children are now in their mid-thirties; at my age, Dad still had a seventeen-year-old in school—my youngest brother—who, inevitably, has different memories of him, a grey-haired man at his high-school graduation, an elderly man at his Harvard commencement. Dad might have enjoyed my travel book, since it was a journey, and factual, but I know that he would not have liked my novels. Without saying so, he believed that most fiction was frivolous— absurd posturing that made the author look ridiculous; immoral, too, unless it was a historical romance, or a certain category of classic.

He loved *Treasure Island* and read it to my brothers and me in our attic bedroom, which we named (in homage) the Benbow Inn. He read us *Kidnapped* and most of *The Deerslayer*, and *The Last of the Mohicans*. These novels had real heroes, and adventure, and a point; he believed them; they lived for him. As for writing, he wrote notes, sent postcards, and for the early years of his marriage—during the Second World War—he kept a laconic, one-line diary. The entry for April 10, 1941, was *Anne had another boy*. That was me.

My mother claimed that I was his favourite. This can't have been true. He was impartial. It was my mother's way of saying that I was not her favourite—and that was true. She was a stubborn, insecure woman—domineering people often are—and she feared me for my defiant aloofness. I knew this and made myself more noncommittal and cooler. It antagonized her that she didn't know what was in my head. Eventually, she did read my work—some of it. On the publication of my first novel she wrote me a letter complaining that she had been overcharged for the book and that the book was (her word) 'trash'. I kept the letter—indeed, still have it after all these years and have often reread it as a goad. She felt that my work did not reflect well on her as a mother and that was all that mattered to her. She often exclaimed in a shrill warning voice, 'The written word is forever!'

So there it was—my father who was proud of me, who never read a word; my mother, who read half a dozen of my books, who didn't like them much, and either told me to my face, or else whispered about them to my siblings. 'Paul's writing filth [or 'porno'] again'— and of course they jeered at me. Of the two, my father's non-reading was the more helpful and humane, as though he was forgiving me for my indulging myself.

I thought of my parents as totally separate beings—my sympathetic but rather formal father, my emotional and talkative mother. Alone with my father I was nearly always happy, but facing them together could be difficult, because my father deferred to her, saw her weaknesses, supported her even in her irrationality. The two sent out contradictory signals. I didn't know what to say. If my mother became sufficiently wound up about something my father would hit us to placate her, though I knew it hurt him to raise a hand to any of us. We were, however, threatened constantly—the chief transgression was insubordination. If he hit us especially hard he'd say, 'That was a love-tap. Next time I'll really haul off and tan your hide.'

It is probable—certain, I think—that my six siblings would disagree with much of what I say here. But it is my contention that each of us had a separate upbringing, that my mother and father behaved differently towards each of us, their sympathies and personalities revealed uniquely to each child, and that we as children were different too. Their child rearing was spread over many years and their circumstances kept improving, from the dire post-war years, to the turbulent Sixties, to the Seventies, when things looked up, to the Eighties, when they began to live in comfortable retirement.

I asked one of my brothers to verify a simple incident in my father's life. He disagreed strenuously with something I regarded as an established fact. I began to think that each of us believes he owns the family story, owns our memories of Dad, our tales, the history of Dad and regards this as beyond dispute. I have often wondered aloud about Mother's oddities and received angry glares from some of them. How dare I? So the Dad I knew might be unrecognizable to the rest of the family, though he was real enough to me. His death was such a blow that for ten years I could not think of writing about him; but now I can describe him and his peculiarities with without becoming upset. I had tried in the past a number of times but got so sad I could not continue.

Because of his natural reticence, perhaps shyness, and his unease in unfamiliar social settings—well, how can a more or less indigent father of seven children be gregarious?—no one knew him well. He had a deflecting and concealing manner, in which he became so supremely accommodating, he made himself almost invisible, a challenge to my trying to recreate what I know of him.

He was proud of his family, tended somewhat to idealize this big happy-family notion, could be deeply contented, was of a reflective even meditative cast of mind and was capable of enormous and infectious happiness. It is possible that he lacked self-esteem—an outsider might suggest this. But I don't think it was the case. He was a man of limited or at least not active ambition, but with a strong capacity for work, great loyalty, honesty, politeness; yet what seemed his sense of unworthiness was piety. He was personally modest, to a degree I have never found in anyone except the most devout lama or holy man, always demurring when he was praised. Yet he was quick to praise other people; he was punctual, deferential, appreciative, sober and correct.

In travelling—especially in Asia—I meet men like my father all the time: shy, conscientious, reliable, uncomplaining, law-abiding, and a bit unworldly and innocent: rickshaw drivers, menials, clerks, shopkeepers—humble men, curious and eager to assist—men who get to a point where they want to help more but can go no further. These are the older men of the provincial towns who know the times of the trains but have seldom been on one; who look a bit fearful and smile nervously in a lobby of a fancy hotel; are often on their way to or from the temple, who want to please, who talk lavishly about their children; not cynical at all but seemingly always in awe of someone bigger, different, wealthy. My father didn't scorn powerful people— he was respectful of them until he had clear proof that they were cruel, or rude, or—one of his favourite words of disparagement—fakers. My father was someone who hardly exists in America any more, but a person of old-fashioned modesty I meet often in foreign parts.

He was the eldest of six children, adored by his mother, respected by his father (for whom he was named), admired by his five siblings— he seemed the most civilized, restrained and decent of them, also the most intelligent. My Grandfather, Eugene Theroux, grew up on the family farm in a Quebec village called Yamaska—ten generations of Theroux had lived there—and then moved south to join his older brothers in Nashua, New Hampshire, to work in the mills. For a time, they lived in Lawrence, Massachusetts. I have a studio photograph of him and his eight brothers in black suits, some of them heavily moustached, looking like a baseball team posed at a funeral. Eugene met Eva Brousseau, who had come all the way from Belleville, Ontario, to work at an adjacent mill in Nashua—the French Canadians were the first real workforce in New England—and he married her.

Around 1905 my grandparents bought—or perhaps built—a small house in the woods outside Stoneham, Massachusetts. In this house my father was born. My grandfather was a night watchman and a worker in a shoe factory. As a child (so my father told me) my father accompanied his father at night, keeping him company 'on his winds'—a watchman patrolled the premises of the empty factory, carrying an L-shaped handle, winding the various clocks. Although my father was a good student, an able athlete—starter on the high school football team—and a fluent French speaker, on graduation from Stoneham High in 1926, there was no question of his going to college. His father brought him to the shoe factory and (so my father related) introduced him to the foreman, saying, 'He's all yours.'

He lived at home, he worked in Wakefield in the factory, and a few years later commuted to Boston—a long way—to work at the American Oak Leather Co. He said he was glad for the work, for any job, and often spoke of all the unemployed people ('college graduates!') selling apples out of crates on the sidewalks of Boston during these years of the Great Depression. This perhaps gave him a life-long craving for steady work, a safe job, no matter the salary, and a scepticism about college degrees.

He was selective in talking about his early life. Obviously he was a conscientious high school student. He would have been a reliable worker at American Oak. Once, talking to a friend, he referred to his father as 'my old man'—his father beat him for it. He said he deserved the beating: he was ashamed. He called his father 'Pa'. His father raised chickens; my father would have helped. One summer, he visited his aunt in Montreal—his mother's sister. He ran out of money. His uncle, a contractor, put him on the payroll of a job—though he was not required to do any work. It was just a scam. He bought a pair of overalls and collected his pay every Friday.

'Imagine. I showed up in clean overalls and all these men who'd worked all week, lined up with me in their dirty clothes. I felt awful.'

He had a memory for these hurts and transgressions, slight as they were. He had a serious respect for hard work—that is, manual labour, getting your hands dirty. He did not regard anything else as work—writing, banking, preaching, fiddling with figures, investing, didn't really count as labour but a more refined sort of scheming.

There is no suggestion of carnality in his early life. He had a few male friends. He would have needed their encouragement in order to range more widely. He drove with them one day to drop off one of their number at Amherst—Mass Aggie, as it was known—and sixty years later still remembered where he'd had lunch that day, in a diner on Main Street. In his rather uneventful life this simple outing counted as an event.

His years of bachelorhood he spent living at home in Stoneham, commuting on the train and what he called 'the electric car' to Boston. 'I handed over my pay packet to my parents every week without fail.' In the winter it was all work. In the summer an occasional outing—Salem Willows, an amusement park; to Nantasket Beach, or the honky-tonk at Revere Beach.

'Your father was a reader!' my grandmother told me in a praising way when I was just a child. 'Albert used to sit there with a book in his hand and a few apples. He would read the book and eat an apple'—and she dramatized that. The book in one hand, the apple in the other. Another unhelpful much-too-neat family story. How old was he? When was this? What was the book?

Reading impressed her because she could barely read, and her husband, my grandfather, could not read at all, had never been to school, though once—mentioned by name in the Stoneham paper, probably a church-related item (St Patrick's Church)—he looked at the mass of newsprint and found his name, put his finger in it, as though to defy the belittlers. Like many illiterate people I have known, he was very shrewd, a reader of faces and gestures, prescient, patient, rather silent and watchful.

On one of the summer outings, my father was introduced by his friend and neighbour Charlie Farrow to a single woman from Medford. She was a college graduate and a teacher, though she gave up teaching eventually. They courted for four years, saving their money, and married in 1937, when my father was almost thirty. They had enough money to buy a house outright. I had thought that because of his work in the leather company, footwear a crucial industry in wartime, my father was exempted from the draft. But it was his asthma and his three children that prevented him from being drafted.

He had few regrets in his life. Not going to college was one. Not having a marketable skill was another. But his keenest regret was not serving in the military—it was mingled shame and sorrow made more vivid because even though asthmatic he was able-bodied. Both his brothers served in the army, three brothers-in-law too, as well as one of his sisters, all of them seeing action and one—Richard Long, 'Uncle Dick', a full-blooded Native American, married to his sister Florence—was captured and kept in a German prison camp for almost three years.

One of the more melancholy aspects of my father's one-line wartime diary is the way the mention of the fall of an Italian city or the bombing of a German one is accompanied by *Rain all day* or *Went to the movies*.

In the early part of his married life, until he was crowded by children and had no spare time and not much money, my father was a moviegoer. He had definite opinions about actors—disliked the cowboy actor Ward Bond; liked Charles Laughton as the Hunchback of Notre Dame, preferred musicals to thrillers; disliked violence of any kind.

His vocabulary was widened if not enriched by the movies of the Thirties and Forties. 'Kiddo', 'Toots', 'Skeezix', 'I'll tan your hide'. The radio, too, of which he was a nightly listener. 'Park ya karkus', 'Taint funny, Magee', and all the catchphrases of W. C. Fields, from

Paul Theroux

'My little chickadee' to 'Who stole the cork out of my lunch?' 'Give us here,' he said, when he wanted something handed to him. 'Give it a rest' when you talked a lot. 'Stop gas-bagging' when you talked far too much. 'Shift' when he wanted you to move. 'He's a faker' described an unreliable person and 'He's a good scout' was the opposite. 'He's a piker' indicated penny-pinching. 'He lit into the woods just as tight as he could jump' a self-conscious Maine expression he liked. 'A lazy man's load' indicated you were carrying too much and would drop some of it.

'Make it *comme il faut*' was his frequent demand. '*Mon petit bonhomme!*' was an expression of praise from his mother, and he used the Quebecois pronunciation 'petsee', as he did with 'clem' in 'crème à la glace'. A frequent Quebecois exclamation, '*Plaqueteur!*', meaning 'fusser', is such an antique word it is not in most French dictionaries, but I heard it regularly.

He was not a coward but he was restrained, overly modest and somewhat shy, deferential, even submissive, especially among strangers. I cannot imagine my father giving anyone a direct order, but I can easily see him taking orders—and going beyond the call of duty: working late for nothing, working weekends, ignoring rudeness or a blunt tone from a superior to keep the peace, or pretending (for his own self-respect) that he had not heard it. He was in a way intimidated by big confident men, whom he half admired and half despised. He would have made a good soldier.

He hated disorder, disobedience, chatter, backtalk, bad posture, idleness, long hair, loud noise, any sort of indecency, foul language, slang, pretence, frivolity, showy wealth, nudity, coquettishness, falsity, silliness, superior airs and obvious overbearing intellectualism as opposed to subtle wit. He deplored ostentation of any kind. He loathed lengthy explanations and long-windedness.

He liked silence and space; he had a boyish admiration for heroism, especially heroism accompanied by modesty. ('Anyone would have done what I did.') He was fascinated by new scenes—a place he'd never been, a new road, a new bridge. New buildings did not interest him.

He was easy to please. He liked his mother's Quebecois food, strong tea, thick kidney stew, mashed potatoes, pot roast, asparagus on toast, pea soup.

Pea soup and johnny-cake
Make the Frenchman's bellyache.

He was addicted to jingles like that.

We're the boys from Nova Scotia,
We're the ones who choke the fish.
We hate the Goddamned Irish,
We're the boys from Antigonish.

I slept in the long attic room we called the Benbow Inn with my
two older brothers when we were very young. After lights-out we
listened to the radio, *The Green Hornet*, *Mr and Mrs North*, *The
Shadow*, *The Great Guildersleeve*.
'Turn that thing off!' Dad would call out from the bottom of the
stairs, which were steep, like a ship's ladder.
One night the radio wouldn't turn on. It was an antique, with big
bulbous vacuum tubes that glowed in its innards. One of them was
missing, and because of this the radio was unworkable. A note had
been tucked in its place, my father's scribble:

Lives there a man with soul so base,
Put him last in the human race.
He'd stoop to steal a radio tube,
And treats his kids like little boobs.

Mildly, quietly anticlerical, he found most priests unbearable in
their piety, obtuse and out of touch. 'What do they know about
raising a family?' He smiled in reproach at the notion of priests
having maids and housekeepers, to cook and clean for them. I think
in a compliant way he resented authority, though he never defied it.
He avoided conflict all his life.
He was somewhat despised by my mother's ambitious,
competitive, sententious and parvenu family but he quietly endured
their boasts. He didn't respect them enough to stand up to them.
Anyway, he was a passionate FDR Democrat and they were
Republicans with a sentimental love of Italy, even in the war. He was
a classic under-achiever in a world that didn't know the word. He

167

was intelligent, fluent in French, always up on the news, totally dependable, a fast learner with a phenomenal memory.

Yet he began his working life in a shoe factory, among cutters and stitchers, and on his marriage had only risen to the rank of 'shipper'— the mysterious word I wrote on the specified line 'Father's occupation'.

Shipper meant the stock room, the mail room—writing labels, sorting mail, tying parcels, and in my father's case, wrapping up crates of new shoes. But so what? He seemed to find it companionable, and often mentioned his work mates, Chester Pyne among them, and another man, a Syrian immigrant, who taught him some Arabic greetings. You might guess at his training when you saw my father take a ball of twine and quickly tie a parcel, making the knot, slipping the loop and snapping off the extra twine in one motion.

For a period in the late 1940s he was a travelling salesman, selling cowhides—sole leather—to the faltering shoe factories in north-eastern Massachusetts and southern New Hampshire. Most were Jewish-owned—my father did business with Jews all the time (I knew it from their names) but I never once heard him make an anti-Semitic remark. Later he began sentences, 'When I was on the road...'

He had almost no interest in making big sales but he was attracted to the serene monotony of the long drives, the freedom of the open road, meeting familiar contacts at warehouses and factories, eating at roadside diners, making side trips to historic sites—the House of the Seven Gables was one, old sailing ships moored at Gloucester and Portsmouth, the Rebecca Nurse house, the Old Man of the Mountains, Mounts Chocorua and Monadnock, battlefields of the Revolutionary War, equestrian statues on the village green in small towns.

My brothers and I sometimes went with him. I don't remember any sales but I do recall an all-afternoon tour of a cigar factory in Manchester NH (the '724' brand). He may have resembled Willy Loman in this phase of his life, yet he was happy and (unlike Willy) he took his boys with him some of the time for company.

One day my father went to work and found the door locked; the company had folded. Without any notice, obviously to avoid creditors, American Oak Leather Co. went into liquidation. This was in 1949. He had the idea of opening his own shoe store—he even leased an empty shop—but was saved from this certain failure by a chance to run a shoe department in a just-opened men's clothing store in Medford Square, O'Brien's. He worked there for thirty years, earning such a small salary that eventually, when there were only a few children at home, my mother went back to teaching.

My father's goodness was usually exploited. He was grateful for a safe job but his innocence made him rather fragile in some ways, bewildered by the cruel world, which threw up unexpected problems.

I had a serious problem early in 1961. I was nineteen. My girlfriend was pregnant. I went to my eldest brother—the eldest in such a family occupying the role of a wise counsellor, except in my case. He was frightened rigid by the news. 'Tell Uncle Jim... Maybe Father Foley will help.' My drunken uncle, our unforgiving pastor.

I fled with the girl to Puerto Rico. When we returned to Boston, she went to a home and then delivered the baby at the Mass General. I visited her there. A very cute baby boy. 'He looks like you.' She gave the baby up for adoption; we found out almost forty years later that he had gone to a childless couple—a wealthy grateful family who became his benefactors, and this boy, educated at an Ivy League college, became an innovative businessman and ended up a multi-millionaire.

At the time of the birth my parents were informed and they were stunned. They realized I'd endured almost a year of exile, a kind of poverty, miserable fear and desperation. But only I had seen the baby.

'What have you got to say for yourself?' my mother said afterwards. I had nothing to say. She said, 'You should be ashamed.'

Later, trying to shame me further, she said, 'I told Dad. He went to bed. I found him lying there, crying his eyes out.'

My father's sorrow was something I had never witnessed. I had hurt him deeply. He never said a word of this to me; never alluded to it. It was a foretaste of his way of dealing with my writing—not something to mention or discuss.

I was relieved. What was there to discuss? But when I had needed them they did not help, could not help, simply were not there, except—in my mother's case—to blame. It was a great lesson to me, a motto for my escutcheon—I am alone in this world.

M y father had a wide knowledge of the process of tanning leather, of shoe making, of shoe styles, all the elaborate names (cordovan bluchers, brogues, wing-tipped, pebble grain). But this was really a sort of dilettantism—anecdotes, the fruit of talk with old timers and work in factories.

His real life was lived between his long spells of work. First was his family. Yet having fathered such a large family—seven children—it was as though he didn't know what to do with us. Such a sprawling family meant great activity and confusion and responsibility—but he seems to have been mellow enough, optimistic enough, not to worry too much about how he would support all these children and a temperamental wife. He was gentle and protective, with occasional episodes of anger, usually provoked by Mother: instead of defying her, he turned his wrath on us. We were a jostling, rivalrous, teasing and talkative bunch but we were not rebellious. I was always somewhat shocked to be disciplined—because I studied, I read for pleasure, I kept to myself, didn't smoke or drink, didn't have a car or even a bike; my only indulgences were my secret fantasies of life as a backwoodsman, tracker, skier, marksman, scout; my tendency to escapism in reading.

The church was important to my father's life. His faith, his sort of devotion I have seen among pious Muslims, among Buddhists in Burma and Vietnam—humble and hard-pressed men with an unswerving belief that goodness is inherent in humans. He would have subscribed to the You-too-can-be-a-Buddha notion of enlightenment as possible through prayer and meditation; kneeling and prostrating yourself in places of worship.

One of my father's church-related activities was the choir, of which he was a member until a few years before his death, which would have been sixty or more years of hymn singing. He had a strong, confident, rather tuneless voice, with a gravelly character, and even if there were thirty other people singing I could always discern my father's voice.

The church choir became the cause of one of the strangest episodes in my father's life. For two years in the early 1950s he performed in the church minstrel show. This antiquated and quaintly objectionable entertainment involved a number of white middle-aged men in blackface, wearing fuzzy and ill-fitting wigs and outlandish vests and frock coats in a variety show that was both slapstick and songs. He was 'Mr Bones' an 'end man', and the others were 'Tambo' or 'Lightning'. Because he practised so often and so loudly I knew all the words to the songs he sang in the successive years: 'Mandy (Is There a Minister Handy)' and 'Rock-a-bye Your Baby (with a Dixie

Melody)' and 'Rosie (You are My Posy)'—in the general imitation of Al Jolson, who had also performed in blackface and was a musical icon when my father came of age in the 1920s. 'Nobody' was another song, written and made famous by Bert Williams, who unlike the other minstrels of his time (around 1910) was a real black man; and the song was broad and bitter.

The stereotyping, the lame jokes, the mockery, the heavy satire of Dad's minstrel show—the embarrassing wrongness of it—were obvious to me, and probably to many people at the time. My father had black acquaintances and shoe customers, yet this was just fun, a parallel activity, and was not regarded by him as offensive. He was tolerant and humane and would have been indignant and hurt if anyone had characterized the show as racist. The first minstrel shows had begun in the 1830s and continued through the nineteenth century, many of them satirizing slave owning and the supposed nostalgia of the slaves for plantation life, as well as commenting on events of the day. Such shows were regarded as subversive in the South, but were an entertainment fixture in the North, where they flourished until the 1930s. After that they evolved into vaudeville and burlesque shows, and only amateur players—like my father and his fellow churchgoers and choristers—put them on. They were finished by the late 1950s but they had been dated and doomed long before then.

I had found it excruciating to watch my shy father doing a soft-shoe shuffle, or rattling a tambourine and singing 'Mandy', wagging his white-gloved hands. His jokes were not funny. 'You should see my brother—he walks like this.' He loved performing. Playing a role gave him latitude and allowed him to overcome his reticence. In blackface, as Mr. Bones he was a man in a mask, liberated in this role.

That was the happiest and most assertive I have seen my father, followed by times in the late Fifties, or early Sixties, singing with his friends on summer evenings over a cookout in the back yard, eating hamburgers and singing along with the Mitch Miller LP. Then, I remember being upstairs in my room, reading a book, probably a bootleg Henry Miller, and listening to the music and the loud voices, belting out these songs.

In college, in '62 and '63, I went home on some weekends but we never talked about the past, about the child I had fathered. We did not talk about my studies, my grades—nor about money;

nothing about the future. These were my problems. My father never gave me money—he had little to give; nor did he offer any career chat, no suggestions or advice. I worked full-time in the summer to save, and did odd jobs in Amherst during the semesters.

Now and then he would drive me up to Route 2, where it crosses Route 128. He would wish me luck ('Be good,' was his usual salutation, or rather grandly, 'Remember who you are') and out I'd get to hitchhike to Amherst. He might park nearby and watch me standing with my thumb out until a car stopped. Then he'd beep his horn and head home. Why did he not give me the dollar or two to take the bus?

He was not an effusive letter writer but he was a regular sender of notes. When I was in Africa he would jot me a note, like a memo, nearly always from his little workstation at the store. He was excited by my having joined the Peace Corps and when I had first said I was going to Africa—Nyasaland—he said, 'Wonderful. Imagine that!'

No intimation that I was abandoning him or that I would be in danger. Probably it was something he wished he'd done himself, a fantasy of departure—just push off and hit the road. Though he had no interest in Africa.

He wrote me notes. My mother wrote newsy or sanctimonious letters about her doings. I published my first novel in 1967. My mother wrote to say it was 'trash'. My father said nothing.

I got married also in 1967. He was pleased to meet my English wife. Later, when we had a child and were home for a visit, he held this baby boy and I could see how uncertain he was with babies— he was at a loss, holding him awkwardly, as the child screamed, no idea how to pacify him or what to do, and when in relief he handed the kid back to me, I understood something of his reticence as a parent of small infants, though he was wonderful as we grew older and became his companions.

In the 1970s he visited London. He was lost in the huge city. He could barely understand Londoners' English, and leaving the shop of the cockney butcher he marvelled that I was able to hold a conversation. 'I couldn't understand a word he said!'

Most London restaurants were cramped, the tables close together. In Wheeler's in Victoria, other diners a few feet away, my father (against all the rules of English restaurant etiquette) tried to strike up a conversation with the man at the next table—much to the man's consternation and annoyance. My father did this later at the café at the Royal Festival Hall and again in a restaurant in Old Compton Street. And when he was rebuffed, my father just laughed. He believed that ignoring someone who was right next to you was ruder than attempting to banter with them.

He had a smile for everyone, never looked for trouble and was genuinely interested in the details of other people's lives. Uncomplaining, he asked for very little, was so unimpressed by luxury he ridiculed it—'Waste of money!'—and hardly cared about comfort. Discomfort was something true to him. If he'd had the money he would have made a great traveller in the old style, as a wanderer, not as a scholar. He always encouraged me in my travels and unlike most people was a patient listener to traveller's tales.

His chief burden was ill health, and his adult life was dominated by asthma—audible breathing difficulties and sometimes choking fits so severe he seemed on the point of gagging to death. His asthma was the formal reason we could not have a cat or dog, but in fact my mother hated pets. 'What's the point of them?' was one sally and 'Do you want to kill your father?' another.

For relief my father used a nebulizer, an old-fashioned glass retort worked with a rubber bulb, producing a dense medicinal vapour which he inhaled deeply. The brand name was DeVilbiss. This seemed to ease his breathing but all that inhalation of mist and medicine may have soaked and shredded his lung tissue. Certainly he had little lung capacity and in his seventies was plagued by emphysema, though he had never smoked; it was this that eventually killed him. He simply suffocated. I know, because I was with him when he breathed his last, with great effort—'agonic breathing', the nurse called it, just before he expired—like a man trapped beneath a heavy stone.

Because of his asthma he could not walk fast, exert himself in games or bend deeply; dusty places were unendurable to him, so were humid days. We climbed Mount Washington in 1953, but he didn't make it to the top. His lungs were clogged, clotted—and my recurring memory is of him squeezing the nebulizer and panting.

Much later he used a small aerosol inhaler. I am convinced these clumsy remedies destroyed his lungs. He lived his whole life in a harsh climate—damp winters and humid summers. 'I should go to Arizona,' he would say with the same mild chuckle as when he said, 'I'd buy a new car this year but I don't like the *lines*.'

'Lines' was a word that fakers used, and it was laughable to Dad that anyone would be fool enough to buy a car for the look of it. Cheapness and dependability were all that mattered to him. He never bought a new car. He never bought a new suit for that matter. He wore the cast-off suits of Harry O'Brien, his boss—good suits that he got altered to fit him. Buying anything brand new was to him a waste of money, something foolish, pure vanity. He sometimes even refused hand-me-down suits as 'too dressy'.

It alarmed me to hear him choke, to see him redden, at times unable to draw a breath. And so I would watch helplessly until he somehow cleared his throat and wheezed and poked the nebulizer into his mouth. He had the loud gargling phlegm-gathering hoick that I have heard delivered into a spittoon, or on to a pavement, with the same slushy gusto by a Chinese peasant.

One of the theories of asthma is that it is sometimes self-induced, psychosomatic, the result of low spirits or repression, the heavy breathing a kind of grieving. I can believe that repression contributed to my father's asthma. He could not express himself fully, because of his wife's weak ego and need for attention, and her own complaints; but though my father clearly suffered he did not use his asthma as an excuse, and often made himself ill in his exertions. But if any of us children needed a favour, a ride somewhere, a sympathetic ear (provided the problem was not too great), my father was willing. 'Where are you?' he'd say to the stranded midnight caller and would immediately set off on a rescue mission. He never had any money, but if he had been wealthy he would have eagerly shared it, saying, 'How much do you need?'

Memories, fragments, generalizations—what do they add up to? This recollection of mine seems insubstantial, yet that itself is a revelation. I thought I knew him well. On reflection, I see he was strange and he seems to recede as I write, as sometimes when I asked him a question about himself, he backed away. In writing about him like this I realize I do not know what was in his heart. He is just like those skinny old men in Burma and Thailand and Vietnam who inspired me to think of him.

What were my father's passions? I don't know. Did he have any fantasies of success? I draw a blank. Ambitions? I have no idea. He enjoyed fishing, beach-combing, tinkering in his shed or in the basement. These are trivial things. What were his dreams? I don't have a clue. Did he ever cheat on my mother? I doubt it, but how would I know? He had stereotypes of some ethnic groups, Italians and Irish, the loud, pushy Boston tribes, but nothing serious. He was tolerant in matters of race, an intuitive humanitarian, and was proud of the fact that Boston sent black regiments to fight in the Civil War—the bas-relief on Beacon Street that commemorates one of them was one of his personal landmarks. There is no better example of how vivid a Yankee he was in his beliefs and how little sympathy he had for the South in that war, nor did he have any romantic notions about the South generally. But if he had secrets, or personal hurts, he did not share them. His most remarkable outward eccentricity was his habit of talking to himself. He murmured constantly, in a private and unbroken narrative.

One memory we shared—a family story—was of my father looking out the window on a winter afternoon and staring hard, and after a long pause uttering (in an almost theatrical manner) one word—'Never!' Then nodding in satisfaction.

What had he been thinking of? What question, what issue? Perhaps he saw a face, heard or remembered something? The word was said with King Lear-like decisiveness, in his characteristic accent: *Nevah!*

He did not hover over me or anyone. True, he did not guide me either, but neither did he impede me. Now and then he would give me a word of warning but it was general, usually a well-meant platitude. He was not sagacious but he was gentle and he knew his limitations. He was greatly in awe of my eldest brother—his trips to China, his hobnobbing with politicians, his audience with the Pope.

My father never spoke a word to me about sex. He never taught me to throw a ball. He did show me how to skip a small flat rock on the sea and how to bait a hook with a worm, how to play a stone-throwing game called 'Duck on a Rock'. My homework was a mystery to him. I wanted a bike and a dog. I did not get them. I wanted a gun—I got a Mossberg 22, in a swap from my friend Eddie Flaherty. My mother said, 'I hate guns.' Dad said, 'Watch where you point that thing.' He never took me to a baseball game, nor a ball game of any kind. Nor a movie. It is possible that he took me to a restaurant but if so I have no memory of it—nor do my older brothers remember any restaurant or dining out.

I never introduced my father to any girlfriends, nor any woman I knew, until I was married and brought my wife home. Twenty-odd years later, on my divorce, he said nothing. But, was there to say? Only 'Everything works out for the best,' his stoical motto. He never gossiped, he never used profanity, nor told an off-colour joke. Scantily dressed women on TV embarrassed him; he'd leave the room.

He was a gardener—not a fancier of flowers but a grower of vegetables. He cultivated beans when I was young—Kentucky Wonders, pole beans; he grew tomatoes and squash. He was methodical. He knew how to space the plants, how to fertilize them, was a diligent waterer and weeder. He nearly always succeeded in producing a good crop. He must have learned these skills from his father, who was also a vegetable gardener.

A shy man himself, he would dare us his children to take certain risks, as though on his behalf—trespass at the Boston Navy Yard, where we were shouted at by an armed sentry; or crouch on a rock and let the tide come in and isolate us. 'I'll give you a quarter!' He saved string, scrap wood, old screws, nuts and bolts, jam jars, coffee cans, cigar boxes, orange crates. He threw nothing away. Garbage he buried in his garden, though the racoons usually dug it up. He never passed a trash barrel or a wastebasket without looking in and seeing if there was something usable to salvage. He believed that people were foolish in most of the things they discarded. The day I received my Honorary Doctorate from the University of Massachusetts I was walking down a campus sidewalk in my robes with my parents and noticed that my father had dropped behind. Nor was he anywhere to be seen—at least not immediately. He was ultimately revealed between two solemn academic buildings as a pair of kicking legs: he had tried to retrieve something from a big steel barrel he'd looked and tipped himself into it. He was up-ended and stuck. When I helped him out he was red-faced from being upside down but still clutched a fistful of yellow pencils, which someone had thrown away. 'Pencils!' he gasped. A find.

Those'll come in handy some day...

My mother was a worrier. He was not. His serenity irked her and made her even more fretful. He had no solutions, therefore (he seemed to think) it was pointless for him to contemplate any problems. His fatalism was rosily tinged with optimism. He believed there was justice in all things and that there was always a price to pay: that if you had a swimming pool you—or someone else—would probably drown in it; if you had an expensive car you'd probably crash it; if you had a lot of money you'd lose it or be robbed; a ridiculously expensive tie would have soup slopped on it; and to all such happenstances he'd say, 'Serves them right.'

He also believed that goodness was rewarded. My brother Alex sees this as Micawberish. I agree with this. 'Something will turn up.'

He prayed. He was devout, even pious. He felt that God would provide answers—surprises, happy endings. Faith was a shield. God protected the devout.

Everything's going to be all right, was his general and often irrational view, his response to querulousness. The odd thing is that not much in his life was all right: he never had money, we had no space, we had no idea where we were going or what we were doing; pure chance sent us to college; we had to grub for our tuition, and nearly all the useful advice I got in my life was from strangers.

Dad was nearly always out of his depth. He seemed to know this, and so he hated scrutiny or searching questions or anything personal. The truth would have been devastating. This made him a natural listener and appreciator of other people's lives and problems.

He was easygoing, humorous, undemanding and, because of his gratitude and lack of complaints or snobbery or ego, he was easy to be with. Yet he had no idea how I was living my life, and he would have been profoundly bewildered if I had told him I wanted to be a writer. He would have said, Why? Or, How? Or, What will you write about? And, Where's the money going to come from?

All art was to my parents an indulgence, superfluous, something that other people did, necessitating a private income. It did not strike me as odd that they felt this way. I felt this way myself and it worried me.

Behind her back, we satirized Mother, mocked her parsimony, her catchphrases ('You'll be in a peck of trouble', 'I'll bet you dollars to donuts'), her explosive temper, her little-girl snivelling, her vanity, her repetitions, her studied piety. She was, to some of us, a bore and a burden, fussing about nothing, though to some of the other children she was a reliable ally—a source of money, adept at the sort of bribery and backhanders that are common among weak people. It was a divided family. Satirizing mother was an act of defiance. It meant you were a rebel—strong, or else pretending to be strong.

Yet we never satirized Dad. It wasn't that we didn't dare to—we were habitually disloyal to each other, as Mother was, mocking us secretly to one another ('He's put on weight in all the wrong places'). We could easily have jeered at Dad. But we spared him. And it was odd, because he had his obvious faults—he too was repetitive and predictable, his catchphrases were no less hackneyed than Mother's, he could get flustered, especially in a car—he was a terrible driver, he learned late, and always made beginner's mistakes, letting the clutch out too fast, braking too hard, not using the rear-view mirror.

Did we spare him because he was so kind to us, unselfish and loving? That would have been an admirable reason, but even sweet kindly people were mocked by us; almost no one got off the hook. Yet Dad did. Perhaps we saw his innocence and goodness, but I don't think it was that. I think at bottom we pitied him, felt genuinely sorry for him, because he was not the wise and revered patriarch he wanted or sometimes pretended to be. He was henpecked. He was ill at ease. He was too preoccupied to worry, and in alarming ways he had accomplished so little as a working man. He was a clerk—barely a clerk. Our mockery would have done more than hurt him; it might have destroyed him. And he wanted us as friends. He had no idea how to help us and yet, as I said, if he'd had money or influence or power he would have shared it. He gave us his love, which is a great deal; he had nothing else to give. But he gave his love unselfishly, in the best way, without burdening us with it, or expecting anything in return, a rare thing, a gift not many people know.

He was an example of self-control and stoicism. So I could never tell what was on his mind or in his heart. I do not know even now. I set down all my memories of him and he remains an enigma, or else—perhaps there is no more to know? He was raised in a large poor family. He went to work. The Great Depression lay like a black frost all over the country. He raised a big family, while the country was at war. He didn't prosper, yet he didn't go under. He survived and ended up counting his blessings. His spiritual life, his church-going, accounted for much of his spare time and his most serene moods. Other kids' fathers had cronies, golf partners, drinking companions, confidants, belonged to social circles, or were members (like Harry O'Brien) of country clubs; they hunted or tinkered with cars or collected stamps. None of these activities interested my father. His life was either his family or the church. Work was too tedious to talk about. He attended the Holy Name Society, and Novenas, the First Friday, High Masses, Benediction, and he usually sat towards the back of the church with his head down, the embodiment of the humble Publican in the parable of the Publican and the Pharisee, praying with his eyes cast down, twisting rosary beads in his fingers, or in the choir, singing his heart out.

In the course of writing this I have reread Edmund Gosse's *Father and Son*, and J. R. Ackerley's *My Father and Myself*, and Henry James's *Notes of a Son and Brother*. A number of biographies, too, trying to answer the question, What are other writers' fathers like? For one thing, other writers' fathers were often themselves writers. Two books that astonished me were *The Life of Kingsley Amis*, by Zachary Leader, and *Experience*, by Martin Amis. I say astonished, because if there was a man who was the opposite of my father in every way it was not nutty Philip Gosse or jolly Roger Ackerley or grandiose Henry James Senior, it was outrageous Kingsley Amis.

Amis led a messy but highly productive life. He had great and lasting friendships with other writers; he was in part a public man, his life is there in his books, he seems to have been an amiable drinking companion, not an angry drunk but a witty one for whom alcohol was creative fuel. For many years he drank heavily, often as much as a bottle of whisky a day. His hangovers were a daily event; he was phobic and a philanderer—he had sex partners and casual women friends. Panic attacks plagued him. Air travel was one of his phobias, he never boarded a plane in his life. He could not bear to be alone in a room. He raged, screaming, 'Fuck!' at his wives and children. He made quite a lot of money but saved very little, ran up debts, was burdened by overdrafts, went through two traumatic divorces, overindulged himself in food, made racist remarks to amuse his pals, was amusingly foul-mouthed and was old at sixty, ill later on, and dead at seventy-three. He received a knighthood. He left behind him a mountain of paper, a long shelf of books, a whole archive of documents.

That man was more foreign to my father than almost anyone I can imagine; my father would more easily have got on with a Bedouin or a Zulu, and in fact in Cairo got on very well with the hawkers in the bazaars, but would have been baffled to the point of non-comprehension by Amis.

If I had said to him, 'Kingsley Amis wrote sixty books—worked every morning, wrote poems, reviewed books, wrote essays, appeared on television, won the Booker Prize, published novels...' my father would have said, with economical sarcasm, 'Really?' and he would have underlined it with, 'Ha!'

No book, no poem, no prize, no gong or title, could justify a life like that, in my father's eyes. Just the drinking would have roused my father's scorn; just the women; just the swearing. Amis did not believe in God. 'It's more that I hate him.' My father believed in a loving God who, propitiated with prayer and good works, might bail him out. But my father wasn't judgemental, he did not offer gratuitous opinions about people who were debauched or dissipated. Pressed for an opinion about Amis, he would have frowned and thought, 'For what does it profit a man to gain the whole world and lose his soul'— words he lived by, but would have only said, 'A wasted life,' and then perhaps tried to temper it, as he often did, in a familiar phrase: 'He's more to be pitied.'

In some ways I know I resemble my father. I yawn like him, growling. I scowl like him at small print. I talk to myself all the time. When I am bored I feign interest in just the way he did: 'Is that so?' I snort and clear my throat like him, his gargle is now mine and so is the reflex to say, 'Serves him right,' because my father without knowing the concept believed in karma, just as he understood the subtleties of the atma concept in Hinduism, though he would have said 'soul'.

My father hated talkers, gabbers, gasbaggers and ear-benders, and so do I. My father had a way of inhaling deeply through his nose when he was impatient, and I do it too. Sometimes, I feel I am my father—never mind the writing; I have a similar temperament, a relative serenity, like to be left alone as he did, will sometime agree to anything to keep the peace, because he felt (as I do) that you can't really change the narrow stubborn mind of a person who is set in his belief, and anyway why bother?

If something is seriously wrong—my father believed—there's not much you can do to fix it. The world is large, you are small, nothing matters enough for you to get steamed up about it, and in a profound sense nothing matters except your immortal soul.

My mother was demanding, thin-skinned and impatient. She was an exasperated mother, all right with babies but hopeless with children who had a will of their own. She struggled with us, replying with her own assumptions, and when I pointed out they were illogical she accused me of defiance.

She was the sort of hoverer who would repeat, 'Be careful! You're going to drop that!' so many times that at last you bobbled the thing and dropped it.

She so completely dominated Dad that even at his most browbeaten he was uncomplaining, always at her beck and call. She became more of a pest as they grew older, rejoicing in the charade of theirs as a marriage of equals, when anyone who knew him well could seen that it was a pure tyranny—she did the talking, he did the listening, he took the blame, and when Dad became mortally ill she blamed him for that too—rolled her eyes at his pain as though he was faking, or at least exaggerating. What a trial it was for her to have this sick, coughing and spewing man in the house.

'I could kill him,' she said once out of his hearing when he was acutely ill and suffocating with emphysema.

If there was a lesson for me, these family experiences resolved themselves in my horror of weak and vain, nagging and castrating women. As soon as I sense an echo of my mother in a woman's voice I recognize the snarl of a she-wolf and I flee. Needless fuss, denial, an utter absence of logic, no memory for the hundred things I've done well but only the one thing I've failed to do, ultimately a cynicism and a merciless refusal to see my pain—when in my life I've heard those things—or heard something as subtle as a sniff, a snort, a harrumph, a certain tilt of the head—I have mentally shut myself down and vowed to end the relationship, because I do not

Paul Theroux

want to become the person that my father became in his old age, reduced to a dependency on an unhappy woman who not only didn't know what she wanted, but needed most of all someone to blame.

That was my father's example to me. In a way I think he was hinting at it all along—'Don't do what I've done, don't live my life, don't make the mistakes I've made.' Now I see I was constantly trying to protect him, rather than the other way around. I spared him the details of my life. He would have been wounded by any revelation of immorality; offended—more than offended—by an off-colour joke. He once stopped and shamed (of all people) a priest who was telling a coarse joke. 'Is that a blue joke, Father? I don't want to hear it. The boys are here'—because we were listening—'It breaks down discipline.'

He would have been appalled by getting wind of instances of my wayward behaviour. I had a mediocre school record. I was arrested by the police at a campus demo in 1962 in Amherst. I had fathered an illegitimate child. I was kicked out ('terminated early') from the Peace Corps in 1965 for a number of transgressions, my first wife and I split up in 1990, I wrote umpteen books—and these events or topics were never mentioned at all, and perhaps in my father's mind they never happened. Or was it because they were faits accomplis, there was nothing to say?

In some ways he was more like an uncle than a father to me. He did not want to know too much of me. He craved companionship without intimacy. He did not want to reveal too much of himself. He wanted us to think well of him. And I did, respecting his wish for restraint and remoteness, admiring his faith and his good heart.

Apart from his episodes of being Mr Bones, he did not burden me with his personality, or his hopes for me. He never pushed me, nor gave me advice. He left me alone and by implication he gave me to understand that he just wanted to be left alone too. ☐

AGAMEMNON'S TRUTH

Javier Cercas

The truth is the truth,
whether it's Agamemnon who speaks it or his swineherd.
Agamemnon: 'Agreed.'
Swineherd: 'I'm not convinced.'
Juan de Mairena, *Antonio Machado*

TRANSLATED FROM THE SPANISH BY
ANNE McLEAN

Javier Cercas

Javier Cercas

CARLOS IGLESIAS

'I want to tell you everything,' he said. 'You'll understand.'
'Of course.'
'I'd better warn you, it's a long story. You only know part of it.
The bit that matters is what you don't know.'
'Don't worry,' I said. 'Tell me all about it. I've got lots of time.'
'I don't know where to start.'
'Start at the beginning.'
He half closed his eyes in a gesture of fatigue; he thought for a
moment, staring blankly at the table between us and the jug of water
and empty glass; he said: 'It began with a letter. I don't have it here,
but I know it off by heart. I received it a long time ago, a year or
so after publishing my last book.
'*The Speed of Light.*'
'No,' he said. 'That's not mine.'
'What do you mean, not yours?'
'I mean not mine. My last book is *Soldiers of Salamis*. Have you
read it?'
'Yes,' I said. 'I liked it. But I liked the other one better.'
'Yeah,' he said without hiding his disappointment. 'Just like
everyone else. Anyway. As I was saying, it all started with a letter; I
know it off by heart. "Dear Javier Cercas," it began. "My name is
Javier Cercas, just like you. I'm writing simply to let you know of my
existence; I've known of yours for a while now. I'm a literature
aficionado, and when your first novel came out I bought and read it.
I liked it. Then I read the second and liked it less, as with the next
one. As for *Soldiers of Salamis*, I regret not sharing the general
enthusiasm it's provoked: it struck me as a facile, dishonest cheat of
a novel. Sorry for speaking so frankly, but I suppose having the same
name as you gives me the right, don't you think? Ha, ha! As far as I
know, we're not related (my entire family's from Granada; yours, I've
read, is from Extremadura), but we have a lot of interests in common,
especially literary ones. I write reviews for a local magazine; I sign them
with my own name and as long as you don't sue me, I'll keep doing
so, but if I decide to publish a book one day I'll sign it with my second
surname: you got there first, after all. Here's a bit of biographical
information: I'm thirty-eight years old (a year younger than you), I
work as a porter at the faculty of literature at the university, I'm
married and have two children. Regards. Signed: Javier Cercas."

'The letter left me puzzled. Javier Cercas is not a common name; Javier González is, or Pérez, or Martínez, or even Javier Miralles; but not Javier Cercas. Cercas isn't a common name at all. In fact, up to that moment I was sure everyone called Cercas came from the tiny dwindling little village in Extremadura where I was born, and that we were all somehow related. That, at least, is what my mother always claimed, and she possessed a prodigious memory and an exhaustive knowledge of the mysteries and ramifications of the family. But my mother was dead, so I couldn't ask her. Goaded by curiosity, that very day I consulted my father, my sisters, relatives in Extremadura and Madrid: everyone was surprised at the coincidence, but no one had ever heard of any Cercases in Granada, much less a Javier Cercas. Then I remembered a novel by Paul Auster that begins when an urgent voice phones the protagonist asking for Paul Auster. I also remembered a Philip Roth novel that began with a cousin of Philip Roth's phoning Philip Roth in Manhattan to tell him there's another Philip Roth in Jerusalem. I thought of Poe, Dostoevsky and Borges. I realized the letter was a joke. A literary joke, of course: someone was having a laugh at my silly propensity to infect my life with literature. However, at the end of the letter was an address (Av. Salvador Allende, 13, Ed. P. Verona, B6, 10, 18007, Granada) and an email address (j.cercas@udgr.es). Although I knew it was all false, I wrote an email to my supposed namesake in which I pretended to believe it was all true. In it I thanked him for his letter, told him of my surprise at discovering the existence of another person with exactly the same name as me and my desire that we should one day meet. "I'm only sorry," I concluded, with the aim of taking some enigmatic revenge for the disparaging opinion about my books expressed in his letter, "that you don't like my novels. Although, of course, having the very same name as me and wanting to be a novelist, it's only natural, don't you think? Ha, ha!"

'Several days went by, but no one replied to the message, so I decided to settle my doubts. I called directory enquiries and, unable to avoid feeling slightly ridiculous, asked the operator for the phone number of a man called Javier Cercas, living in Granada, at number 13 avenida Salvador Allende. After a moment, the operator told me they had no customer of that name living at that number of that street. "Is there anyone with that name anywhere in Granada?" I insisted. After another moment, the operator informed me: "No." My suspicions confirmed, I was smiling inside, wondering which of my friends or acquaintances would have been responsible for that little joke, when a tiny remnant of uncertainty gave me an idea. I called directory enquiries again, asked for the number of the faculty of literature at the University of Granada and dialled it. "Faculty of literature, how can I help you?" chirped a woman's voice. "May I speak to Javier Cercas?" I asked. "One moment, please," she answered. Incredulous, I waited, and after a while my namesake picked up the phone. I identified myself; his reaction was not warm. "I looked for your home phone number," I said for something to say, as if to apologize for calling him at work. "But I couldn't find it." "The telephone's in my wife's name," he answered. "Ah," I said. "Well, I just wanted to thank you for your letter." "You already thanked me by email," he said. "Oh, you received it?" I asked. "Naturally," he answered. I didn't ask why he hadn't replied to my message: by that point it was already evident that he was not very happy that I'd phoned him, which bothered me a little, because after all he'd been the one who got in touch with me first. I tried to be accommodating, however. "You know, I thought it was a joke," I admitted cheerfully. "What?" he asked. "Your letter," I answered. "Why would it be a joke?" he asked. "Well, our name's not a very common one," I explained. "I thought we were all from the same family, or at least from the same village." "Well, now you see you were mistaken," he said. The conversation continued along the same lines for a while, but little by little I managed to assuage my interlocutor's acerbity or initial distrust. I asked about his work, his wife and children, his literary tastes, the reviews he'd published. "You write novels, don't you?" "No," he replied. "Not yet." "Not yet?" I asked. "I mean, maybe one day I will," he clarified. "Well, actually I have done, but I didn't like the result. Anyway, I suppose I demand too much of myself." The comment struck me as petulant: the classic bravura of someone who can't write, doesn't know how to write or doesn't want to write, but whose vanity prevents him from recognizing it. Of course, I didn't say anything, but nor was I able to repress a hint of compassion for him. We kept talking, and eventually said goodbye with a modicum of courtesy (more, in any case, than the beginning of our conversation presaged), vaguely saying we'd keep in touch. Naturally, we didn't keep in touch.'

'You didn't?'

'No. Not in the weeks that followed, at least.' He leaned towards the table, picked up the water jug, filled his glass and took a sip. Setting the glass back down on the table, he warned, 'Now the story starts to get complicated. Complicated and long.'

'Don't worry,' I reassured him. 'Go on.'

'I was going through a bad time,' he continued after a silence. 'My latest novel had been very successful: people had liked it; the critics as well. I know you're not going to believe me, but the truth is there's nothing better than success. Nothing or almost nothing, as long as you know enough to keep the idea out of your head that you've stolen your success from someone who deserved it much more, and that all success is disgrace and humiliation, and that it's always contaminated in some way by stupidity; besides, I assure you that success has many things to teach. Looking no further than myself, it taught me that I possessed a fabulous capacity to do damage... Anyway, I'll spare you the gruesome details. What happened is that I lost my wife, I lost very dear friends. At first I attributed this to the fact that, strange as it seems, it's often more difficult to love someone when things are going well for them than when things are going badly, because the other's happiness deprives us of the dirty pleasure of compassion. I also frequently thought of something Pascal once said: "No one is entirely saddened by a friend's misfortune"; or what amounts to the same thing: no one is entirely delighted by a friend's happiness. What I mean is that at first I thought my wife and the friends I'd lost hadn't been able to bear my success; with time I've arrived at the conclusion that my wife and the friends I'd lost hadn't been able to bear me, simply because I'd become unbearable. On the other hand, my novel's success allowed me to give up my job and devote myself to writing full-time, but during several months of non-stop work I wasn't able to write anything that didn't seem derivative or simply bad, so at some point I decided I wouldn't write again. The surprising thing wasn't the decision (one of those decisions dictated by frustration that are revoked as lightly as they're taken); the surprising thing was that I didn't feel the slightest anxiety. Just the opposite: I felt relief, as if I'd freed myself of a responsibility I'd assumed only due to a misunderstanding. I'll explain why.

'I'd dreamed of being a writer my whole life; it was an exclusive dream, and that's why I'd always written compulsively, as if it was a necessity or even a therapy, just as if I harboured an irrational suspicion that, as soon as I stopped writing, I'd turn into a monster. Well, as soon as I was successful—as soon as I thought I knew for sure that I was now a writer—that suspicion evaporated, perhaps because I'd already turned into a monster. I no longer wrote out of necessity, but out of inertia, and therefore the result could not possibly be necessary, but only inert, derivative or simply bad. Stunned, I realized I could live without writing. The worst thing was, by this point, I couldn't stop being a writer, because everyone—publishers, readers, critics: everyone— considered me a writer and, since you're never entirely what you are, but what others choose for you to be, this situation condemned me to a fraudulent condition: a writer is only a writer when he's writing— not before, not after—and, although happily I no longer wrote, I remained, obliged by circumstances, imprisoned in the humiliating role of a man of letters that disgusted me and impeded me from becoming entirely who I then thought I wanted to be.

'That was more or less the situation I found myself in when, a few days after talking to the man who had the same name as me but wasn't me, someone from Granada city council phoned to invite me to participate in a writers' festival. By then it had been a while since I'd started turning down all the engagements that forced me into my humiliating man-of-letters role, so I turned this one down too. I did it instinctively, but as soon as I'd hung up the phone I remembered my namesake in Granada and couldn't avert the superstitious thought that fate has her own rules, and the next day, after a few hesitations, I found the phone number of Granada city council, called and accepted the invitation. The event was to be held in a month's time; the week before I called my namesake and proposed that we make use of my visit to Granada to have dinner together. He told me he couldn't, that he had a previous engagement the night I would be spending in the city; then I suggested we see each other during the day, or the next night, but he said he couldn't make it then either. I understood that he didn't want to meet me, but I insisted again and again, until finally, I don't know how, I managed to overcome his resistance. We arranged to meet for dinner. "How will we recognize each other?" I asked before hanging up. "Don't worry," he said. "We'll recognize each other." So a week later, after participating with three other novelists in an anodyne round table at the Palacio de los Condes de Gabia, claiming an inescapable family commitment I avoided the dinner the organizers of the event had planned and went to Los Manueles, the restaurant where we'd arranged to meet. It was a place with a self-consciously Andalusian ambience, with a long bar crowded with people drinking beer and eating *pescadito frito*, at the end of which I made out a man on his own, who looked up from the menu when I was just a few metres away. At that moment I felt a vertiginous emptiness in my stomach, I felt I couldn't get any air and was losing my footing, and I'm sure I would've fallen flat on my face if the man hadn't stood up, steadied me, dragged me over to his table and sat me down opposite him. "Drink this," I heard. I drank: it was whisky. I had another drink, and only when I began to feel the warmth returning to my body did I dare to look at the man in front of me. More than look at him, I studied him, and the alcohol kept me from fainting this time, because he was exactly like me, my living portrait, as if, instead of having before me an individual of flesh and bone, I had only the clean surface of a mirror. "You're..." I stammered. Shrugging his shoulders he nodded. "It's incredible," I said. "Incredible but true," he pointed out in a voice as foreign and as familiar as my own voice heard on the radio; then, with disconcerting naturalness, he continued: "I know what you're thinking. How is it possible? I've only got one answer: how should I know? In theory, there are no two faces alike in the whole world; in theory there should be no two faces alike in all of humanity. But that's in theory; in practice here you have it, and for all we know there might be a guy in Bogotá right now with the same face as Napoleon Bonaparte." I tried to say something, but I couldn't; one part of me had already accepted the evidence, but another part refused to recognize it, as if I suspected that my life had suddenly turned into a dream. To bolster my courage I downed the whisky in one gulp. "How long have you known?" I asked. "Since I saw a photograph of you in the newspaper," he answered. "And why didn't you tell me before?" I asked. He shrugged again. "What for? A person's got enough to worry about with the things that go on every day, let alone having to worry about weird things as well. And don't forget you're the one who insisted we should meet." A waiter came over to take our order and, while I scanned the menu as quickly as possible, I heard a peculiar noise; I looked up: the waiter, his eyes watery, was making an enormous effort to hold in his laughter. At that moment I thought of Pascal: "Two faces which resemble each other make us laugh, when together, by their resemblance, though neither of them by itself makes us laugh." I wasn't hungry, or perhaps I couldn't decide what to have, but my namesake ordered for us both: he ordered salad, croquettes and *pescadito frito*; he also ordered wine. As soon as he turned around, the waiter convulsed with laughter. "Does anyone else know?" I asked sadly. "No one, as far as I know," answered my namesake. "Except the waiter, of course." He smiled for the first time, and it was as if I was seeing myself smile. "Lots of people know there's a guy with the same name as me who's a writer and, when your books started coming out, people asked me if I'd written them; luckily your publishers don't put author photos on their covers and a few who've seen you in newspapers have told me we look alike, but nobody's gone any further, I suppose because when the obvious is incredible it ceases to be obvious." We began to eat in silence, picking morosely at our food and sneaking sidelong glances at each other, but after a while an unexpected complicity had grown up between us brought about by the visible secret we shared, to the extent that, when we left the restaurant, I realized I'd told my namesake things I hadn't even had the courage (or temerity) to tell myself; I now know that he'd done the same with me. I suggested we go for a nightcap and, although he'd barely tasted the wine during dinner, he accepted: it was obvious he was now amused by the conversation, even enthused, especially when he managed to restrict it to my affairs. We went to El Diván de Tamarit, a nearby bar with comfortable armchairs and stools in front of the bar and a big mirror behind it, where very soft music that I didn't recognize played. We sat on two stools. I ordered a whisky; he ordered tonic water. After a while I ordered another whisky and, while I was drinking it, I looked at my namesake in the mirror; he looked old, fat and sad: it was as if I was looking at myself, because he was also looking at me. Thinking of Pascal, I was about to burst out laughing, but at that moment an idea so explosive crossed my mind that for a second I thought it wasn't mine; unfortunately, I didn't discard it. I took another sip of whisky, and before turning away from the mirror noticed that I was smiling. "You're not happy with your life, are you?" I asked as if stating a fact, suddenly noticing my furry-sounding voice and instantly regretting the way I'd put the question or statement; the next instant I understood there was no other way to put it. "Who is?" my namesake smiled. "But

Javier Cercas

there's nothing to be done." "That's not true," I said. "There is something we could do: we could change it, change our lives." "Sure," he said. "I could leave my house, walk out on my wife and kids. Don't be a fool: at our age you can't change your life any more without destroying all sorts of people. And I'm not strong enough and far too lazy to do that." "Maybe it's not necessary," I said. "I mean maybe it's not necessary to harm anyone." He looked at me and said: "I don't understand." I sighed, downed my whisky and succinctly explained my plan. It consisted of trading places: he would be me and I would be him. My namesake now looked at me with genuine curiosity; then burst out laughing. "You're crazy," he said. "You're crazier than I thought." I insisted: I told him the swap would obviously not be forever, just for an agreed amount of time; I told him, if I were him, I'd be less unhappy than I was, because I'd recover something I'd lost, and that, if he were me, he'd also be less unhappy, because he'd get something he'd always wanted. "It would only be for a while," I concluded. "When we get tired of being who we're not, we can go back to being who we were." "You're crazy," he repeated. "Don't you realize that, supposing I accepted, which is impossible, we'd be discovered straight away?" "Why should we be found out?" I asked. "Physically we're identical: no one would guess that I'm not me and that you're not you. And as for the rest, they'll only find us out if we don't prepare ourselves conscientiously, not if we do: really, all we have to do is spend two or three days together and you tell me all about your life, your work and your family and I'll do the same. What we don't learn in those days we'll pick up with time and with care, naturally. Think it over, it would be an extraordinary experiment, and at least it would free us from the weariness and boredom of being who we are. Besides, it'll be for a short time: when you get tired of being me or I get tired of being you, we'll swap roles again and that'll be that, no one will have noticed anything, it'll be a secret just between the two of us." I paused. "Well?" I dared him. "What do you say?" He stared at me for a few seconds, with a mixture of wonder and irony; I looked away: I noticed we were alone in the bar and the music wasn't playing any more. "Let's go," he finally said. "You're drunk."

'It was true. I knew it as soon as we stepped outside, but still I insisted on walking home with him. Instead he drove me to the hotel. We didn't speak along the way; I stared blindly at the sleeping streets

The perfect gift.

A gift of *Granta* is perfect for friends and relatives who share your love of reading; there is no risk of sending something that they have already read, and the pleasure will extend all year!

Buy today and you can give four issues of *Granta* for only £24.95* – that's a saving of 50% off bookshop prices.

GRANTA

'The most
influential literary
magazine in the UK'
Observer

Yes, I'd like to give Granta as a gift.
Please reserve the following subscriptions:

Number of subscriptions	Delivery region	Price per subscription	Saving
☐	UK/USA	£24.95	50%
☐	Europe/S. America	£29.95	40%
☐	Canada & rest of world	£34.95	30%

BILLING DETAILS All prices include delivery!

Title: Initial: Surname:

Address:

Postcode:

Telephone: Email:

GIFT ONE DELIVERY DETAILS

Title: Initial: Surname:

Address:

Postcode:

Telephone:

Email:

Please start with ☐ this issue ☐ next issue

GIFT TWO DELIVERY DETAILS

Title: Initial: Surname:

Address:

Postcode:

Telephone:

Email:

Please start with ☐ this issue ☐ next issue

PAYMENT

[1] I enclose a cheque payable to 'Granta' for £_____ for _____ gift subscriptions to *Granta*

[2] Please debit my ☐ Mastercard ☐ Visa ☐ Amex for £_____ for _____ gift subscriptions

Card number: ☐☐☐☐ ☐☐☐☐ ☐☐☐☐ ☐☐☐☐   07EBGRA0

Expiry date: ☐☐ / ☐☐   Signed _____   Date _____

Please return this form to Granta Subscriptions or telephone +44 (0)1256 302 873
PO Box 6712, Brunel Road, Basingstoke, RG24 4FP, United Kingdom

OUR GUARANTEE: Your subscription is 100% risk-free. You can write and cancel at any time, for any reason and claim a refund of the cost of all un-mailed issues.   G R A N T A

Please tick if you would prefer not to receive occasional offers from compatible companies by post ☐ by phone ☐ by email ☐

of Granada, going over and over my plan, so when he stopped the car I insisted again: I told him my flight the next day was at half past twelve, and that I'd be at the hotel till eleven. "If you change your mind, call me," I said. "I haven't got any commitments, I can stay as many days as we need: we can shut ourselves up in my hotel room and swot up on each other's lives, until we know the other's as well as we know our own. Think about it," I concluded. I don't remember what his answer was (undoubtedly it was negative), or even how we said goodbye (undoubtedly it was politely), but I do remember that I kept drinking and smoking in my hotel room, facing the television I didn't turn on, and that the next day I woke up with an apocalyptic hangover and an equally vague and guilty memory of what had gone on the night before. As I had breakfast I glanced through the local papers, saw an interview I'd given and a quite detailed report of the round table discussion in which I'd participated. I didn't read them through to the end: when you read what you said in a newspaper and you've read the same things that you said ten times in ten other different newspapers you feel nothing but utter revulsion, as if it wasn't you who said what you'd said, but an unscrupulous dummy that lives inside you and has no sense of the ridiculous and has usurped your voice and your words. At least this is what I thought as I leafed through the papers, and immediately thought of my namesake and the unlikely proposition I'd made a few hours earlier. I smiled: I remembered his shocked face and wondered how I would have got myself out of it if he had let himself get as carried away as I did by the insanity of alcohol and, instead of refusing my offer, he'd accepted. It wouldn't have been the first time in the last little while that, after a night on the whisky, tormented by guilt, I had to rush to put out the fire I'd started the previous evening, but luckily, thanks to my namesake's good sense, on this occasion there was no wrong to right. Almost happy, I looked at my watch: there was just half an hour till the taxi would come to take me to the airport. I took a couple of aspirin, went up to my room and was just getting my things together when the phone rang. I picked it up; it wasn't the taxi: it was my namesake. I hadn't yet recovered from the surprise when I heard him say that he accepted my proposal. "What proposal?" I asked, knowing perfectly well what proposal he was referring to, but trying to play for time. "The one you suggested last night," he

Javier Cercas

reminded me. "That we should trade places. That I should be you and you should be me." Noticing that the phone had started shaking in my hand, I stammered: "Really?" "I think so," he said. "I've been thinking it over all night and I've arrived at the conclusion that, well, it could be fun and even healthy, I think it might do me good. Besides, it'll only be for a while... Yes: I want to give it try. You haven't changed your mind, have you?" "No, no, of course not," I lied. "It's just that, well, to be honest I didn't expect you to call and..." I looked at my watch: the taxi was about to arrive and I still hadn't finished packing my things. I don't know why, I thought of my late mother and of my father living in the old people's home and my wife and my son and the empty office I had to return to and didn't want to return to, I thought about all that and, as if I were taking revenge on someone, without knowing I was making the most transcendental decision of my life, said: "Okay." And I added, noting that the phone was no longer trembling in my hand: "I'll wait for you at the hotel."'

He paused, staring at the almost empty glass on the table: a self-absorbed or melancholy smile floated on his lips, and for a moment I had the impression that he'd forgotten me; he hadn't forgotten.

'That was how it all began,' he finally said, without appearing to have emerged from his abstraction. 'It was madness. Imagine the scene: two identical men, who've just met, confined for hours and hours in a hotel room, tirelessly exchanging stories, habits, abilities, confidences, addresses and infinite, endless details of their lives and of those who surround them. If it wasn't so laughable, it would be a bit frightening, which is how it strikes me each time I remember it. Anyway. We thought shutting ourselves up for a couple of days would be enough, but we didn't feel the slightest bit sure of knowing each other until four had gone by, because even the blandest life of the blandest of men is impenetrably complex. We proceeded with caution: no one was waiting for me at home, so I didn't have to make excuses for my absence; as for my namesake, the first day he told the university he was ill, so he spent the eight hours of his workday with me and went home at the usual time, without awakening any suspicions. We soon realized that the most difficult thing would be to exchange habits, because we were both men of habit, and opposite habits besides: I smoked and he didn't, I drank and he didn't, I bit my nails and his were intact. I won't go on: it was a problem. I trusted that, in my case, the change of life would enable a change of habits; as for him, he opted for a strategy that would demand less effort: he would carry on not smoking, drinking or biting his nails, and would attribute the sudden end of his vices to an old determination to change too long and too often postponed. It wasn't difficult, on the other hand, to absorb the details of his work routine, but that of his family was a different story, obliging me to take lots of notes and memorize lots of information concerning the rules of domestic life, the pasts and presents of his wife and his two children; the opposite must have occurred to him, because mimicking my non-existent family life would be a piece of cake, but my work was another thing altogether. We resolved this difficulty by opting for the simplest solution, which was to cancel all the engagements I'd contracted for the following months, except for writing an article every second week for the Sunday supplement of a newspaper: since it was a significant source of income that was worth hanging on to, we agreed I'd carry on writing the article and would send it to him by email and he could send it to the paper by the same route, so they wouldn't notice any change in the return address. We also agreed that, since it was the safest, email would be our habitual means of communication, and only in very exceptional cases could we have recourse to the telephone. On the afternoon of the fifth day, at the time he usually went home from work, we traded clothes, I handed him the keys to my house, my office and my car, and he handed me his; we said goodbye. "Well," I said, shaking his hand. "From here on in you're me. Enjoy." "Same to you," he said. "And good luck." I went out into the hall, got to the elevator, called it; before it arrived I turned around. My namesake was still at the door to the room. He looked serious. "Good luck," he repeated.

'That's how my new life began. It's true that it wasn't entirely new, and in more than one sense it amounted to a retreat to the one I'd left behind, a family life with a wife and children and an eight-hour workday; but it's also true that it couldn't have been newer, because everything in it radiated the undiminished gleam of the first time, so even the most insignificant gesture was steeped in the prestige of adventure in my eyes. With unusual ease I gave up my vices: I quit smoking and drinking and biting my nails, and slipped into my namesake's habits as if they were a made-to-measure suit, which to my surprise made me stop feeling like a fraud, just as if my true identity

Javier Cercas

wasn't the one I'd abandoned, but the one I was now usurping. I remember the day I arrived at my new house, just minutes after having taken leave of my namesake at the hotel. It was a modest apartment in a modest building on Avenida Salvador Allende. When I opened the door no one came to greet me. Following the sound of a television, I walked into the sitting room: on an imitation-leather sofa, two boys were watching Japanese cartoons. Hi, I said. Neither of them turned around, but the elder one answered: Hi. I went to the kitchen: a dark-haired, plump woman, wearing tracksuit bottoms and a tank top straining to contain her full breasts, was dumping a steaming saucepan of boiled spinach into a colander. I said hello, went over and kissed her on the cheek. "Javi," she said in an almost surly tone of voice. "Do me a favour and drag those kids away from the TV and into the shower." It was the first time since my mother's death that anyone had called me Javi; I didn't find it disagreeable. The woman wasn't disagreeable to me either; my namesake had described her at length, and reality didn't betray his description: she wasn't pretty, but, perhaps because I'd expected something much worse, I didn't think her ugly either. I obeyed: I dragged the almost kicking and screaming boys to the shower; then we had dinner, all together, in front of the television, almost without speaking, while I contemplated my new family out of the corner of my eye. Then the kids went to bed and, once the kitchen was cleaned up, the woman sat down next to me on the sofa, lit a cigarette and zapped through the available channels until stopping at a game show. We watched the game show; once in a while she'd make a comment that didn't require a response; I kept quiet, very quiet, unable to follow what was happening on the screen, feeling the warmth of her thigh against mine, breathing in her unhappy-housewife scent, until at some point I noticed I was getting hard. I tried to calm the erection, but the effort did nothing but make its determination firmer. I thought of my namesake, of certain intimacies he'd told me about during the time we spent together. I brushed her hair away from her face. She turned and looked at me with surprise, almost displeasure. "What are you doing?" she asked. I smiled. "Nothing," I said. She turned back to the television, and I immediately put my arm around her waist. I don't know if I tickled her, but now she was the one who smiled. "Keep still," she said. Anyway, after a little while we were screwing on the sofa. The truth: it was a glorious fuck; she came several times: first we did it face to face and then from behind, and when I was about to come...'

'You don't need to go into details.'

'Sorry. Anyway, like I said: it was a glorious fuck, I don't think I've ever enjoyed one so much... You don't believe me, do you?'

'I didn't say that.'

'No, you haven't said it, but that's what you're thinking.' He looked me in the eye. 'Let me ask you a question. Have you ever screwed a wife and mother you've never seen before, who would never even dream of being unfaithful to her husband, and who doesn't even know she's being unfaithful to him while she is? Of course not. Well, I can assure you it's the most exciting thing there is.'

'I believe you.'

'No, you don't believe me. But it doesn't matter... I don't care if you don't believe that; you believe the rest, don't you?'

'Of course.'

'That's what matters.' He leaned over the table again, poured himself some more water, drank again. Then he went on: 'The days that followed were as extraordinary as the first. It was all exciting, brutally exciting, from the moment I woke up in someone else's house beside a woman who was not my wife and had breakfast with children who were not my children until I returned to the same house and had sex with that fat, not very good-looking woman I fancied more with every fuck, after having spent the day at the university carrying out my porter's work (opening the faculty, sorting and delivering the post, answering the telephone and doing the thousand and one little routine jobs that kept the faculty running smoothly), striving to carry out the same surreptitious, clandestine exercise with the people I worked with as I practised at home, an exercise that had all the attractions of an adventure with none of its real dangers, and that gave me the same satisfaction as a delinquent might derive from getting away with a crime. Because that was how I felt: like an unpunished criminal, like a spy and an impostor and a usurper and a voyeur of my own life, but never like a fraud, which is how I used to feel when I hadn't yet stopped being who I was. I also felt happy: not only with my new life, which wasn't entirely new because in a certain way it amounted to a retreat to my previous life; but also (or perhaps to an even greater extent) because no one suspected I was an impostor.

'No one suspected my namesake was an impostor either, or at least that's what I deduced from his almost absolute silence. I heard, in effect, very little from him, and the little that I heard did not disprove this conclusion. Every two weeks without fail I sent him my article, accompanied by a brief message or just a greeting, and he replied in the same way. At first I thought it strange that he didn't ask about his family, but I decided to put it down to a perfectionist zeal to conscientiously embody his new character, cutting himself off from everything that bore any relation to the old; on the other hand, I often asked him about mine, and he answered with antiseptic brevity, except for the vague optimistic comments on the excellence of our change of life with which he tended to begin his missives. However, with time our email correspondence became less laconic, until it acquired the level of fluidity or friendliness that one day (by then more than five months since we'd changed places) my namesake confessed that for the last several weeks he'd been living in the same house as my wife and my son, as if they were his son and his wife. Understandably, my first reaction at this news was surprise; incomprehensibly, the second was jealousy. Making an effort, I suppressed them: it was true that I had begged my wife in vain several times to come back to me, but it was also true that, if I was living with my namesake's wife, it was entirely logical that my namesake should be living with mine. This reasoning not only reassured me (or at least partially reassured me), but also the extraordinary image of my namesake on my sofa screwing my wife, a married woman and a mother he'd never seen before, and who thought she was going back to being faithful to her husband while she was actually being unfaithful to him, excited me as much or more than if it had been me who was having sex with her. So I accepted the wife swap as one more ingredient of the experiment I had risked undertaking. That wasn't all we risked. A few weeks later my namesake asked my opinion of a text he'd just written. I read it. I was surprised to find it wasn't bad; to please him, I told him it was really good and, undoubtedly carried away by euphoria, he asked me if I'd let him send it to the newspaper just this once instead of the text I sent every two weeks. Without even thinking it over I accepted, and two weeks later the same thing happened again, and again two weeks after that, so I ended up cutting the umbilical cord that still connected me to my previous life: writing. Why did I do it? I don't know. I suppose because I was fed up with writing, and not doing it was a sort of cavalier form of liberation; and, besides, because reading my namesake's articles, each one fresher, funnier and more clever than the last, satisfied me like a long-delayed personal revenge, proving once more that writing is not a question of intelligence, sensitivity or talent, but of pure and simple obstinacy. Anyway. The thing is these unexpected exchanges had the effect of solidifying the experiment and the smooth and happy way my life went on: up till then, blocked by the unquenchable obsession of writing, I'd been unable to enjoy my wife and son, whom I considered hindrances that kept me from fully realizing my vocation; now, instead, freed from the tyranny of literature, my family was a constant source of satisfaction, to such an extent that, though I knew it wasn't mine, I had no option but to think of it as if it were. Of course, they noticed. I mean my wife and my sons noticed that their relationship with her husband and their father had changed, but, since it had changed for the better and since people never wonder why good things happen (only bad), they accepted the fact with no concern or questions, and only on very few occasions I surprised my wife spying on me with inquisitive eyes, as if searching mine for someone who wasn't me. Unlike my real wife, she wasn't a curious person: she hardly ever read, only liked predictable or bland films and TV programmes she could doze in front of on the sofa, but she enjoyed that smooth placidity that is the irresistible charm of certain charmless people. I knew that she was unaware, because my namesake had hidden the fact, that a thousand kilometres away existed a man with the same name as her husband and who was a writer, and one afternoon, after work, I bought a copy of my latest book, took it home and showed it to her, pretending to be astonished by the coincidence of the name. My wife was astonished without pretence and grabbed the book out of my hands. "I loved it," she told me two days later, her eyes wide and shining. "It's so moving, so funny…" She paused and added: "And so strange." "So strange?" I asked. "Yes," she answered. "While I was reading it I kept thinking that it was the book you would have written if you'd really wanted to be a writer. It's silly, but that's what I thought. There's something else I thought as well: why don't you get in touch with him?" "With the author?" I asked. "Of course," she said. "Who else?" "What for?" I asked again. "No reason: just to tell

him you've got the same name as him. I'm sure he'd think it funny."
"That's ridiculous!" I said, feeling a tickle of satisfaction in my
stomach. "Why would it be ridiculous?" she said. "Try it and you'll
see he thinks it's funny. Besides, he's a writer: maybe he can help you
publish the books you've got in the drawer." I was about to ask:
"What books?" but I stopped myself in time and settled the
conversation: "No way." That very night I wrote an email to my
namesake reproaching him for never having mentioned the
manuscripts he had hidden away and asking him if his wife had read
them. He answered my two points immediately; the question clearly:
his wife hadn't read them, because, he wrote, she never read anything;
and the reproach evasively: he hadn't told me about the books he had
hidden away because they weren't up to the standards he set for
himself. The answer irritated me so much that I replied with a threat:
if he wanted to continue the experiment he'd better tell me where the
books were and let me read them. He gave in without any resistance:
the two books (a novel and a collection of stories) were in two folders
with blue covers, in a bookcase in the back room. That very night I
got hold of them, and over the following days read them avidly and
saw with relief that they weren't as good as I'd feared for a moment;
not that bad either: the stories were better than the novel, but both
belonged to that type of book that a second-division publisher (of the
sort that claims to specialize in the discovery of new talent, which in
reality is almost never new or talented), would perhaps not disdain
to publish, but would publish without the least conviction. Of course,
I didn't say any of this to my namesake, and nor did I rule out the
possibility, which at some point I actually came to consider seriously,
of asking him to let me submit his novel to my editor, as if it were
mine, to satisfy my contractual obligation with him.'
    'With whom?'
    'My editor. Didn't I say that?' I shook my head. 'I thought I did.'
After a pause, as if he were telling a timeworn story which bored
him profoundly, he explained: 'I had signed a contract with my editor
that committed me to submitting a novel within three years. It was
a mistake, because there wasn't much of the allotted time left and I
hadn't even started to write anything. Nor did I have any intention
of doing so. So when I saw that my namesake had an unpublished
novel I thought that maybe... But I didn't dare.'

'Why not?'

He hesitated for a moment, shrugged his shoulders.

'I don't know.'

'So then, how did you get out of the predicament?'

'I didn't: they got me out. That's what I was going to tell you. But first let me tell you something else, because if I don't you might not understand how it all ended. I think I already explained that my father lived in an old people's home; he had Alzheimer's, or some kind of senile dementia. Our relationship had never been very close, at least until my mother died; then it changed a little, but by then it was too late. Anyway, I visited him once in a while, perhaps not as often as I should have, but I did visit him... The thing is one night, when I checked my email as usual, I found a message from my namesake telling me that my father had died suddenly and his funeral would take place the next day in Sant Narcís church. The next day I called the faculty from the airport to say I was ill, took a plane to Barcelona, hired a car there and at noon parked in the Plaza de Sant Narcís, in front of the church. Several groups of acquaintances milled around the door. After they'd gone in, and though the day was warm and cloudy, I put on some dark glasses, pulled on my overcoat, put the collar up and followed them. Inside the church there were a lot of people, but I soon spotted my sisters and their families, my wife and son in the front rows; also, just like one more among them, I recognized my namesake. He was in the front row, sitting very straight and dressed in black, and during the whole ceremony he remained perfectly still, and when at the end people went over to express their condolences he doled out kisses, handshakes and embraces with the same heavy-hearted ease with which he would have done had it been him and not me who had just been orphaned, but it wasn't until later, at the moment when they were walking towards the door, hidden beside a confessional, when I saw my wife and my son and my sisters go by a few metres away and especially when I made out the unmistakable irritation of tears in the eyes of my namesake, that I felt for the first time a wounding nostalgia for my other life, for my previous and true life, for my wife and my son and my home and my work as a writer and also for my father, and the sadness and nostalgia got mixed up with a murderous rage towards my namesake, as if it had been him who'd stolen my life without warning and not me who'd insisted that he lend me his in exchange so that I could do the same for him. Surreptitiously I followed the cortège to the cemetery and surreptitiously I attended the burial and surreptitiously I returned to the airport and to Granada and to my surreptitious Granada life, and for a while, for reasons I wouldn't have been able to explain, I still tried to recover the excitement of the novelty of the first days of my new false life, but it was in vain: my false job bored me and so did my false family life, my false children and my false wife, perhaps because the tension of clandestinity no longer existed and so I could no longer feel like a voyeur or an unpunished criminal, because with time and habit that deceitful life had irremediably turned into my real life. Nevertheless, I didn't decide to put an end to the experiment until one afternoon I arrived home and found my kids watching TV and my wife reading a book. She didn't give me time to ask her what she was reading; she showed me: the book was called *The Speed of Light*; it was by Javier Cercas. "It's just come out," she said, smiling. Incredulity left me speechless: making no effort at pretence, without even a single word, I snatched the book out of her hands and locked myself away to read it. I didn't sleep all night, and the next day, arriving at university, the first thing I did was phone my namesake. It was the first time I'd done so, because we'd decided we'd only use the telephone in case of emergency and by previously agreeing a time by email. My namesake answered perplexed and furious, but I was even more so. "You're a son of a bitch," I told him. "How dare you publish a book under my name?" He must've noticed I was more furious than he was, because he calmed down and asked me to calm down. "I don't feel like it," I answered. "You promised me that if you published a book one day you'd do so under your second surname. Tell me, how could you publish a book under my name?" "Let me remind you your name is also mine," he answered. "Oh please, don't give me that," I replied. "I am me and you are you. You've used me." "And you haven't used me?" he answered. "Come on, Javier, please, be reasonable. Tell me something: have you read the book?" I said I had. "And what did you think?" I'd thought the book was surprisingly good (better, undoubtedly, than either of his; better, I fear, than all of mine); of course, I refused to admit it, and instead of answering his question I demanded explanations again. "I really don't know why you're so upset," he reasoned. "You've stopped writing, you don't really want to do it any more, right?" He didn't let me answer. "So what's wrong with me doing it for you? Besides, your editor was putting the pressure on; as soon as I gave him the two books the problems were over." "Two books?" I asked. "What two books?" "The other one's a mixture of things: columns, articles, essays; I think I'll probably include a story as well. It's called *Agamemnon's Truth*, it'll be coming out pretty soon, I think. So your editor was very happy. Instead of acting like a lunatic, you should be grateful: I've got you out of a spot." Maybe to show him he was mistaken and didn't yet know what a lunatic was, I started to act like a real lunatic, but the very violent argument didn't resolve anything, probably because it was all impossible to resolve. "Well, that's enough," I cut him off. "It's over. Remember our deal: when one of us gets tired of being who he isn't, we'll go back to being who we were. Well, I'm tired of it now." "It's not possible," he said, and I noticed with satisfaction that his tone of voice had changed. "Think about it. Now we both lead the life we wanted to lead: you've recovered what you'd lost, and I've achieved what I've always wanted. We're both satisfied. Why change?" "I'm not satisfied," I said. "Not any more. But even if I were, I'm tired of it. I want my real wife and my real son and my real work back, I want my real life back." "But don't you realize your real life is the one you've got now?" he reasoned. "Don't you realize? Even if you wanted, your wife isn't your wife any more, your son isn't your son any more, your books aren't your books any more. Your life isn't your life any more: it's mine. I'm you. Don't you understand?" "You're a son of a bitch," I repeated. "The only thing I understand is that you're a son of a bitch and you don't want to comply with what we agreed. Well, you are going to comply, whether you like it or not." "Oh, really?" he asked, and I noticed his tone of voice had changed again: now it had turned ironic, almost sarcastic. "And how are you going to make me?" "I'll tell everyone the truth," I said, and I noticed I was shouting. "I'll tell your wife and your kids and your friends and your workmates, and my wife as well and my son and my editor and the newspaper..." He didn't let me finish: down the telephone line his roar of laughter sounded frank and clear, identical, I thought then, to one he'd let out that night in Granada, in El Diván de Tamarit, just after I suggested we swap identities. "But, hey," he said, "don't you realize no one's going to believe you?" "They'll believe me," I assured him unthinkingly. "They certainly will believe me. If things aren't back in place within two weeks, I'll start telling everyone. I'm warning you. And that's my last word on the subject." Without giving him time to answer, I hung up. Of course, it was my last word, or at least the last I exchanged with him. Over the next two weeks, in a state of nervousness that edged closer and closer to panic, I waited for a message, which did not arrive. Meanwhile my wife wouldn't stop talking about the Cercas novel, I read a couple of enthusiastic reviews of the book (in one of which the critic admired the unexpected change of direction the author had taken in his writing and the surprising capacity to avoid his two worst vices: gratuitous humour and the propensity to sentimentality) and I heard him give a couple of radio interviews and couldn't distinguish his voice from mine. When the two weeks I'd given him were up, I sent several ultimatums by email, but he didn't answer them; he didn't answer his phone when I called either: he'd changed the number, and directory enquiries told me the new number was unlisted. By then I'd admitted I couldn't tell everyone the truth, for the simple reason that, as my namesake had understood long before I had, no one would believe it: my real wife wasn't going to believe she'd spent more than a year living with a false Javier Cercas, nor would my son and my editor and my friends, and my false wife and my false sons and my false workmates would never admit that the man they'd been living and working with wasn't the Javier Cercas they'd always known. Desperate, I understood I was a prisoner in a hermetically sealed nightmare; I understood there was nothing I could do. Nothing except what I did, of course. Don't make me tell it again, please. Everyone knows the story, I've never denied it. All I want is to be understood, I want them to know why I did what I did. I had no choice. They say I lost my marbles, that I went crazy; let them say what they like, but I'm asking you to take me seriously. Think it over seriously and you'll realize there was no other solution. And you'll understand I'm not mad. I'm perfectly sane. I know I must be punished: I've killed a man and I must be punished. I'm not asking for forgiveness. All I ask is that they don't take me for a madman, that they believe me, that you at least believe me, that you believe that all I've told you is the truth, the pure truth, that's all I ask. You do believe me, don't you?'

'Of course.' □

GRANTA

A WOMAN WRONGED
Jeremy Seabrook

Jeremy Seabrook

In 1949, my mother, having nursed her husband through tertiary syphilis, divorced him. In the same year, Aunt Em's husband died of TB. It seemed only natural that they should seek consolation for their loss in each other's company. My mother, my brother and I moved into the little terraced house in West Street, Northampton, in 1950. It was a cramped and confined space. My mother soon came into conflict with her sister.

Aunt Em was a woman whose purpose in life was clearly indicated to her by events, and she never hesitated for a moment in fulfilling it. Four years older than my mother, she was a good woman, in a way my mother could never claim to be. My mother's life was shadowed by what she saw as her wrongdoing; and even though this had been as a result of her husband's infidelity, that, too, produced great guilt in her, since she felt she had been unable to prevent him from straying. It must have been her want of sexual attraction which had sent him off on his journeyings in search of the fancy woman whose poisonous gift to him was a disease which inspired a revulsion equalled only by Aids later in the century.

There was no such stain of guilt and remorse in the life of Aunt Em. She married her husband in the early 1920s, when he was invalided out of the Royal Navy with tuberculosis. He had become ill in Novaya Zemlya, rescuing White Russian refugees in 1917 and 1918. In 1924 he was given two years to live; and it was under sentence of death that she married him. He lived a further twenty-five years. She never said so, since she was a modest and self-effacing woman, but love kept him alive. Indeed, his survival became locally well known, and gave hope to many other TB patients who might have expected to die within a short time of diagnosis. He had spent a few months in a sanatorium, where the beds were wheeled at night on to freezing verandas, since fresh air was then considered the only palliative. At his entreaty, Aunt Em had taken him home, not to die, but to thrive on her devotion. It gave her a passionate belief in the healing capacity of love, not as sentimental theory, but as a devoted and disciplined practice over the years. Accordingly, she behaved in the same way with everyone; and while some regarded her as a pushover, others who had been recipients of her thoughtfulness took her for granted, assuming that kindly was simply the way she was. But she knew this was no chance attribute; it had required self-control

206

and hard work, although as she grew older it came to her more naturally.

Uncle Frank, too, was a significant figure in our lives, yet another man to whom access was forbidden, and also because of sickness, although of a quite different order from the shaming affliction that kept us apart from Sid, our putative father. Frank's was sickness as nobility and sacrifice, contracted in the service of his country. We rarely visited the house, where he sat in bed for many years, breathing with the vestiges of a single lung. TB was still widely feared in popular consciousness, even when it had become curable. A number of ancient scourges remained well into our childhood, although by this time partly as superstition: we were afraid of breathing in the effluvia from the drains, especially after a long summer drought, when the smell was particularly potent—the aftermath of epidemics of cholera and typhoid which had raged within oral tradition, if not quite within living memory.

The figure of the self-sacrificing woman was familiar in the streets. There were thousands of them in our town, many unmarried, compassionate and for the most part accepting of their fate, since their contribution was widely acknowledged by the community. When they died, people shook their heads and declared them saints in shoe leather, hoping that their heavenly reward would compensate them for the years of self-disregard and dedication to others. Aunt Em looked after her mother as she grew older, since she lived in the same street. Her elder brother also came within the scope of her care, since he had remained at home, a characteristic male incompetent who was lost if his dinner was not set in front of him when he reached home for his midday break.

You could distinguish them at that time in the town, as they scanned the stores for some small luxury to tempt the taste of their infirm or sick relatives, with their ten-to-two walk, lisle stockings and wicker shopping baskets. They were always in a slight hurry, since they were preoccupied with the one they had left—would she have had a fall or had she tried to get out of bed, would she have wandered out of doors in her nightdress, would something terrible have happened to him in her absence? If their self-denial was choiceless, this only made it more poignant. These women tended the victims of

Jeremy Seabrook

industrial accidents—the man crushed by a beer barrel falling from a dray, the worker maimed by the collapse of scaffolding in a high wind—as well as the war-mutilated and the weak, the elderly children only ninepence in the shilling, the emotionally disturbed and the other casualties of industrial life. Some remained unmarried because a fiancé or follower had died in the First World War. Our next-door neighbour, whose betrothed was one of the last to die in 1918, had prepared everything for her wedding; and for the rest of her life, her trousseau remained, the pillowcases mildewy, the lace eaten away by sunlight and moths, the china cups criss-crossed by tiny cracks, soap hardened and flaking, utensils corroded by rust in the damp spare room where she had hoarded her unfulfilled life. This woman, too, had given herself to the care of her mother and brother. When we knew her, she had already passed into the dress of old age: the black skirt and blouse, hair tied in a shiny silver bun, so that she looked like an animated photograph from an old family album.

These charitable women often comprised a significant portion of the dwindling attendance at churches and chapels. Sunday mornings, sedate and solitary, they made their way to places of worship, where they thanked their maker for granting them the privilege of serving Him in the shape of his wounded creation, to whom they ministered with such unremitting devotion. They had at least two consolations, which many of their successors—of whom there are still plenty—lack. One of these was public recognition. They were known to everyone, and people often looked upon them much in the way that they look today upon celebrities and heroes—they were deferred to, admired and loved. They were not products of publicity machines, but walked among the people in flesh and blood; they were not shadows projected across the world for public consumption and profit, but performed tasks and duties which served as a model to others, and as an inspiration to them to strive and to endure. It is difficult to exaggerate the succour which this provided them, and how it lightened the burdens of their altruism. Today, the millions of 'carers', as they are now self-consciously called, are often objects of pity, at best unfortunates whose lives have been blighted, at worst, losers who have not been able to get out from under the charge of duty they have been landed with.

The second great comfort was undoubtedly that they were rarely alone in their commitment to the weak and sick. More often than not, they were part of a wider network, people who would take over their role regularly, if briefly, so that the work was not overwhelming. Once a week, Aunt Em visited us, knowing that her mother was sitting with Uncle Frank; another afternoon she went to the cinema with her sister, since the neighbour had promised to take her husband his afternoon cup of milk at the usual time. Such women were part of an invisible but tenacious mesh of humanity, which didn't have to call itself 'caring', since that was its unselfconscious purpose.

A few men also fulfilled this role, but it was more rare: the husband of the woman who had had a stroke, himself elderly; the brother of the brain-damaged girl who went everywhere with her, and wouldn't even go out courting unless he could bring his sister along. Next door to us an unmarried man lived with his elderly mother. As she became more frail, she could no longer walk. Her legs became badly ulcerated and eventually had to be amputated. He worked in a factory; and since Aunt Em lived next door, it was no hardship for her to look in from time to time. The son never went out. He said that since she had cared for him when he was helpless, it was only natural that he should perform the same service for her. When people asked him when he was going to get married, he would say, 'My mam is my only sweetheart.' And people didn't sniff and think of him as a timorous poof, although by some definition he might have been. On the contrary, women looked at him with a wistful tenderness, and wished their own sons were a bit more like him.

Uncle Frank died just before Christmas 1949. We spent that Christmas with her at the house of my other aunts, and Aunt Em came to meet us through the hoarfrost of the bright morning. In the deserted streets she was a lonely figure, for there were no solitary walkers on that day. She took hold of my mother's arm, while my brother and I fought for the hand that was free, in its glove knitted by her dead husband's bedside. I was ten and this was my first encounter with the need of adults for compassion—something until that moment unheard of, since I had wanted all the attention available in the world for myself. It was a disturbing moment and she gripped our hands firmly, in recognition of the small consolation we offered her. This was the first intimation I had of the meaning of loss.

I had never before been in the company of a bereaved person, let alone this sweet woman who, even when she was sitting in our house drinking tea, was always quite clearly also elsewhere—wondering, perhaps, whether the neighbour had remembered to give Frank the two rich tea biscuits he had with his afternoon milk, always fearful that *something might have happened* in her absence. This was not an irrational thought: it was her constant attention, if not attendance, that had prolonged his life beyond all expectations; who knew what disaster might not occur if her restorative presence were removed, even though she was scarcely bent on reckless self-gratification in the dutiful visit to her kinsfolk?

I observed her closely, not so much out of pity as because I expected to be in the same condition of loss when my mother died. I wanted to know what I could learn, in order to prepare myself in advance. I could detect very little in her bearing that would help: some moments of abstraction, a weakening of her ready smile, a slight soreness about the eyes. When I thought of the bottomless grief I anticipated for myself, I concluded that her love for Uncle Frank had probably been of a more measured kind; and anyway, they had only been husband and wife. It wasn't as if she had been his mother, supreme and irreplaceable. They had been already adults when they met, and I assumed that adults were not subject to the hostage-taking of the feelings of others in the way that mine had been taken into the custody of my mother. But her loss threw its pallid mantle over the festival, so although the game of Newmarket on Christmas afternoon took place as usual, the gusto with which pennies were lost or won was muted; and when Aunt Em got the wishbone from the chicken, she gave it to my brother and me, as it was clear to everyone that the only wish she could possibly make would be a vain and wasted one.

Since Uncle Frank had received a naval pension for sickness incurred in the course of duty, this continued for his widow. In any case, he had saved and invested money, so that she was better off than any of her sisters. Indeed, much of his life was devoted to making sure that his wife would not want when he was dead; and he became proficient in using the surplus from their modest requirements to amass for her a comfort that would reward her years of selflessness.

Aunt Em's bereavement occurred at the same time as my mother's divorce—even the manner of their separation from their respective husbands contained a kind of moral lesson. It was perhaps inevitable that we would provide a focus for her need to protect others. After Frank's death, I would go alone on a Saturday to Aunt Em's house, where we had what she called 'lunch'. I marvelled at the ceremony of this meal. She would decorate a fillet of cod with a sprig of parsley and a circle of tomato—culinary ornaments which my mother would have scorned—and set napkin rings at the side of both plates, and often had on the table a spike of bright yellow winter jasmine or a Christmas rose. These were the remnants of small festive touches by means of which she had celebrated with Uncle Frank his survival to share yet another day. She was delicate and understated in everything she did; her eyes shone when I walked in the door, and to this day I cannot remember any such spontaneous exhibition of pleasure at the sight of my often miserable person. After lunch, we went to the cinema. At the same time, every Saturday we were enfolded in the curved Art Deco walls of the Savoy, usually entering the auditorium in the middle of a film, any film. It was the custom of people to go to the pictures as though these were discrete and unconnected images in an album. In any case, the plots were formulaic, and it was not difficult to catch up. People were without discernment in their visits to the cinema. It might be a murder film with Edward G. Robinson, a costume drama with Stewart Granger, or a saga of female pirates with Jean Peters, or even a British misnamed 'thriller', achromatic (in every sense) efforts in which women in fur coats walked through a deserted Mayfair at three o'clock in the morning, followed by the shadowy individual you knew was about to murder them. After the pictures, we went on the bus to Kingsthorpe, then walked the last mile to White Hills, past the Recreation Ground, the fever hospital and the cemetery, to my mother's butcher's shop, where my mother would be cleaning the slabs on which the meat had stood and wiping down the stained silver rails from which shanks of dead animals hung. The house always smelled of animal fat and the spices used in sausages. Aunt Em brought some little treat, vanilla slices or a Bakewell tart, and she remained with us until Monday morning.

Partly as a result of the success of these weekends, and in consequence of my mother's inability to carry on with the shop—she was about forty-five by this time—it was suggested that we should go to live with Aunt Em. That was, after all, what families were supposed to be there for in those dim times, unilluminated as they still were by a later wisdom that taught the highest duty is to oneself. Aunt Em, all generosity and gentleness, opened what had been a sedate house of sickness to her sister and her children; and if she ever regretted it, she never spoke a word of disloyalty about any of us. The most extreme expression of her displeasure, when she wanted us to conciliate our mother in a rage over some symbolic but trivial affront, was, 'Well, you know what she is.' The house had been fumigated after Uncle Frank's death, so it posed no risk of infection; a kind of purification ritual which, however, did not rob it of its quality as a shrine to my aunt's undead tenderness for him.

When they first lived together, my mother and aunt took pleasure in each other's company. They used to play nap in the evening, a card game which involved a mild element of gambling. They talked together constantly—memories of childhood, the conduct of neighbours, how much Em had paid at the grocer's for half a pound of butter, and where it might be had more cheaply. They kept rigorous accounts, and at the end of each day reckoned up their dues to one another to the last halfpenny. Since they were to spend thirty-five years together, longer than either of them had lived with her husband, it seemed that they had done the right thing, and might settle into an easy companionableness.

It was not to last. Just as our mother had put my brother and me in our place, lowly, subordinate and unobtrusive, she set about her sister, whose shortcomings cried out—to her at least—to be addressed. And she devoted herself to this with the moral vigour and practical efficiency which had always distinguished her.

Since Aunt Em's husband had spent his years of idle debilitation looking after their financial affairs, it was perhaps inevitable that his views tended to become conservative over time. The social consequences of this very modest shift were more far-reaching than any mere political change of colour. For Aunt Em, who made friends effortlessly, had become part of a group of women who visited each other's houses every Tuesday afternoon to play bridge and take tea together. There were delicate sandwiches and such dainty cakes as the severe 1940s permitted, and rose-patterned tea sets in the shape of funerary urns. Aunt Em had met these friends either through her attendance at the Saxon church of St Peter's or at the Old Guides Association, and they were of a more genteel disposition than most of the women of West Street. They all lived in houses much bigger than ours, close to the park, addresses associated with superior social standing. Aunt Em was attracted by their manners—the fact that they didn't swear, and were as remote as could be from the working class in which she had originated. Ideology in the 1950s was as much a matter of temperament as it was of conviction. Certain social types were drawn to forms of behaviour and social observances rather than to ideas about how society should be ordered; this, in part, accounted for the conservatism of the decade. And when she was with her friends (my mother used the diminishing term 'pals'), she did indeed become a different person. She had an affected little laugh, and her voice (never harsh) became even softer, as she imitated the vowels and inflexions of her companions.

It was my aunt's turn to entertain once a month and on those days my mother remained in the kitchen, washing or scouring, or engaged upon some other domestic activity designed to contrast with what she regarded as the wasteful pastimes of the women in the other room, and she clattered a bucket noisily in competition with the tinkle of teacups, laughter and the bids of the card-players. In fact, the bridge was not serious, but rather an excuse to meet, to remember their youth and share the pity and sweetness of life.

My mother decided to put a stop to these frivolous parties. She objected on two grounds—that the parties trivialized life, which was sombre and serious (Aunt Em knew all about that), and the guests thought their arse didn't hang in the same place as everybody else's, that is, that they were snobs. They were, she declared, vapid and artificial. They were stuck up. They were only patronizing Aunt Em, because by deigning to visit her little house in West Street they could better relish their own success in Park Avenue North or Christchurch Road.

They stopped coming. Aunt Em explained that now her sister and her boys were living with her, there really wasn't enough room. They understood perfectly. Little by little, her pretensions were crushed. She

Jeremy Seabrook

became a shadow in the house in which her radiant but unobtrusive gladness had sustained Uncle Frank for a quarter of a century. She went about the business of emptying the chamber pots (we had an outside toilet) into a green enamel bucket every morning, making the beds and sweeping the snow in winter. My mother took over the preparation of meals, and did away with the small decorative touches with which her sister had transformed these bare necessities.

Aunt Em and her sisters had inherited the popular culture of late Victorian Britain, including many popular songs from the music hall, hymns of Moody and Sankey and nineteenth-century poetry. They received more recent cultural offerings through radio and films, but what they had learned as children, often at meetings of the Plymouth Brethren or the Salvation Army (where their presence had as much to do with the annual treat or the iced bun at Christmas as with religious teachings), remained with them, and these would be sung or recited at Christmas. Aunt Em, with her efforts at refinement, was usually called upon to render them, often stories with a pointed moral, calculated by Sunday School teachers to touch the hearts of poor children, even if their spirit or soul remained out of reach.

> Skylark, Skylark, when you go up in the sky
> Skylark, Skylark, winging your flight so high
> If among the angels, Mother you should see,
> Ask her if she'll come down again
> To poor dear Daddy and me.

Aunt Em recited songs and poems of this kind in the little-girl voice of a classroom of perhaps fifty or sixty years earlier. She had always longed to go to 'elocution lessons' and, in the absence of any such opportunity, had cultivated her own version of polite recitation. My mother detested these performances, although she may not have rejected the sentiments. She thought her sister needed to be brought down a peg or two.

The house of love became a house of correction. My mother also put a stop to one of Aunt Em's most charitable actions. When their mother died, their brother Harry had stayed at home, but, incapable of boiling an egg or making a cup of tea, Aunt Em had offered him a hot midday meal three days a week, which he ate during the break from the shoe factory where he worked.

Harry never married. For many years he had been engaged to a young woman in the factory. He and his fiancée set up a joint savings account, into which each paid a proportion of their weekly wage. After eight years, Floss suggested they should see what their savings amounted to. It appeared not only that Harry had never paid a penny into the account, but that he had carefully withdrawn every penny his fiancée had paid in—cash long spent on drink, snuff and the horses.

Harry was 'uncouth', as even Aunt Em admitted. When they were young, there had been little time for the refinements of table manners, and Harry continued to eat with noisy and messy enjoyment, spreading the remains of his oxtail stew across the table, and spitting things he didn't relish on to the wooden-block floor, from which all carpets had been removed during Uncle Frank's illness, since it was thought these harboured germs. On days when Harry came, the tablecloth was covered with newspaper. Aunt Em thought it her duty to feed this rough and ill-spoken churl, but my mother disagreed. 'I don't want to be slaving for him,' she said, 'without word of thanks.' Thanks, she well knew, were what men thought beneath them to offer up for the services of women, wives, mothers or sisters. My mother said she found him disgusting. We, as children, were repelled and fascinated. He had lost a joint of his middle finger in an accident with one of his leather-cutting tools, and he would use the stump as a resting place for pieces of food, which he then popped into his mouth. His fingers were stained a dark orange by nicotine, and he exuded the smell of the animal hides with which he worked. It was made clear to him that he was no longer welcome; and in this way, my mother established the convention that she didn't want anything to do either with people who thought they were better than others or with people who showed they were worse. In fact, she didn't want much to do with anybody at all, apart from her sons and her sister, who all fell under her control.

A unt Em's real crime in my mother's eyes was that, in spite of her vanished happiness, she was still animated by a compassionate interest in the lives of others. Since the modest sociability of her home had been shattered, she had to seek affirmation elsewhere. It was because of her love for Uncle Frank that he had provided her with

Jeremy Seabrook

the means to live; and she had no qualms in doing so, since she had
discharged all the obligations prompted by love and duty, and a great
deal more besides. Although my mother had the tangible fruits of her
success in life, in the form of her subdued and sullen sons, Aunt Em
exuded the self-confidence of those who have been happy. This galled
my mother beyond endurance.

She went on pioneering coach tours of Italy, and came back from
Capri with the story that Gracie Fields had graciously descended from
her villa and sung 'Sally' for her admirers gathered below. She
continued to go to church until, suddenly, it became too dangerous for
women to venture out alone after dark. She visited the Women's
Institute, and came back with jars of jam, pickles and bottled fruits,
and the Women's Gas Federation, a social organization created by the
Gas Board, where she learned to make the lightest of Victoria sponge
cakes. These activities were as far away as can be imagined from the
dissolute and wasteful occupations my mother considered them to be;
but her behaviour towards her sister became punitive.

Aunt Em also had a fur coat, which she fetched out of its mothballs
every November. It was tied at the waist with silk ribbons, so that no
buttons disturbed the soft fabric. It was an extravagance, no doubt,
and quite inappropriate to West Street, for which gaberdine and felt
were considered quite good enough. My mother mocked her
pretensions and told her she was putting herself at risk of being robbed
if she insisted on parading herself about in such a get-up. It reeks of
money, she said. Eventually, Aunt Em set the offending garment aside
and reverted to less showy wear. I found the coat after her death,
with the label of the exclusive local furrier who had provided it
inside, its brown silk lining still as good as new, the fur sleek and
shiny; by that time, of course, the wearing of fur had been disgraced
for other reasons than that it made people look like Lady Muck.

Then, thanks to the providence of Uncle Frank, we were able to
move into a slightly bigger house: only two or three streets away,
still a terraced house, but to eyes practised in the subtle social
distinctions of our town, a significant rise in the world. Constructed
on the site of old orchards in the 1880s, these houses had longer
gardens, and the extensions built on the back as shoemakers'
workshops made spacious kitchens. The lavatory remained outside,
and was not enclosed until the late 1960s, when to have to go out

216

of doors to shit was to occupy unfit property, condemned under sweeping plans for slum clearance.

My mother remained in the house, more and more reluctant to leave it. Even when she went out shopping, she was seized by an urgency to be home as soon as she could. She suffered from something more than agoraphobia: a fear of not being securely within the safety of the four walls which held her entire life—her twins and her wandering sister, who, perversely, preferred the world outside, the meretricious distractions and trumpery of making jam and cakes in public rather than in the secure privacy of her own kitchen.

Aunt Em maintained contact with a new generation of the family— a practice widely discontinued as its members had scattered. She remembered the birthdays of great-nephews and nieces, and visited them from time to time, creating a surrogate of the crowded home-place of her youth, when five or six sisters had shared the same bed. She was a true conservative, in the sense that she wanted to preserve the family, to halt the disintegration which so many others were viewing as a liberation from the ties of duty imposed by blood. As it turned out, her efforts were not reciprocated: they probably regarded her as a tiresome old aunt with nothing to do and time on her hands; and none of those to whom she had regularly sent small gifts at Christmas and on birthdays made an appearance at her sad small funeral.

As time passed, television began to colonize their lives. First of all, the cards were put away, and brought out only when I visited with my partner, when they still enjoyed a few hands of whist. But their evenings of nap or cribbage ceased. At first, they consulted the paper to see what was worth watching on TV, but later, it became the constant companion of both, not merely an accompaniment to their lives, but a sort of relation, bringing to them surrogate gossip, news, information and scandal which they had formerly exchanged with each other and people in the neighbourhood. You could feel the disintegration, not only of the local community, but of the social fabric of the town itself, as the 1970s set in. The locks were strengthened on the doors, and extra bolts fitted: into the deserted spaces where the cats howled at night and the dustbin lids clattered in the wind, and the dark of evening pressed with new menace against the rattling windowpanes, it seemed that evil spirits were hovering—the muggers, rapists and burglars who had been kept away when the streets were still populated. When the evening paper came, they turned first to the Deaths column, to see which of their acquaintances had pre-deceased them; and their comments on these departures were the only time they came alive to one another. 'She was only sixty-two, no age at all.' 'I saw her in town only last month, and I looked at her and thought Yes, my lady, you've got the shadow of the grave on you.' 'She never had much of a life, did she—he knocked her about for years.' 'There was always something wrong with him. You couldn't put your finger on it, then he got pinched for touching them kiddies.' 'Of course they were a TB family, she should never have married into them.' Their conversations became a valedictory lament for the decayed social relationships of the provincial town. And the role of television not only turned them away from one another; its insistent excitements, its passions and dramas, came as an oblique criticism of their own uneventful lives: lives that would previously have circled around local happenings—the house fire in the next street, the discovered marital infidelity of a neighbour, the woman caught shoplifting, the stolen bicycle and the unknown father of a young woman's baby—were now caught up in exaltations of a far grander order, as murders, gangland robberies, international espionage and epic love stories emanated from the TV and absorbed their attention in a way that made their own lives appear parochial and unsatisfying.

At the same time, my mother became more complaining about the mild trespasses of her sister, just as she had habitually lamented the shortcomings of my brother to me and my failings to him. I have to do all the work, she doesn't lift a finger, all she thinks about is her holidays, her whole life is a holiday—a monologue of discontent; even though, since my mother felt insecure the moment she walked out of the front door, it would have been absurd had she not kept herself occupied with the daily chores against which she nonetheless managed to sustain an unassuageable resentment.

I remained in thrall to my mother to such a degree that I faithfully reflected her judgement of Aunt Em; and I saw her through my mother's eyes, so that her mild aspirational snobbery and posturings became her chief characteristics, hiding the warmth and kindliness of her heart, her generosity of spirit and charitable openness to the world. Later—I wonder if it was too late—I bitterly repented this usurpation of my perceptions by my mother, and came to love Aunt Em more deeply. I have loved her more since her death, which is probably a measure of the guilt I feel for my disregard of her truly exceptional qualities while she lived. The dead do not leave us alone and our relationship with them is not frozen at the point when they cease to live. They continue to work on our feelings and our understanding of them, a provisional immortality that lasts at least as long as those who remember them remain. I thought Aunt Em shallow and thoughtless. I despised her library books—she read Georgette Heyer and Lady Eleanor Smith, while my mother at that time was absorbed in books that I had brought her, *Old Goriot* and *Madame Bovary*.

Aunt Em lived to see herself transformed, in the eyes of others, from the noble and generous creature she was into a pathetic old woman; such was the lowering of the esteem in which that generation of selfless women was held as the twentieth century wore on. She remained with my mother until the end of her life. When they could no longer stay in the house on Palmerston Road, they went together into a nursing home, where they shared a room. After a few months, they complained of the claustral oppression of this building, which was a big red villa surrounded by sombre evergreens—the kind of seclusion appropriate for the enjoyment of his wealth by a former boot and shoe entrepreneur, but less so for elderly people, for whom it represented an abstraction from the life they were to leave soon enough anyway.

They were transferred to a purpose-built home, with picture windows overlooking a golf course, where people were constantly coming and going. My mother, immobilized by Parkinson's and arthritis, sat in her chair, elbow resting on the arm, her thumb on her right cheek, her fingers shielding her eyes from the world, a symbolic posture of withdrawal, from which she would not budge. Aunt Em maintained a wan cheerfulness, as the visitors became more rare, outings ceased to occur and friends ('so-called friends' my mother called them, vindicated in her conviction that it was better not to have such relationships, since they were sure to let you down in the end). A few stragglers of our extended, but now dispersed, family brought them the gift of their company, and the old ladies always said 'Thank you for coming' as they left, like the little Edwardian children they had been.

Jeremy Seabrook

Aunt Em became ill. There was something wrong with her bowel, an obstruction of some kind. She remained in the general hospital for a few weeks, but there was no treatment that could reasonably be given to a woman of ninety. The geriatric ward to which she should have gone was being closed down in the 1980s cuts to the health service; and so she was sent back by ambulance to the home. It was a sleety November day and the old lady looked with weary eyes at the wet trees, their black branches covered with icy silver beads. It was to be her last view of the world. When she arrived, my mother refused to have her back in the shared space, and she was placed alone in a separate room. She died that same night.

Born in 1899, she was cremated on a fine December day in 1989. Many of those at the funeral were friends of mine from childhood; but few of those upon whom she had expended her sympathy and compassion were present. Of course, many were dead; but all the comforting myths in which she had believed, about bread cast upon the waters, proved to have been simply untrue. Her pity for and patience with the sufferings of others, which were uncelebrated in that busy and self-absorbed town, were not less significant than those of people in more exalted places, but for this sweet wronged woman they had to be their own lonely reward. ☐

MORNING SWIMMERS
Gerard Donovan

Gerard Donovan

In the first week of May, before the water in Galway Bay changed to a mild summer blue, Eric Hartman and John Berry drove to Jim's house and announced that they had gone swimming that morning, at eight o'clock, by the diving tower at the end of the promenade in Salthill. The three men had grown up together and still lived in the same town, though in recent years Jim had seen them less, or, as they put it, they had seen less of Jim.

It was still early morning and Jim walked the kitchen in pyjamas and crooked glasses, bringing cups of tea to the white table.

Eric said, 'You should come with us, make it three.'

John said, 'Yes, the water's cold, the concrete is cold, but once you're in the water it's not too bad.'

They said nothing more as Jim sat with his cup. He scratched the hair that still felt for the pillow he hurried from when he heard the doorbell. It had been five or six weeks since he'd seen either of them. This was the way it is with even boyhood friends: sooner or later another life always comes with its bags, even in the late years.

Jim said, 'I'm not a man for cold water, but I heard the bay is warmer in January than summer, with the Gulf Stream from Mexico.'

Eric said, 'Always the man for facts. Are you up for it then?'

Jim looked at the floor between his feet and saw the tower. It was a cold place, the tower and the concrete shelter at the end of the promenade, completely open to the elements, completely without comfort in the face of the strong wind off the bay. And that solitary journey to a cold dunk in the frigid water drew solitary people to it every morning: as a child he watched the old bony swimmers leap into the water and swim around the base of the tower and run shivering for the towels they draped on the railings. One man used to leap straight from the sea on to his black bike, cycling home instead to change, stopping wet on the way to buy a newspaper. Perhaps all those memories made him want to agree to go with them, or perhaps the recent loneliness that visited him in the mornings had taken to staying a little longer by the week.

And so it came to pass that at eight in the morning, four times a week through the summer and well into fall, the three of them swam in the waters of the Atlantic, fast pink arms in the churn of the dark seas.

Today Jim had come twenty minutes early. The water was slate grey and a blustery wind seemed to push the sunlight off the boulders that ringed the tower. He had not slept well, and as he drove along the seaside he saw rain showers blowing in from the Aran Islands and knew he did not want to wait for the other two. The routine had taken over the excitement, he understood that, but lately their conversation shared the same fate as the time trapped in his watch: it always came around to a point where it used to be. He parked his car farther down the promenade than usual and walked the extra distance to warm himself. Because the November sunrise had found the clear part of the sky, he wanted to swim while the sun could shine on his skin, even a sun without heat, any sun, because this time of year was unforgiving: you ran in and got the thing done. But if he kept coming, doing this, perhaps by spring he would feel differently.

He undressed down to the swimming trunks he wore underneath and picked his way on flat feet across the stones to the water, found a patch free of seaweed, bent at the knees and launched himself. The cold clamped him at the head and the chest and dragged ice along his body as he entered fully the green silence, opening his eyes to the salt and the waving seaweed, the fat tendrils' ballet in a slow current. He thrashed his arms, twisted his neck, rose to the surface and kicked his legs until a seed of heat burned at the numbness. He made a tight circle around the tower and hauled himself on to a rock, gasping and saying incomprehensible things just to ward off the brutal chill. A gust sliced spray off the rocks after him as he grabbed his bag and ran to the shelter to change. He placed firmly in his mind the dry promise of the towel, the second sun gleaming from the dashboard in the car on the way home, the hot shower of water from pipes.

Inside the shelter, he took the towel and entered the only cubicle even though he was the only one there: Jim liked the ounce of privacy. He wrapped the ends of the towel in his fists and see-sawed it along his back with his toes curled off the damp concrete, dabbed his chest and legs, noticed the strings of blue veins under the skin. He threw the towel down and reached for the underpants. That was the good thing about the harsh concrete of this place: you didn't want to hang about and think.

He was drying his feet when he heard his name spoken at the door of the shelter.

223

'Remember what Jim said—last July, was it?'

'What did he say?'

Jim smiled as he recognized the voices of his friends. He dredged the toes of his left foot with the towel.

John said, 'Don't say anything. Is that Jim's car parked outside?'

'I'll look,' Eric said. 'No, he's not there.'

Jim had a hand on the cubicle door to push it open and tell them he had beaten them to the swim, but then John shouted, '"Listen, today is going to be the best day of our lives!"'

Eric laughed. 'Will you keep it down, will you? He could be along any second.'

Jim stopped. Was that something he had said once? He said that once. He should put his pants on first before leaving the cubicle.

'I mean,' John said, 'he's out there on the rocks and says that to us about the best day of our lives. What was that all about?'

'I could hardly stop myself from laughing out loud,' Eric said. 'He stands in his wet trunks with his arms up in the air and says, "Look at the clear water, the sun in the clouds," and then he says—'

'Don't—'

'—"Christ, lads, isn't it great to be alive!"'

Inside the cubicle Jim pulled his pants on. The rest of his clothes were in the plastic shopping bag outside the cubicle. He couldn't very well walk out now to get his shirt and socks. His friends were talking about him and they would be embarrassed. He would be embarrassed.

John got his breath back. 'I felt like saying, "The best day? We're going swimming, Jim. What are you doing?"'

'I wouldn't mind but he's the one who got winded,' Eric said, 'tried to go out a hundred yards and ends up floundering. Lucky the man didn't get blown out to sea altogether. Thinks he's still a young fellow.'

Inside the cubicle, Jim smiled. They were talking about him behind his back and he was listening behind theirs. He'd wait another minute before springing the surprise. They'd all laugh about it later in the bar, a little friendly elbowing. How many get to hear what their friends say about them?

As he waited, carefully silent in the cubicle, Jim remembered that day of his extra-long swim: it was midsummer and he felt brave enough to explore, to go farther, stretch the circle out in a wider radius to the bigger waves and be helpless and brave in all that water. He was tired of the same path his friends dug out of the waves to follow. It was something he decided at the moment he dove in and so could not tell the others, who always swam as a pair a little behind him. He took a left turn and in two minutes was already far enough out that the tower had shrunk two or three inches and his friends were half the size. It was more than he bargained for. How tired he got! He didn't say anything at first, but when the cramp tugged at his calf, he wanted to call out to the others, but they might laugh at him or not notice the call coming from an unexpected place, so far to their left where no one ever swam, and so he trod water to get his breath and watched his friends circle the tower and pick themselves out of the sea. Then he felt the first tug of a different current push him out a few inches more, an indifferent hand pushing him out into the open and anonymous sea and beyond the magnet of the tower. The terror of those inches! The sea yawned under him. He kicked and thrashed his way parallel to the shore until the tugging stopped and he was able to head for the beach, coming from the waves fifty yards downshore. He wound his way back to the shelter along the sharp rocks in the surge of sun and the relief that he was on dry ground, and when he reached the tower his friends were already in the shelter, but his relief had turned into joy. He stood on the flat lukewarm stone, and that was when he shouted that today would be the best day of their lives, that it was great to be alive after all.

Jim buttoned his pants. Outside the cubicle, his friends were not finished with him.

Eric said, 'Ever think Jim was a little, you know, off?'

'As in?'

'Don't know really. Off.'

'Daft?' John said.

Eric said, 'Daft. Good daft, I mean.'

'No wonder his wife—'

'Wait. I want to hear, but check again first.'

Jim moved away from the door. No wonder his wife what? He hung the towel at his shoulders.

Eric's voice sounded again after footsteps: 'Nothing. He's late today. Maybe he's not coming.'

'We better get in and swim. Looks dark out in the bay.'

Jim heard bags rustle and shoes thud as they undressed. If he opened the door now, he would mortify his two friends. At this point he would gladly have taken the embarrassment he passed on previously. Best to wait until they left the shelter for the swim and then to get his bag, dress quickly, go outside and wave at them as if he'd just arrived. Two swims for him today.

'She's not bad-looking at all,' John said.

'A quiet one, though.'

'Heard she's seeing some fellow from Dublin, some archaeologist or other.'

Jim leaned against the wall of the cubicle. His breath left his body and his heart seemed locked in another chest, a strange chest, where it beat instead.

'Get away—where did you hear that?' Eric said.

'Everyone knows it—the birds are singing it. I hear it's a bit of an open marriage there with Jim and her, you know.'

'I heard—'

'Ask no questions, that type of thing. She takes this archaeologist to a hotel out of town.'

John coughed. It echoed around the shelter, a cold being caught and repeated in another throat, and then another, the way things spread. Jim placed a hand on the cubicle wall and lowered himself to the bench and felt the cold stone under his feet, how cold.

'Strange enough,' Eric said, 'because I never see Jim with anyone. How long has this been going on?'

'The word is a couple of years,' John said.

Jim took the ends of the towel and placed them over his ears. Archaeologist? The wind blew under the cubicle door and up inside the pant legs. He felt years blowing in with it, ageing him on the spot. His testicles tightened and the wet hair dripped frigid dots down his neck. Then he heard the whisper of pants sliding off.

'She's a bit of a flirt, all right,' Eric said, with the cough that told Jim the pants were indeed off. Eric always coughed right then.

John said, 'If I had her body, I'd be a flirt too.'

'Jim hasn't a clue, does he? I don't think he knows about it at all.'

'Don't think so—head in the clouds. You've got to like him all the same.'

'Jim's a decent sort,' Eric said. 'A good man. Always something different.'

As he sat, Jim looked around him, looked down at his stomach. Despite months of exercise, the folds of fat were still there. His chest too seemed flabbier, little pouts around his nipples. Another blast of wind shook the door of the cubicle and fried his skin cold into goosebumps. His legs looked thinner, less muscular. The swims had done nothing more than expose how much a body can shrivel, what lay ahead of him. Yes, he was older, as if he had not noticed until his body said, I am fifty-two, and this is you.

His wife was surely happy. Denise and he lived a marriage without questions. His Saturdays were a stroll through the bookshops, a coffee on Shop Street, mingling with the crowd, the smell of fish and pizza on High Street down to the Spanish Arch, and from there a short walk to the swans at the Claddagh. You can judge a marriage by Saturdays, Jim thought. The inside of the shelter darkened. He moved his shoulders; must leave soon. But he did not want to make his friends feel bad.

Eric said, 'At some stage you have to wonder if Jim can do the business.'

'Not true at all,' John said. 'Remember Lucy at the department dinner? I heard Jim and she went into the bathroom and she came out fixing her dress. Jim walked out a little later and headed for the bar.'

Jim shook his head. I never touched that woman. I went to the bathroom to escape her. He stood and waved his arms to get warm.

Eric said, 'Interesting. No one ever told me about that, Jim and Lucy.'

'Is it raining yet?' Eric said.

'No. We're okay.'

'I hate this part, taking off my shirt. Kills me.'

In the cubicle, Jim felt colder than the wind. He stepped up on to the seat and did weightlifting movements, bending his knees and bringing his backside down to his heels, and back up again, breathing softly. He leaned to the wall and shivered, one hand on the towel to keep it from falling. He was fine in here as long as he didn't make any noise, as his friends never used the cubicle. They always used the same part of the shelter, with Eric on the inside and John nearest the door, and undressed in the same order: pant leg, shirtsleeve, that stupid cough, the same breathing, the same little jumps between the cracks on the concrete as they bounded for the water. And since they always faced the wall as they got ready, they wouldn't see him if he put his head over the cubicle door.

Lifting himself on his toes, Jim looked.

As expected, John Berry's black left sock was coming off on schedule. Go on, John. Now the top shirt button, that's it, and use your index and thumb—excellent. And now another little cough as you take it off. Jim placed his right knee against the door hinge and his left foot flat across the bench, while holding the towel with his right hand and using two fingers of his left on top of the cubicle wall for balance.

John removed the shirt and coughed. 'It's a lot colder today, that's for sure.' The fat around John's waist bobbed as he hung the shirt on the third hook from the left. Jim remembered watching him eat bacon and cabbage at Eric's one night, carefully tearing fat from a glistening rind. John Berry folded his pants and placed them in the bag, giving them the usual tug to get the wrinkles out. 'I don't know. He must know about his wife and the archaeologist. I don't see how not. I would, I can tell you. In a second.'

Jim tried to list all the archaeologists he knew.

Eric said, 'Maybe it's one of those sham marriages. One of them is gay, but they stay together.'

'Remember Lucy. Unless he goes both ways. Why, Eric, do you fancy him?'

'Stop!' Eric shouted.

They laughed as John froze at the level of his eyes behind the cubicle.

Eric said, 'How about just you and me do the next windsurfing trip? I don't know about Jim this time.'

'Yes, just the two of us. Remember him explaining how the nature spirits live in the west? He sat one night by the Cliffs of Moher and waited for them to come out.'

'He saw them dancing in the moonlight.'

'Like this?' John Berry raised his left arm and danced in a circle, then pulled his stomach in and stood sideways. He looked himself up and down. 'I have a question.'

'Yes?'

'Do you think I've lost weight?'

'What? A bit, around the waist, yes.'
'Are you sure. Are you being honest now?'
'I am, I think, yes.'
As far as Jim could tell, John weighed himself every day. He did not need anyone to tell him. From his high perch in the cubicle Jim saw that John had lost some hair at the crown, and the fat around his jaw squeezed out a second chin. His knees swelled with arthritis.
'This is the first time Jim's missed a swim,' John said. 'Maybe there's trouble with the wife.'
'Maybe she's seeing that lecturer fellow at the university again.'
'Again? It never stopped,' John said. 'They were at it last week, from what I hear, in the college bar, off in a corner.'
Eric swung his arms. 'Poor fellow doesn't know half the things she does behind his back. She even came on to me once.'
'No,' John said.
'At the annual department party.' Eric folded his sweater. This was the order: after folding his pants, he hooked his thumbs under his loose white oversized underpants, turned to the wall, bent as he lifted his right leg and then the left, put the underpants in his bag and hoisted up his swimming trunks. Then off with the sweater.
Jim waited long seconds as both men rubbed their hands and paced the shelter. To show himself now would bring confrontation, old denials, new defences. He swallowed and felt the draught of that November morning sweep along the concrete and swirl about the cubicle, rubbing a dull red blade across his ankles. His left foot slid on the wet seat. As he fell, his right knee scraped the hinges. The only thing was to let go. The seat sprang like a see-saw and slammed against the wall.
'Jesus,' Eric said.
Jim draped the towel over his head and chest. He opened the door.
From under the towel he saw John Berry's black nylon socks and brown shoes under his swimming trunks. He always put the socks and shoes back on for the run to the sea.
'Ah Jesus,' Eric said from the shelter entrance.
'What?' John said, joining him.
'Looks like rain.'
John turned. 'Excuse me, what's the water like today?'
The simple disguise of a towel and some distance. Jim revolved

his wrist in a 'so-so' fashion, the misery of it. He took the bag and turned back for the cubicle.

Eric said, 'John, come on, let's do the swim before that cloud comes down on us. Let's run at it today and just dive in.'

John Berry and Eric Hartman charged out of the shelter.

They would run to the sea and crouch, blowing into their hands. At the last second before diving in, John removes the shoes and socks. They both swing back their arms, bend at the knees and tip over like milk into tea. They swim once around the tower, bodies static but busy, insects in a toilet bowl.

Inside the cubicle again, Jim grabbed for the plastic grocery bag, his shirt, his pants, socks, shoes and jacket. It was true that Denise and he had an arrangement. Their personal life was complicated, but only if viewed from the outside. Passion was something he could live without, and he supposed she felt the same. But if he were ever to meet someone he would tell Denise. While not romantic together any more, they slept in the same bed, and she hadn't said anything about an archaeologist or a lecturer. Or it was all malicious gossip?

She would have said something. Jim stood and tightened his belt over the shirt. Yes, she had come home drunk a few times. Yes, she did appear depressed. He'd asked her if anything was wrong. She said she felt tired. Jim lit some candles and massaged her head. 'You are very good to me,' she said, and touched his hands.

Jim placed the wet gear in the bag and sat again in the cubicle. Something you hear through a stall door, from a chance conversation on the street, a phone quickly put down when you enter a room, something you hear that depresses you for an hour and maybe for the rest of your life. He had minutes to get out before the two returned to the shelter, but Jim could not find the will to move. Instead he saw images of Denise, not with another man, not of her naked body, but of her not telling the truth. He watched her in the kitchen not telling the truth, in the garden not telling the truth, watching television not telling the truth. The images slid back in time, and in a few seconds she was not telling the truth ever, all the way back to when they first met. Even then, when he brought her to a film on a rainy Friday after classes and she was still doing her degree, she was not telling him the truth. His stomach moved and he heaved. He cupped a hand over his mouth and clenched his thighs as another blast of wind scoured the shelter, this time carrying in rain on top.

In the final minute of John Berry and Eric Hartman's morning swim, Jim remembered the day of the midsummer wild swim, when he said those words about it being the best day. He had turned and seen them smiling to each other in the cave of the shelter.

'Well, why not?' he called. 'Why can't today be the best day?'

'You might be right,' John's shadow said back to him, 'but I wouldn't bet on it. Not today.'

Now it was too late to leave the cubicle. Jim sat until he heard both men enter the shelter in a swish of feet and shivering.

'Very cold today, John. Jim missed it.'

'He's probably out looking for his wife.'

Jim grabbed the inside bolt and burst out of the cubicle, a blur of hair and glasses and a shout: 'Don't you two have anything better to do?'

Eric said, 'Jim.'

'Is this what goes on behind my back?'

John took a towel. 'No, Jim.'

Eric said, 'Was that you earlier?'

'Yes, I heard it all,' Jim said.

'Fun, that's all it was.'

Jim said, 'Eric, you can't keep your mouth shut. That's why no one tells you anything, nobody except this fellow here.' He pointed at John. 'And John, your wife wants to leave you.'

'Now look,' John said.

Jim said, 'And ask me how I know that.'

'She doesn't want to leave me.'

'Because she told me. She told me months ago, when I was picking you up that day your car was in for service.'

John shook his head, looked at the ground.

Jim said, 'All those pills.' He walked to the door of the shelter. The rain was picking up and he felt it swamp his shoulders.

'You'd better leave,' Eric said. 'You're saying foolish things.'

John took a step. Eric stopped him. 'Leave, Jim. We know you're upset.'

'You know nothing about me. Don't talk to me again, either of you.'

Jim walked the promenade to his car, started the engine and turned the heater up to a blast. Over Galway Bay, the heavy cloud combed the water into fluff and rocked the car with a gust that spattered drops on the left window. He watched Hartman and Berry run from the shelter with their bags. He felt fists rummage in his kidneys.

He knew, yes, he did, but he loved her too much to say anything. And she had been kind to him the morning of the strange and dangerous swim when he got home and could not wait to tell her about it, since they did not have such moments any more, he and Denise, when he could tell her something new. She said he was foolish to try that, but she laughed too and smiled at him, a smile he knew from a long time before. And he thought briefly that there might be hope.

Fifty yards away through the downpour he saw his friends raise a hand to each other and shrink to unlock their doors. John Berry dragged his jacket over his head. Jim sat with his hands on the steering wheel, waiting for the car to warm up. The shower stretched the bodies of his friends across the glass, melted them down the windshield and finally made them strangers. □

HUNTER'S MOON
Thomas Lynch

Some days on his walk Harold Keehn thought about his wives. Some days it was caskets. Others it was the heartbreaking beauty of the natural world such as he had come to know it. Often as not the consolidation of these topics was seamless and the names and particulars would race through his brain like a litany in code that only he could cipher. *Elizabeth, goldfinch, Primrose Maple, hemlock, Helen, Mandarin Bronze, osprey, glacier, eighteen-gauge Permaseal, Autumn Oak, chickadee, trillium, Joan.* The list always ended with Joan, his third wife, whom he'd buried last April in a Clarksville Princess Mahogany with a tufted dusty rose velvet interior, in Mullett Lake Cemetery, between two blue spruce saplings he'd planted there. The naming gave him a sense of mastery, as if he'd had some say in all of it.

When she had died in early January her body was kept in the cemetery's stone winter vault, waiting for the frost's hold on the ground to give way in the spring and the grave to be opened.

'We don't dig much after the deer season opens,' is what Harley Flick, the local sexton told him, when the graves were arranged for last November, when Harold knew the end was near.

When the racing of names got out of hand Harold would stare intently at the path in front of him, count the cadence of his footfall or breathing and pray for his mind to go blank and hush. Then he could hear the air in the leaves, the lapping of water, the brisk movement of wildlife in the undergrowth. He could imagine the larval stages of next year's hatch of dragonflies and hexagenia, caddis and stoneflies, the imperceptible growth of antlers and turtle shells, the long pilgrimage of hatchling and fingerling, the return of the grayling and wolverine. He would try and sense his body's oneness with the pace and nature of the world around him. Better not to think too much, he often thought.

He thought it unlikely he'd ever marry again.

He did three or four miles a day, along the abandoned railroad bed through the woods, between his place on the south-west corner of the lake and the village to the north; or south along the west edge of the river mouth, circling the wetlands, where carp spawned in late May and early June, under the interstate and up to the highway, then back again. Some days he'd do more if the weather was fine and his knees didn't ache, or the sciatica hadn't hobbled him, and he was glad for the time out of the house, where he found the days, though shortening now, impossibly long. On the best of days he could imagine himself walking all the way to Cheboygan, on out the Straits Highway at the north end of town, along the edge of the big water to Mackinaw City, over the bridge to the Upper Peninsula and into whatever oblivion God had in mind for him. Maybe to Munising or Seney or Manistique—he loved the sound of northern names. And the names of tribes that had named those places: Algonquin and Huron and Chippewa. Or walking south all the way down the mitten of Michigan along the old railway lines through Gaylord and Grayling, Saginaw and Bay City, all the way to Rochester, where the tracks passed alongside the house he'd lived in years ago with his first wife before the names of things made much difference to him.

Time occupied for him a kind of geography, the north of which he thought of as the future and the south of which he thought of as the past, and where he was at any given moment was the immediate present tense of his personal history, the known point on the map of what he'd call his life and times. It kept him from feeling entirely lost. Some days the future was west and the past east and the moment was shooting craps out in Vegas or some other fantasy, but it always suited him best to think of the whole miserable business as linear. The prospect of time bringing him back around to the point he set forth from was a crueller joke than he could imagine, though the faces of clocks, the evidence of the sun and moon, the repetition of themes in his own life were, of course, disquieting. 'Today is a gift' the sign outside the Topinabee Church read this morning when he'd gone for his oats at the Noka Cafe, 'that's why they call it the present!' Better than last week's bromide, Harold thought: 'Fresh Spirits Have No Expiration Date!'

Harold stood on his porch, stretching both arms to reach the ceiling, then he dropped his sweat pants and pissed in the general direction of the neighbours' place. Everyone was gone this time of year, back to their jobs and schools and schedules. There were some colour tourists and weekenders, but mostly he had the place to himself. He spread his legs, bent at the waist, touched his palms to the ground, feeling the backs of his thighs stretch, having to bend his knees ever so slightly now. Then he stood up straight and stretched his arms over his head again, easing the standing pain in his lower back and right buttock. Then he hitched up his pants, did a couple of slow squats to loosen his knees and side-to-sides to ease the tightness in his groins and stepped off the porch, pursing his lips to suck in the air. The decadent smell of leaf fall, the crunch of his foot fall in the road's top gravel, the sparkling light of the advancing afternoon, the sweet crispness in the cooling air, the sore pads of his feet, the ringing in his ears—these were all familiar.

If he was hungry after his walk, he told himself, he'd drive into Topinabee for a slab of whitefish or a burger at the Noka. That might kill the time left until nightfall. Once it was dark he could fall asleep watching some cable news or old reruns. Always good to have a plan.

He could hear the dog barking in the distance—Larry Ordway's bat-faced mongrel bitch—frenzied and barking at God knows what. Harold looked along the roadside for a proper stick.

If he'd remained married to Elizabeth, today would be their anniversary. Was it forty years yet? He'd lost count. October 29— the day the stock market crashed and the Great Depression got under way. The day, he'd heard on the radio this morning, the National Organization for Women was founded, the day he was married for the first time, that late October during Vietnam. That figures, he thought, thinking how Elizabeth had left him broke, depressed, vanquished and confused about women, suffering a kind of post-traumatic stress.

She had left him for a woman.

It all seemed a bit of a blur to him now, and feeling the nerve ends in his right leg warm to the pace he was keeping up Grace Beach Road he was glad for nature's forgetfulness, how the pain in his ass could be dulled some and the numbness in his legs could be walked out. The afternoon light angling through the woods, the blue sky, the bird noise in the trees, the air rushing in and out of him: life as he knew it, here in the moment, in the gift of the present, such as it was, was nothing but a walk in the woods of northern lower Michigan, in mid-autumn.

They'd had a ranch house on three acres in one of the best suburbs north of Detroit. He was a sales rep for Clarksville Casket. All of Michigan—over 400 funeral homes—was his territory. They had a daughter, Angela, a dog, Maggie, a rosy future. And even if he'd married Elizabeth because he thought marriage was sensible and inevitable, and because he figured as well her as any other, even if he found her, while very attractive, not entirely admirable, even if she had married him to get out of her crazy mother's house, even if they both woke some mornings wondering if they each might have done better for themselves, they had assembled a life. If he had not loved her completely, utterly, irretrievably, he thought then and he thought now, coming to the intersection of Grace Beach and Grandview Beach Roads, he had loved her sufficiently.

Larry Ordway's dog was in full fury now, the sharp blasts of its barking amplified by the general silence in the rest of the world, through which Harold's approaching footfall in the gravel was all the more discernible. Harold's grip on the stick tightened in anticipation of the dog's charge down the driveway in real or feigned attack. One never knew what to expect of the bitch. He wanted to be ready for all contingencies. From half a mile off, the dog's distemper sounded menacing. Maybe a raccoon trapped, or skunk or deer, or some late-season cottager going by on a bike or on foot. The dog was a pest—another in a line of disagreeable mixed breeds that had guarded Ordway's empire over the years. It was an empire of sheds and outbuildings, scrap vehicles and rusting implements surrounding his doublewide in the woods at the side of the abandoned railroad easement. The current mutt kept sentry at the top of a long drive that gave on to the road where it curved to cross the tracks. It would come snarling and barking down the drive, chasing off everything that came into its view.

Angela, their daughter, was lovely and bright; their lives seemed full of possibilities. They had a manageable mortgage, good credit, good friends, made love twice a week, belonged to the local Congregational church, where Elizabeth sang in the choir and was known for a casserole she brought to funeral luncheons and potlucks. Harold ushered for Sunday services. They were the happy young couple with the pretty child.

When Elizabeth turned thirty she went back to school to finish the degree she'd abandoned when she got pregnant. Angela went to day-care. Elizabeth commuted to the university and took classes in English and Women's Studies.

Harold was gone a part of most weeks working his way up and around the state, calling on northern and western accounts. Other times he worked Detroit and the suburbs. He'd go as far west as Lansing, as far north as Saginaw and still be home in time for dinner. He'd check the death notices in the Sunday papers to try and get a sense of who'd be in their offices and when. He'd try to see his best accounts every other month, others once a season, others twice a year, some just at conventions and some he'd call or send a card to now and then. Some bought better over lunch, others after a few drinks, some over coffee in their offices. Harold had learned to cultivate his relationships with the primary buyers—most often the owner or the owner's son. He'd listen to whatever he had to listen to—their theories on why one unit sold and another didn't, their bad-mouthing of the competition, worries over the cremation trend, stories of the latest strange cases: double suicides, remarkably obese cases, multiple fatalities at industrial sites or on the interstates, anything. One week he'd work the city among the ethnic firms—Poles and Romanians, blacks and Jews—then the cushy suburbs of Grosse Point and Bloomfield Hills, up through Pontiac to Flint. Another week he'd work the firms in tri-cities and all the small farm towns in between, spending as much time with the Woolevers in Midland and Cases in Saginaw and Penziens and Stapishes in Bay City, with their multiple rooftops and hundreds of calls, as with the Struthers firm in Reese, who did forty funerals a year, but all of them copper or bronze or premium hardwood, paid for in cash by old German farmers. Then he'd take a run out through Ypsilanti and Ann Arbor and Jackson along I-94 to Kalamazoo and Muskegon, then up to Grand Rapids and up the west side of the state through the rich resort towns, Traverse City and Charlevoix, Petoskey and Harbor Springs. Once in the spring and once in the fall he'd try to make it through the UP. He'd buy drinks for his accounts at their district meetings and their yearly golf outings and pop for lunches and dinners with his best accounts. He loved the long hours alone in the car and the vacant landscape and the open roads. He'd been through the CB Radio craze—his handle was 'Boxman'—and car phones and cell phones, all the gadgets. The drive along Route 2 to the west, then north to Seney, then up to Munising, then west to Marquette was a favourite drive. His accounts up there ordered caskets by the truckload and were accustomed to infrequent deliveries. They'd back up their best units in basements and garages and keep six months' worth of inventory on hand and borrow from their colleagues in the next county if they ran short of a particular unit. And the drive along the east side up the Lake Huron shore from Pinconning and Standish, where he'd always lunch at Wheelers for the way it hadn't changed over the years, still serving malted milkshakes in big silver tins and burgers with fried onions and real French fries. Then through Au Gres and Oscoda, Greenbush and Harrisville, all the way up to Alpena and Rogers City, along the long blue edge of the state. He'd listen to radio preachers or farm stations that gave the price of sugar beets and alfalfa. Or Paul Harvey or Rush Limbaugh or public radio—it hardly mattered. He called on every firm in every town, promising each to keep their 'line' of Clarksvilles 'exclusive' to prevent comparison-shopping between competing firms. If one bought a Tuscany 20 gauge, with lilac crepe for little old ladies, he'd sell the other firm a Silver Rose with pink velvet. If one took the Pietà or Last Supper, the other was pitched the Praying Hands or Old Rugged Cross. He kept sales charts on them all and pushed them to beat last year's averages, convincing them that the more they spent on caskets, the greater return they'd eventually realize on their 'investments'. He left stacks of notepads, pens and packets of breath mints, each with Clarksville's logo and his contact particulars imprinted. He gave his best accounts custom-made coffee mugs and playing cards with their firm's name embossed next to 'Clarksville & Keehn—a Winning Team!'

Elizabeth hadn't exactly left him. She'd put him out. She kept the house, their daughter, the newer of their two cars and showed him the door.

'You're welcome to stay if you want to,' she told him, 'but I'm sleeping from now on with Eleanor.'

It happened so fast it was a blur to him now. He'd gone from the more or less happy paterfamilias to a man living at loose ends. They'd been married twelve years and it was over in months. Or maybe he was only the last one to know. Either way, he found himself paying the mortgage on a house he no longer lived in, payments on a car he no longer drove, and support for a daughter, now ten years old, he saw all too rarely. That he was paying alimony to a woman with whom he no longer slept vexed him especially at the time. His consortium had been taken over by Dr Eleanor Dillingham, who taught a course in American Women Poets at the community college.

'Poetry,' she had been quoted as saying, 'like suicide, is something more women attempt and more men accomplish. It is time we changed all that!' The required reading for the course was a book about a madwoman who lived in someone's attic and began, 'Is a pen a metaphorical penis?'

The thought of Dr Dillingham making love to Elizabeth both excited and disturbed Harold. He could understand their attraction to each other and wondered at the time why they couldn't include him. He found Eleanor oddly fetching himself. He moved out the first weekend in December that year.

One of his accounts gave him the use of rooms over the funeral home garage where he could put a phone and sleep when he wasn't on the road. He took night calls and helped with the removals in trade. A grieving family gathered around the deathbed of a loved and lamented head of the household sent twinges of regret and anger through Harold, but the face he showed to mourners was commiseration. With no particular home to return to, his trips got longer and longer. His sales began to increase as he spent more and more time on the road. Money began to roll in again. He opened an account for his daughter's college fund. He wanted her to go to Alma College, a Presbyterian school in the middle of the state where he called on the Dewey Funeral Home and where the male students looked like young Republicans. Or Albion, where there were mostly Methodists and they didn't teach women's studies. Or maybe Calvin College, where modest Dutch Reform girls and boys were monitored for proper conduct.

Come Fridays he'd stay on wherever he was. He'd take a room in Grand Rapids or Ishpeming or Port Huron. He'd coax his last account out for a boozy dinner and offer to help out with the Saturday funerals and sit in the motel watching TV or sit in the lounge listening to the terrible music and hoping to get lucky with one of the local women.

He bought the house on the lake the year after the divorce. He'd heard about it from the account in Indian River who had buried the widow that had lived in it for years. It was old and a little ramshackle but it had a good foundation and 200 feet of frontage and could be bought right from the old woman's children, who lived in Ohio.

Thomas Lynch

Harold saw in it a refuge from the rootlessness he felt—a place
to bring his daughter for those summer vacations and winter breaks
his visitation rights entitled him to. He envisioned her long into the
rosy future, learning to fish and ski and name the species of things
with him, then perhaps bringing a boyfriend up for the weekend.
He saw her wedding on the lawn under a great tent on a blue day
in July or August, and his eventual grandchildren gathered round
the barbecue for family reunions, playing badminton or horseshoes,
or paddling canoes out on the sparkling water, all housed in the
dormer he would in due course build over the big garage—everyone
together, all distance and divisions healed. He saw, however dimly,
all of them circling his last illness, or bearing him to some proper
disposition, then returning to the family home on the lake to toast
his life and times and memory—a man, they would say, who had
played the cards life dealt him, and played them well, and would be
sorely missed.

Quality time he told himself; less is more, if better spent.

It had a stone fireplace in the main room and a good well and a
wide front porch and a screened porch off the front bedroom upstairs
from which he could watch the lake and the stars and the northern
lights. The sunrise poured into the windows; he slept to the lapping
of lake water. He compensated for fewer visits downstate by inviting
his accounts up for a weekend's fishing or snowmobiling or hunting
or cards. He'd take them to the Breakers Bar in Topinabee, get them
a little liquored up, buy them a steak, pitch the latest additions to
the line and take their orders. He'd write off the expenses on his tax
returns. His market share kept getting better and better. His up-line
in Indiana were all full of praise. There was talk of a job at
headquarters, maybe something salaried in marketing.

The business was all about 'protection' then. Just like diamonds and
deodorants, tampons and defence budgets, caskets were sold on the
cold war notion that they could be 'sealed' and 'safe' and would
'protect' the body more or less 'forever' from leakage or embarrassment
or unforeseen dangers. It was the marketing theme. Harold would
spend hours extolling the virtues of Clarksville's gum-rubber gaskets,
'cathodic protection'—a magnesium bar that ran down the bottom of
their heavier-gauge steels which was said to retard rust—and the forty-
eight-ounce Solid Copper Omega, which 'grew stronger through age

by oxidation'. 'Precious metals,' he called the bronze and the copper units. 'Permanent protection.' The more product knowledge his accounts had, the more product they'd buy and the more they'd sell and the better he'd do.

The second summer after he and Elizabeth divorced, Angela came up to the lake and stayed with him for a couple of weeks. She was just on the brink of becoming a teen. Harold could sense the changes coming. He resolved to have her bedroom redecorated when she'd come up next year 'for the whole summer'. But, after he married Helen, she first demurred—a conflict with summer volleyball—and then refused. Angela said that her mother said that her father was an incurable heterosexual, bound to dominate women, a member of the patriarchy, a serial rapist and a hopeless case. Angela told him all of this in a letter Harold figured her mother typed. She was turning thirteen. Elizabeth's anger at his remarriage was something he never understood. That she passed it along to Angela was even more inexplicable. Harold called often but Angela was always 'out'. He sent flowers for her birthday. He sent her cards and letters she never responded to. It hurt him, but he blamed it on her mother. He tried to stay in touch but figured he was best off leaving well alone. She had enough to deal with with all the changes in her little life. He didn't want to pull her into a conflict. He thought the day would come when she was older that she would understand her father better and they could re-establish a relationship. It never happened.

When she was sixteen, Angela was hit by a train. She'd been walking the tracks that ran between Main Street and the Mill Pond early on a Sunday morning. The autopsy showed that she'd been drinking and was pregnant. And though the death was ruled accidental, Harold wondered if she might have thrown herself in front of the train and, if so, which of her parents should be blamed the most. It also occurred to him that maybe the man who had impregnated her pushed her in front of the train. He wondered if it was a man or a boy. Had she been looking for another father figure in her life or just playing around with one of the pimply jerk-offs she'd grown up with? Knowing the cause of death while not knowing the cause of the cause of death sent Harold into a spiral of such steep descent that he resolved to put it all out of his mind, void as that darkness was of any place names he could recognize; he feared the point of no return.

Thomas Lynch

Elizabeth arranged to have Angela's body cremated, to which Harold agreed, but he insisted on putting her in a Melrose Cherry instead of the cardboard casket they always used when there wasn't going to be a public viewing. 'A shame to burn such a beautiful piece of wood,' Elizabeth had said, when they went to the funeral home to identify their daughter's body. She rubbed her hand along the deeply polished finish, averting her eyes from the body in the box. He wanted to hit her. He wanted to put his fist through her face and shut her mouth forever. But he only nodded and thought yes, a shame.

Angela's face was unmarked, all the injuries apparently 'internal'. He and Elizabeth divided the ashes. Each got a little cherub-shaped urn with half their daughter's remains inside. He never knew what his former spouse had done with her half of their daughter. He never asked. He hadn't spoken to Elizabeth since.

Harold didn't know Larry Ordway, or even if Larry was his name. It might have been Lenny or Louie or Lester. All the sign said was L. ORDWAY PRIVATE, scrawled on a white board in blue paint and nailed to a tree stump at the end of the drive. Harold couldn't remember when he settled on Larry or why exactly, or how he'd come to several conclusions about a man he had never met. There was the cross that went up in the woods one year, painted white and gold and ten feet tall and wired for lights, big bulbs, that shone through the dark eerily—a sign of the born-again Christian fundamentalist, Michigan militia type of head-case he reckoned Larry Ordway must be. And there were the mean-spirited dogs always challenging him at the bend in the road, barking, baring their teeth, the current one now five or six years into its miserable life, looking like the hound of hell with its frothing muzzle and pointed ears. Harold had feared it and picked up his pace to get past its purview and kept an eye out even when he was beyond range. He had even taken long detours through the woods to keep out of the dog's way, his fear getting the best of him until once, the week after Joan had been diagnosed, Harold had waited for the dog, growled back at it as it hunched and snarled, and taunted it with waving arms, and timed it perfectly so that when the cur lunged within kicking range, he caught it squarely in its yapping mouth, a perfect punt, flipping it on its backside and sending it yelping back up the drive. It hadn't really challenged Harold since. Its barking was vicious but still it kept its cowering distance. Harold kept a stick handy, just in case, half hoping it would give him another go. Sometimes now, after he'd gotten past Ordway's, he'd hear movement in the dense woods on either side of the railway easement, aside and behind him, and wondered if the dog was following along, waiting to pounce or wanting to make friendly. Harold didn't know but didn't trust the thing. He'd turn sometimes and look behind him. Once or twice he thought he caught a glimpse of the bitch crossing the tracks in a blur, maybe stalking him, waiting for its chance to settle the score.

At Hobo Beach, where the trail ran nearest the lake, Harold stopped to sit and watch the water for one of the eagles that nested nearby or the osprey that nested on a platform placed in the river mouth by the DNR, or anything else that might happen. The rapturous descent of fishing birds, the haunted call of loons, the hovering of kingfishers, the uncommon beauty of common mergansers—these incarnations now remembered, late in the day, late in the year, made him feel a fortunate pilgrim, indeed. Above the tree line on the far side of the lake the fat face of the full moon was emerging. Harvest moon, he thought. No, hunter's moon, then beaver moon, then cold. He ran through the names of moons such as he knew them. There would be moon shadows tonight and light on the water.

All the docks and boat hoists were stacked on the beach, waiting for the coming winter's freeze and deep snows and next spring's thaw—worm moon, he thought in March, pink moon April, May, the flower moon—before being hauled out and reassembled in the water for the high season. The boaters and sunbathers all gone south and the snowmobilers not yet thinking about coming north, the off-season vacancy of late October struck Harold as the best of all times of year.

This golden harvest aspect of it all, a feast for all souls, the sense of finished work and jobs done well—'Autumn Oak' is what he named the clear-finished, hand-polished number with the fallen-leaf appliqué stitched into the cap panel and the tailored beige linen interior when he first beheld it, and his bosses at Clarksville had agreed with him. They even designed an urn to go with it—same wood, same finish, same falling leaves machine-etched into it—a package deal for the cremation crowd. 'The Autumn Oak Ensemble' they called it in the catalogue and sold them by the truckload all over the place—the most popular of Clarksville's hardwood line.

Thomas Lynch

He should have been better to Helen. She had never been anything but good to him. Maybe if he'd been more trusting, less damaged goods, not so angry. Maybe if Angela had lived. He didn't know. He often wished he could do that over again, make it up to her.

They'd met at the convention in Grand Rapids. Her booth for Barber Music Systems was next to Clarksville's on the exhibit floor. By the last day of the convention he worked up the nerve to ask her to dinner. She was younger, plain-faced, smarter and more pleasant than anyone he'd been out with in years. Her father had started the business, which sold background music systems for mortuaries—hours of hymns or new age music to 'Break the Terrible Silence of Grief'. Under Helen's guidance the company was marketing video memorial tributes.

They dated for six months, then got engaged, then got married. They honeymooned at Casa de Campo in the Dominican Republic. He golfed, she sunbathed. It was good but brief. They divorced soon after Angela's death. Helen had the marriage annulled and was soon enough remarried to a man from Forethought Preneed who didn't drink, as Harold had begun to, and didn't sleep around, the way Harold did in the months following his daughter's death. Helen wasn't bitter. She just wanted out. She wished him well, but wouldn't hang around for his 'self-destruction'.

He saw her at conventions after that. She'd always smile sweetly and keep her distance. He'd readied the little speech to make amends and ask forgiveness, to say it had all been his fault and bad timing and the drink, of course, but when he approached her in her booth the year before he retired, her eyes looked panicky, she put one hand over her mouth and the other out straight as if to warn him off. 'I'm sorry,' he said, 'I just wanted to say...' but she looked frightened and her eyes were filling with tears and she was backing away as if from some peril or contagion, so he stopped and turned away and said nothing. He thought maybe he'd write it all in a letter, to let her know he knew how bad he'd been to her. But he never got around to it and thought now, sitting by the lake, watching the moon rise, that he likely never would.

He stood and sighed heavily and stretched and, dropping his pants, pissed in the sand and, after hitching up again, walked back from the water's edge to the trail along the railway bed he'd been on. It was here he'd seen an indigo bunting once, perched on the head of a cat

tail by the water, a blueness he had never seen before or since. He felt
a chill in the evening air. Looking down the long tunnel between the
trees, Harold watched for deer crossing, or porcupine, or beaver. He
looked back the way he'd come for signs of Larry Ordway's dog.
Nothing moved. Once, years back, he had seen what he swore was
a black bear pausing in the clearing with its nose in the air. He knew
that the woods held red fox and grey wolf but he had never seen them.
Signs of life in the deep interior, seen and unseen, quickened in him
the kind of gladness he remembered having as a boy. The emergency
flight of pheasant and wild turkey, the passing shadows of osprey and
vulture and gull, the trees fed on by nuthatch and pileated woodpecker,
felled by beaver, scraped by whitetail bucks, mauled, he imagined, by
bear and raccoon—these apparitions of the world's natural order were
a comfort to him for reasons he could not articulate.

It was Harold Keehn who had convinced Clarksville to market
wooden caskets, the rich grains, the homey cabinetry warmth of it all.
And Harold who came up with the idea of planting trees, saplings
only, pennies only by way of expense, in cahoots with the forestry
department, for every Clarksville casket sold. The Memory Tree
Program had been a huge success. It assuaged the baby boomers'
natural concerns about ecology and conservation and renewable
resources. He'd pitched the whole market shift at a sales conference
in a presentation he called 'Don't Let Your Business Go up in Smoke',
in which he noted the growing popularity of cremation and the natural
consumer preference for boxes that would burn. 'Permanence' and
'Protection' had given way to 'Natural Beauty' and 'Sensible Choices'.
A woman's right to choose, thought Harold, applied to the recently
widowed as well as the recently impregnated, noting the coincident
rise in the abortion and cremation rates. 'If you can't beat 'em, join
'em,' he told his bosses at Clarksville headquarters. 'Give them plenty
of choices.' They called their cremation catalogue 'Options by
Clarksville' and filled it with urns and cremation caskets.

Had it not been for the drinking and carousing that everyone
knew about but no one mentioned, he might have been given a vice-
presidency, stock options, an office at headquarters in Indiana. As
it was they thanked him for his insights and cut his territory. He
didn't care. Inflation kept his commissions high. He had nothing to
save for. His dead daughter's college fund went into a couple mutual

funds and swelled during the 1990s. He had more than he'd ever need. His place was paid off. After Angela had died, after Helen left, very little mattered until he met Joan at an AA meeting in a church basement in Topinabee.

She had looked to be about the age Angela would have been if she had lived. She always listened to Harold carefully when he talked at the weekly meetings. She nodded and smiled when it came to his turn to tell how he was powerless over alcohol and his life had become unmanageable or how he'd come to believe that a power greater than himself could restore him to sanity or the particulars of his searching and fearless moral inventory. She would nod and smile and at the end she would squeeze his hand after the Our Father or the recitation of the Serenity Prayer and give him a hug and tell him, 'Easy does it, Harold.' She was so happy, it seemed, so very happy. And whatever calamity or sadness brought her to AA, details of which she shared frankly on occasion, she seemed to inhabit a permanent present tense, free of the past and future, afloat on the moment she occupied. She was pretty and had a graceful body and eyes like the blue of the indigo bunting he had only seen once. When Harold asked her if he could take her out to dinner, she said she'd rather bring him dinner at home. It was a chicken and rice casserole, and pecan pie for desert. She stayed that night and the night after that and on the weekend they moved her out of the rooming house in Cheboygan, her entire estate fitting easily in the trunks of their two cars. There had never been any talk of marriage. They were companions and occasional lovers, generous with each other in ways that were new to Harold. He took her walleye fishing and built fires in the fall and winter. She read to him in bed and cooked him breakfast. He took her on sunset cruises along the lakeshore in an old wooden inboard he bought for such occasions, savouring the changing light and night skies and the silence that would sometimes settle between them. She quit her job at the marina, where she did payables and receivables. He did most of his business by phone and fax. They went to dinner in Petoskey and Mackinaw City and Indian River, movies in Gaylord and Cheboygan. She abided his long walks, his long silences, his darker moods. Whenever she touched him, or talked to him, or looked at him, Harold felt alive. And though he never could figure out why she came and stayed—she was twenty-three years younger and might have had a more exciting life—his gratitude was manifest and he treated her accordingly.

He bought a small RV and they would leave just before Memorial Day, driving around the country on no particular schedule, returning after Labor Day, when all the summer neighbours had returned to their downstate lives. He kept a list of the place names they had been to. She kept albums full of photos, each of them posing for the other in front of some diner or park entrance or stop in the road. They had lived together there on the lake for over ten years. The best years of his life, he would always say. The best of hers, she would say in return. Only when her death seemed certain had they agreed to marry so that Harold could be her next of kin. Her family in Lansing was long estranged. None came during her sickness or after she died, though Harold made the requisite phone calls. Whatever happened between her and her family happened years ago, the detachment having achieved a point, apparently, of no return.

Joan's cancer took a year and a half from first diagnosis to the surgery to remove a lung, through the radiation and chemo and eventual reoccurrence—the 'irregularity' they called it when it showed back up—to the morning last winter when, after an awful seizure, because it had grown into her brain, she died with Harold sitting helplessly by.

After the burial he'd ordered a stone with her name and dates on it—Joan Winters Keehn—but he'd never seen it, though he passed the cemetery often enough: he never thought of her as there. But some nights over the past months, he'd go out to the motor-home and sit at the table where they'd played gin rummy during their nights on the road; or he'd crawl into the bed where they had slept in their summer travels, pressed to one another, his right hand cupping her small left breast in their genial embrace. Some nights alone out there in the RV in the driveway, he'd wonder if it was time to take up drink again. So far he hadn't, on the advice that Joan herself had always given out, that there was no sadness that couldn't be made more miserable by the addition of a Class-A depressant. Still, the brand names of whiskeys were beginning to make their way on to the lists of names he kept—Jameson's, Bushmills, Power's and Paddy—with the names of birds and the names of caskets, the names of moons and towns and tribes and names of his lost wives.

Harold Keehn could imagine Adam in the garden, that first index finger working overtime, assigning to every new thing he saw fresh, orderly syllables—aardvark, apple, elephant, waterfall—as if to name it was to know it or own it or anyway to have, if not dominion over it, some consortium with it. He wondered how it must have been when that first man first whispered 'Eve' and the woman turned to look into his eyes.

When Harold found himself at the south edge of Topinabee, the hum of the highway coming through the woods on his left and the moon on the water on his right, he knew he'd walked too far. How had he lost track of it all? And turning back to go the way he'd come, he wondered if there would be enough light left in the day for the way home. Even at his best pace it would take him nearly an hour. Suddenly he was aware of his body and its pains and aches. His knee was grinding, his feet aflame, the small of his back full of crippling twinges. He was fatigued. The air was getting colder now and the wind off the lake increasing. He resolved to keep, in spite of everything, a steady pace.

He'd quit the casket trade at the right time, Harold thought. It was no longer the permanence and protection of the metal ones, or the warmth and natural attractions of the woods. Now it was all gimmicks and knick-knacks. Interchangeable corner hardware—tackle boxes for fishermen, plastic mum plants for gardeners, little faux carrots and kitchen utensils for women who cooked, all moulded in plastic—how silly, he thought. And 'memory drawers'—the little box within the box to put farewell notes and mementoes in—smarmy malarkey thought up by 'focus groups' and test markets. Back in his day it was the salesman on his rounds who came back with the best ideas. What the public wanted in a casket, Harold had told the honchos at home office, was a way to 'get a handle' on it all—a death in the family—the once-in-a-lifetime aspect of it all. Trouble was, it was the ultimate one-to-a-customer deal. And hard enough to get folks enthused about even the one.

Now he was aware of the angling lights that lit the way before him. The golden rays of evening washing through the trees on his right and the silver of the moonrise over the lake on his left illuminated the track of railway bed before him. It took his breath away, the beauty of it. His chest was heavy. He sighed.

When Joan's Princess Mahogany was moved last April, from the stone winter vault to the freshly opened grave, the seams of the boards in the casket lid were splitting where the epoxy had dried in the cold interior of the holding tomb. Condensation, desiccation, extremes in freeze and thaw: even the best of boxes will eventually rot, he thought. Everything in nature disappears. Harley Flick let Harold bury his daughter's ashes, the half that he had kept in the house these many years, in the room she never came to stay in, in the same new grave as Joan was buried in. He poured his daughter's ashes over his third wife's casket, where they filled in the open seams in the lid. Then he borrowed Harley's shovel and filled half the muddy grave himself before Harley finished the job with his John Deere backhoe.

When Harold turned off the railroad easement by Larry Ordway's cross, the dog lay dozing in the road at the bottom of the drive and hardly budged when Harold walked by. He'd let his stick go miles back. Turning down Grace Beach Road, on the last leg of the journey, he looked back and saw the dark shape of the dog behind him. It was not barking or bothered or giving chase, just following him at Harold's own pace, silhouetted by the last light of the sun behind it. He was aware of his heart racing and his breath labouring and the general ache of his body sharpening and the fatigue of the long walk overtaking him. If the dog attacked he could not fend him off. But the dog did not attack, only followed Harold home, footsore, winded, aching, spent.

Harold slumped on the bottom step of his front porch, watching the last light pour out of the day and the moonlight widening over the flat surface of water and the darkness tightening all around him. He avoided the impulse to name some stars that appeared in the firmament, or to name some fish swimming unseen in the dark waters, or whatever living things moved in the woods. He wouldn't be going to Topinabee. He didn't want a drink. He wouldn't build a fire tonight. In his flesh he felt entirely quenched. It was enough to let his vision blur watching the water and the moon and to find Larry Ordway's dog, if Larry was Ordway's name at all, curled beside him free of menace, watching nothing happen, thinking nothing of substance, void of memory or purpose or expectation. Neither the names of breeds nor the names of dogs nor the names of their owners troubled him anymore. The dog kept watch all night and did not howl at the rising or the falling moon. □

THE CLASH WITHIN
Democracy, Religious Violence, and India's Future

MARTHA C. NUSSBAUM

"This is an extraordinarily interesting book on a very difficult subject. Martha Nussbaum's commanding familiarity with culturally related political issues across the world, past and present, combines immensely fruitfully here with her involvement and understanding of India."
—Amartya Sen, Harvard University
Belknap Press / new in cloth

DRY MANHATTAN
Prohibition in New York City

MICHAEL A. LERNER

"Mr. Lerner's painstaking research is generously on display in *Dry Manhattan*, and without the usual Jazz Age clichés. Rather, he draws a disturbing portrait of the 'dry' movement and how it exploited the country's fear of immigrants, then arriving from Europe in vast numbers."
—Russ Smith, WALL STREET JOURNAL

"[An] exceptionally interesting book."
—Jonathan Yardley,
   WASHINGTON POST BOOK WORLD
new in cloth

WWW.HUP.HARVARD.EDU **HARVARD UNIVERSITY PRESS**

NOW A MAJOR
MOTION PICTURE

Todd McEwen

Todd McEwen

Print on demand? Bah. E-books? Fuck you. None of these high-falutin pansy-ass would-be 'technologies' are going to save literature. Look at it. The book is practically dead—that almost unbelievably perfect human-made thing which brought literature into being, nurtured it, and proudly and beautifully published it to the world for centuries? The only way left to us to preserve all the thought, all that beauty that went before, which we ride around on like a shit-stained kiddy-kar, is to MAKE MOVIES OF IT? Oh, we're looking forward to that.

The Wealth of Nations 1938 dir. Ernst Lubitsch. Leslie Howard, Edward Arnold. In 1780 London, a bewigged coffee-house bore tells everyone what to do.

Das Kapital 1950 dir. Erich von Stroheim. Ernest Borgnine, Robert Coote (as Engels). In 1890 London, an enormous German terrorizes the Establishment with his boils.

Hiawatha 1955 dir. John Ford. Jack Palance, Marlene Dietrich. A man of Chippewa descent is driven mad by rhythmic pounding.

The Prelude 1940 dir. Jean Renoir. David Niven, Margaret Lockwood. Failing to think only of his sister, a north of England man steals a boat and goes to college.

The Raw and the Cooked 1960 dir. Howard Hawks. John Wayne, Sidney Poitier. On safari, a white hunter realizes he does not understand the significance of dinner.

The Origin of Species 1960 dir. George Cukor. Rex Harrison, Trevor Howard, Sabu. A bored aristocrat sails to the South Seas, where he tells animals what to do.

The Theory of the Leisure Class 1955 dir. Billy Wilder. Sammy Davis Jr, Frank Sinatra, Peter Lawford, Joey Bishop, Angie Dickinson. Four philosophers visit Las Vegas and learn how to relax.

Mein Kampf 1947 dir. Henry Koster. Peter Lorre, Ginger Rogers. A ne'er-do-well Austrian artist finds the meaning of life.

Now a Major Motion Picture

The State and Revolution 1931 dir. King Vidor. Charles Middleton, Joan Blondell. A diminutive Russian has plans to dominate the earth but is filled with embalming fluid instead.

Mastering the Art of French Cooking 1960 dir. Jean-Luc Godard. Jayne Mansfield, Jean-Paul Belmondo. In occupied France, a dizzy WAC discovers a sauce that fights Nazism.

Baby and Child Care 1968 dir. Russ Meyer. Leo G. Carroll, Jerry Mathers, Patty Duke, Jay North, Oliver North. A mad doctor finds he has reared a nation of narcissistic monsters.

Civilization and Its Discontents 1940 dir. René Clair. Fred MacMurray, Greta Garbo, Robert Benchley (as Jung). A timid European doctor is haunted by his own penis.

See also the musical sequel:
Vienna Holiday 1950 dir. Victor Fleming. William Powell, Sonja Henie. After a scary dream, Dr Freud falls in love with a pretty skater.

Paradise Lost 1947 TECHNICOLOR dir. Alfred Hitchcock. Don Ameche, Loretta Young. In Yellowstone National Park, a blind, psychotic forest-ranger frames a newlywed couple for littering.

Seven Types of Ambiguity 1965 dir. John Ford, Jean-Luc Godard, Woody Allen, John Cassavetes, Otto Preminger, Roman Polanski, Cecil B. De Mille. Bob Hope, Anna Magnani, James Mason, Judy Garland. Four wacky intellectual castaways keep warm by knitting amazing neck beards.

Wittgenstein's Nephew 1998 dir. Charles Crichton. Matt Damon, Arnold Schwarzenegger. Two wacky invalids discuss philosophy and get wheeled around a hospital.

The Cantos 1947 dir. Douglas Sirk. Adolphe Menjou, Linda Darnell. A caged poet dreams of better days. □